ALL VILLAGES IN ONE PLACE

ALLE DÖRFER AN EINEM ORT

A B C D E F G H I J K L M N O P Q R S T U V W X Y Z

ABSTRACT

A great deal of the work of Myvillages takes place in remotely situated villages, far away from metropolitan centres. The *International Village Show* at the Museum of Contemporary Art Leipzig (GfZK) brings things that have been produced, presented, and questioned concurrently together in one place. The show is a synchronous cross-section of the artistic work of Myvillages.

The Gartenhaus of the GfZK was remodelled for the *International Village Show*. In the Gartenhaus and garden, two villages or landscapes that previously had no connection encountered each other every three months from February 2015 to December 2016. The eighth and final show is dedicated to the presentation of this book – all villages in one place.

In Dörfern, abseits der Metropolen, an entlegenen Orten findet ein großer Teil der Arbeit von Myvillages statt. Die *International Village Show* in der Galerie für Zeitgenössische Kunst (GfZK) Leipzig bringt an einem Ort zusammen, was gleichzeitig weit entfernt voneinander produziert, gezeigt und befragt wird. Die Show ist ein synchroner Schnitt durch das künstlerische Schaffen von Myvillages.

Für die *International Village Show* wurde das Gartenhaus der GfZK umgebaut. In Gartenhaus und Garten treffen von Februar 2015 bis Dezember 2016 alle drei Monate zwei Dörfer oder Landschaften aufeinander, die vorher in keinem Zusammenhang standen. Die achte und letzte Show ist der Präsentation dieses Buches gewidmet – alle Dörfer an einem Ort.

COGGESHALL
KELVEDON
THE TEYS

Andaluces de Jaén

Andaluces de Jaén
aceituneros altivos
decidme en el alma quien
quien levantó los olivos,
andaluces de Jaén.
Andaluces de Jaén.

No los levantó la arada
ni el dinero ni el señor,
sino la tierra callada
el trabajo y el sudor,
unidos al agua pura
y a los planetas unidos,
los tres vieron la hermosura
de los troncos retorcidos,
andaluces de Jaén.

Andaluces de Jaén
aceituneros altivos
decidme en el alma de quien
de quien son esos olivos,
andaluces de Jaén.
Andaluces de Jaén.

Cuantos siglos de aceitunas
los pies y las manos presos,
sol a sol y luna a luna
pesan sobre vuestros huesos,
Jaen levantate brava
sobre tus piedras lunares,
no vayas a ser esclava
con todos tus olivares,
andaluces de Jaén.

Andaluces de Jaén
aceituneros altivos
decidme en el alma de quien
de quien son esos olivos,
andaluces de Jaén.
Andaluces de Jaén.

Andaluces de Jáen is a song based on a poem by / ist ein Lied nach einem Gedicht von **Miguel Hernández** (1910–1942).

AUTOMATIEK

The 24-hour economy is an integral part of the *International Village Show.* The Dutch-style vending machine at the Gartenhaus was initially manufactured for on-the-go sales of hot snacks. Very handy at railway stations, but rarely seen in villages. There we found vending machines for bread in Flanders and condoms in Spain. And the pinnacle of consumerism in German villages seemed to be chewing gum dispensers.

In Leipzig the contents of the vending machine cost 2, 4 or 6 euros. We fix the amount each time by turning a knob and changing the display screen. There are eight shows and the vending machine has 12 compartments. **WF**

Die 24-Stunden-Wirtschaft ist integraler Bestandteil der *International Village Show.* Der Warenautomat niederländischer Bauart am Gartenhaus wurde ursprünglich für den Straßenverkauf warmer Imbisse eingesetzt. In Bahnhöfen ist das praktisch, auf dem Land sieht man es selten. Dort fanden wir dagegen Verkaufsautomaten für Brot, in Flandern, und für Kondome, in Spanien. Der größte denkbare Konsumrausch in deutschen Dörfern war ein Kaugummiautomat.

In Leipzig kosten die Inhalte des Automaten 2, 4 oder 6 Euro. Wir legen den Betrag jedes Mal neu fest, indem wir den Münzeinwurf einstellen und ein neues Preisschild anbringen. Es gibt acht Shows, und der Automat hat zwölf Warenfächer. **WF**

IVS 1/8

Geological Collection
International Village Show in Leipzig
The youngest specimens – the ventifacts – at the top, and the oldest – the greywackes – at the bottom. We fill an extra compartment with darker and lighter lignite because it seems to be popular. All the specimens were collected by Ronny Schmidt of GeoWerkstatt Leipzig.
each euro 2.–

IVS 2/8

Orange marmalade made by nuns from the Convent of Santa Paula, Andalusia
The nuns who make this famous marmalade have no contact with the outside world. The oranges for this special edition came straight from the orchard of the CAAC Museum in Seville.
each euro 4.–

IVS 3/8

Frisian horsemilk soap
ROM chocolate bar
Grindstone from Brezoi
ROM is the chocolate bar that every Romanian migrant longs for.
each euro 4.–

IVS 4/8

International Village Shop 2016
Tea towel calendar
Screen print on linen
each euro 6.–

IVS 1/8

Geologische Sammlung
International Village Show in Leipzig
Die jüngsten Gesteinsproben – Windkanter – ganz oben, die ältesten – Grauwacken – zuunterst. Ein Extrafach füllen wir mit dunklerer und hellerer Braunkohle, denn die ist anscheinend beliebt. Alle Proben hat Ronny Schmidt von der GeoWerkstatt Leipzig gesammelt.
je 2,– Euro

IVS 2/8

Orangenmarmelade der Nonnen von Santa Paula, Andalusien
Die Nonnen, die diese berühmte Marmelade herstellen, haben keinen Kontakt zur Außenwelt. Die Orangen für diese Sonderedition stammen direkt aus dem Obstgarten des Centro Andaluz de Arte Contemporáneo in Sevilla.
je Glas 4,– Euro

IVS 3/8

Friesische Stutenmilchseife
ROM-Schokoriegel
Schleifsteine aus Brezoi
ROM ist der Schokoriegel, nach dem sich jeder rumänische Auswanderer sehnt.
je 4,– Euro

IVS 4/8

International-Village-Shop-Küchentuchkalender 2016
Handsiebdruck auf Halbleinen
je 6,– Euro

A

IVS 5/8

Vending machine owls
Vending machine hares
Vending machine hedgehogs
By Chajim Grosser, Berlin based ceramicist, who visited Zvizzchi in the summer of 2015
each euro 6.–

IVS 6/8

Flower Tattoos
When applied correctly, a tattoo lasts for 3 to 5 days. Twelve different motifs are available.
each euro 2.–

IVS 7/8

Company Drink Miniature Cordials
from Barking and Dagenham (Greater London)
each euro 2.–

IVS 8/8

Geological Collection
International Village Show in Leipzig
For Christmas we are offering one of our vending machine bestsellers: rocks.
each euro 2.–

IVS 5/8

Automateneulen
Automatenhasen
Automatenigel
Automatentiere von Chajim Grosser, Berliner Keramiker, nach Zvizzchi gereist im Sommer 2015
je 6,– Euro

IVS 6/8

Blumentattoos
Im Angebot sind 12 verschiedene Motive. Richtig angebracht, hält ein Tattoo 3 bis 5 Tage.
je Set 2,– Euro

IVS 7/8

Company Drink Miniature Cordials
aus Barking and Dagenham (Greater London)
je Set 2,– Euro

IVS 8/8

Geologische Sammlung
International Village Show in Leipzig
Zu Weihnachten bieten wir einen unserer Automatenbestseller noch einmal an: Steine.
je 2,– Euro

Windgeschliffenes Geschiebe

Braunkohle Flöz I

Braunkohle Flöz II

Beuchaer Granitporphyr

Löbejüner Porphyr – Rhyolith

Permosiles

Quarzit

Grauwacke

Ventifacts
rocks transported by glaciers, often carved into a keel-like shape by the wind

Lignite
a fossil fuel used to produce energy

Beuchaer Granite Porphyry
used to build the Monument to the Battle of the Nations at the beginning of the 20th century

Löbejüner Porphyry – Rhyolith
igneous rock from Saxony-Anhalt

Permosiles
uncovered in 2014–15 when the Karl-Heine-Canal was connected to the Lindenauer port

Quarzite
from the Fischwasser Quarry, which can only be recognized by the hole it left behind, which is now filled with water

Greywacke
more than 570 million years old, unearthed in Leipzig during the construction of the Karl-Heine-Canal in the second half of the 19th century

Windgeschliffenes Geschiebe
von Gletschern transportiertes Gestein, häufig durch vom Wind transportierten Sand zu kielartiger Form geschliffen

Braunkohle
ein fossiler Brennstoff, der zur Energieerzeugung verwendet wird

Beuchaer Granitporphyr
benutzt für den Bau des Völkerschlachtdenkmals zu Beginn des 20. Jahrhunderts

Löbejüner Porphyr – Rhyolith
vulkanisches Gestein aus Sachsen-Anhalt

Permosiles
freigelegt 2014/15 beim Anschluss des Karl-Heine-Kanals an den Lindenauer Hafen.

Quarzit
aus dem Steinbruch Fischwasser, der heute nur noch als ein wassergefülltes Restloch zu sehen ist

Grauwacke
mehr als 570 Millionen Jahre alt, in Leipzig freigelegt beim Bau des Karl-Heine-Kanals in der zweiten Hälfte des 19. Jahrhunderts

B

B

Ballykinlar
entre

B

Ballykinler / Ballykinlar

Northern Ireland, GB

Population / Einwohner: 348

Ballykinler or Ballykinlar, depending on which of the two "communities" one belongs to, is wedged between the Mourne Mountains, the Irish Sea, and – cutting off access to the beach – a British Army camp. The adjacent "Abercorn Barracks" have dominated the village since 1902. The military provided many jobs, allegiances and opposition, again depending on one's national / cultural identity.

The village is a condensed, rural microcosm of Northern Irish society, history, and politics, magnified by the presence of the army. It is hence similar to interface zones in Belfast, with its urban environment of segregated communities.

During "The Troubles", the army operated in Northern Ireland, but they now prepare for deployments in Afghanistan and future areas of armed conflict worldwide. In July 2014, the "2nd Battalion, The Rifles" were relocated to an army camp in Lisburn, Northern Ireland. The Abercorn Barracks and its ground are now only used as a training ground and many jobs in Ballykinler and nearby villages have been lost.[1]

Our main contact in the village is Anne-Marie Dillon, mother of seven children, local resident, artist, activist, and feminist (listed according to her own order of priorities). All ideas get checked with her, as she knows the community and wants to provoke new action and thinking without further polarization in an already segregated Northern Irish society. She tells me to put down my camera when we drive through the village, taking random images is not the done thing.

Ballykinler oder Ballykinlar – je nachdem, zu welcher Bevölkerungsgruppe man gehört – liegt eingezwängt zwischen den Mourne Mountains, der Irischen See und einem britischen Armeelager, das den Zugang zum Strand versperrt. Die Kaserne »Abercorn Barracks« bestimmt das Leben im Dorf seit 1902. Das Militär hat vielen Arbeit gegeben, Bündnisse geschlossen und Widerstand erzeugt – auch das in Abhängigkeit von der jeweiligen nationalen/kulturellen Identität. Das Dorf ist ein ländlicher Mikrokosmos der nordirischen Gesellschaft, Geschichte und Politik, verstärkt durch die Gegenwart der Armee. Es ähnelt den Übergangszonen in Belfast mit ihrer städtischen Segregation der einzelnen Nachbarschaften.

Während der »Troubles« kämpfte die Armee in Nordirland, doch inzwischen bereitet sie sich auf die Verlegung ihrer Einheiten nach Afghanistan und in Gebiete künftiger bewaffneter Auseinandersetzungen weltweit vor. Im Juli 2014 wurde das »2nd Battalion, The Rifles« in das Lager von Lisburn, ebenfalls Nordirland, verlegt. Die Abercorn Barracks und ihr Sperrgebiet werden seither nur noch als Übungsgelände genutzt, und viele Arbeitsplätze in Ballykinler und nahe gelegenen Dörfern sind verloren gegangen.[1]

Unsere wichtigste Kontaktperson im Dorf ist Anne-Marie Dillon, Mutter von sieben Kindern, Ortsansässige, Künstlerin, Aktivistin und Feministin (in der Reihenfolge ihrer eigenen Prioritäten). Alle Ideen werden gemeinsam mit ihr geprüft, da sie die Gemeinde kennt und neues Handeln und Denken fördern will, ohne die rigide getrennte nordirische Gesellschaft weiter zu polarisieren. Als wir durch das Dorf fahren, bittet sie mich, die Kamera abzusetzen, denn es gehört sich hier nicht, einfach ein paar Fotos zu machen.

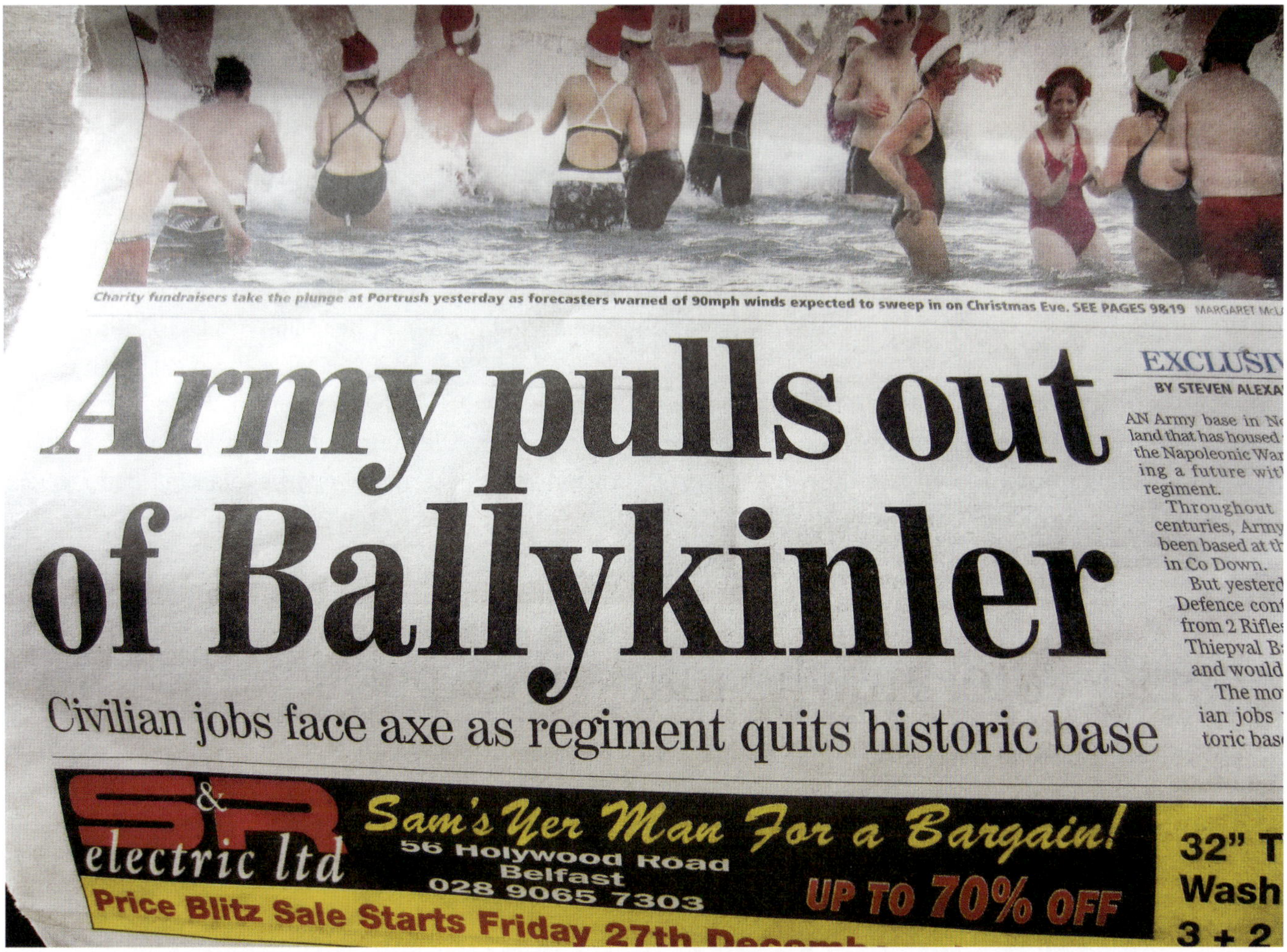

Charity fundraisers take the plunge at Portrush yesterday as forecasters warned of 90mph winds expected to sweep in on Christmas Eve. SEE PAGES 9&19 MARGARET McL

Army pulls out of Ballykinler

Civilian jobs face axe as regiment quits historic base

EXCLUSIV

BY STEVEN ALEXA

AN Army base in No
land that has housed
the Napoleonic War
ing a future wit
regiment.
Throughout
centuries, Army
been based at th
in Co Down.
But yesterd
Defence conf
from 2 Rifles
Thiepval B
and would
The mo
ian jobs
toric bas

S&R electric ltd
Sam's Yer Man For a Bargain!
56 Holywood Road
Belfast
028 9065 7303
UP TO 70% OFF
Price Blitz Sale Starts Friday 27th Decem
32" T
Wash
3 + 2

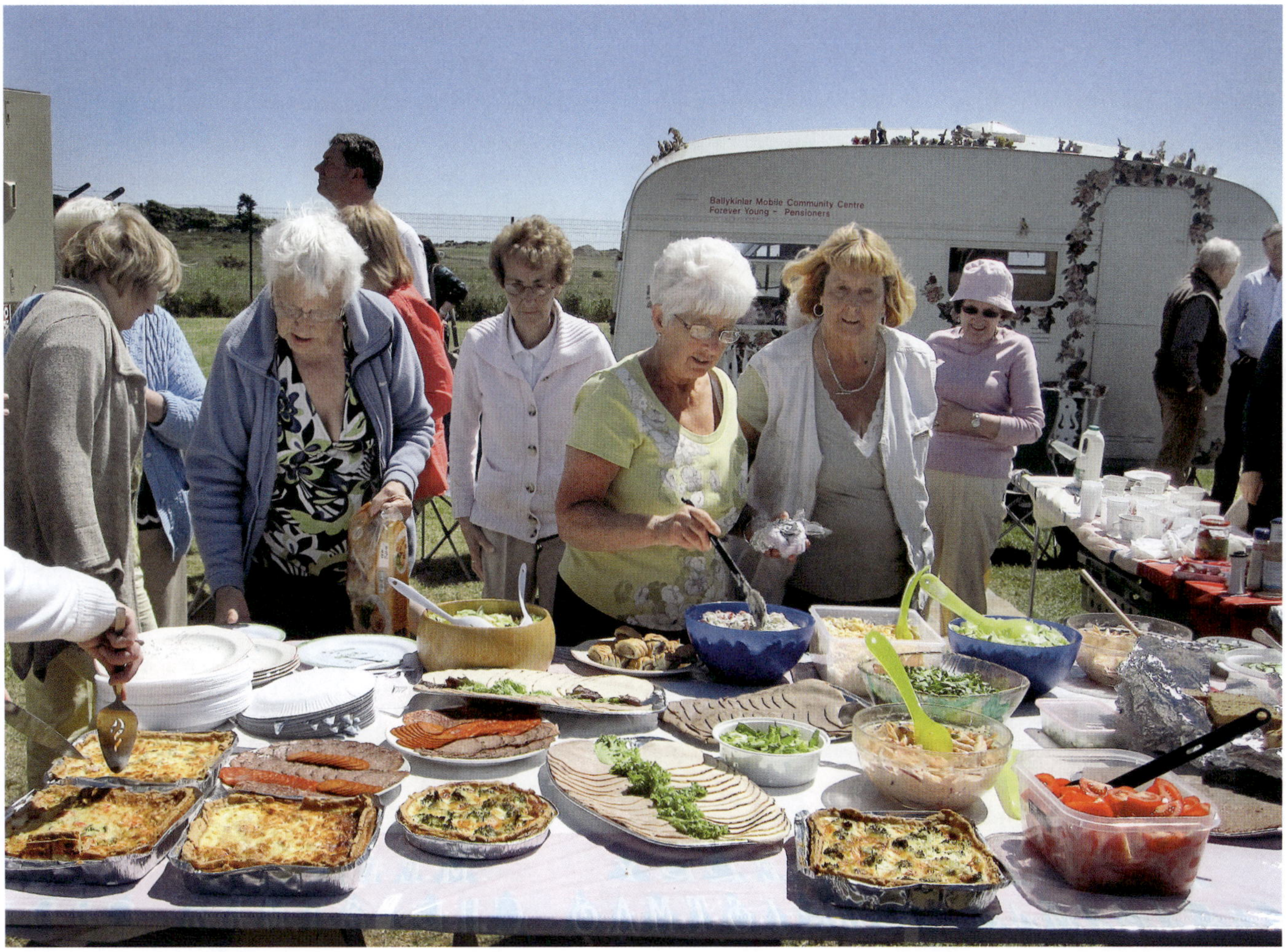

Ballykinlar Mobile Community Centre
Forever Young – Pensioners

B

My position here is simpler: I'm clearly not just a guest, but I'm also a stranger, and therefore not one of "them" or "them". Our collaboration started with the invention and making of the *Caravan Pot*, which commemorates the courageous act by the "Forever Young Pensioners" group of bringing a long desired community centre into existence by simply placing a full size caravan in the middle of the village.

For the second product we wanted to involve the army. When we finally were granted permission to do an arts project, most of the men had been deployed to Afghanistan, and so we worked with the women, who call themselves the "Army Wives".

The drive from Belfast to Ballykinler takes an hour, sometimes longer if you get stuck behind an army vehicle on the narrow country lanes. The drive from the barracks to meet the Army Wives at their community centre can be only two minutes, but may also take an hour, depending on who is available to escort you onto the grounds. Mobile phone reception is notoriously bad there, and at times it seemed impossible to get hold of each other; Facebook has thus become the most reliable form of communication.

The brief for the new product was driven by two strong wishes, to have a reminder of the barracks as a home, and to not have military items enter their homes.

The women have declared their houses in the family quarter of the barracks a military free zone – with the husbands obviously being an exception. Their lives are so dominated by the top-down and military decisions around them that the home is territory to be defended as one's own, be it with scented candles, feminine aesthetics or domestic cleanliness. The new *Twisted Bugle* will sit on the mantle piece alongside other selected decorative items.

We would like to do another Ballykinlar product one day. Let's see what Anne-Marie says. **KB**

1 The first two paragraphs were written by **Peter Mutschler** and **Ruth Morrow**, Belfast.

Meine Stellung hier ist einfacher. Ich bin Gast und eine Fremde, ich gehöre weder zu »denen« noch zu »denen«. Unsere Zusammenarbeit begann mit der Entwicklung und Herstellung des *Caravan Pot*, einem Wohnwagen aus Gusskeramik, geeignet als Blumenübertopf. Er gedenkt des denkmalwürdigen Akts der »Forever Young Pensioners' Group«, ein lang ersehntes Gemeinschaftshaus ins Leben zu bringen, indem man einfach einen Wohnwagen in der Mitte des Dorfs abstellte.

Für die zweite Dorfware wollten wir die Armee mit einbeziehen. Die meisten Männer waren nach Afghanistan verschickt, und wir arbeiteten mit den Frauen, die sich selbst die »Army Wives« nennen.

Die Autofahrt von Belfast nach Ballykinler dauert eine Stunde – manchmal auch länger, wenn man auf den schmalen Landstraßen hinter einem Armeelastwagen hängen bleibt. Die Fahrt von den Barracks zu den Army Wives wäre eigentlich eine Angelegenheit von zwei Minuten, kann aber auch eine Stunde dauern, je nachdem, wer einen auf dem Gelände eskortiert. Der Handyempfang ist bekanntermaßen schlecht hier, und Facebook war die verlässlichste Art der Kommunikation.

Die Vorgaben für das neue Produkt waren von zwei Wünschen geprägt: 1. die Kaserne als ein Zuhause in Erinnerung zu behalten und 2. keinerlei militärische Gegenstände im Haus zu haben. Die Häuser im Familienquartier der Kaserne wurden von den Frauen zu einer entmilitarisierten Zone erklärt, die Ehemänner bildeten dabei offenkundig eine Ausnahme. Das Leben der Frauen wird dominiert von den hierarchischen Befehlsstrukturen rundherum, das Haus dagegen verteidigt als eigenes Territorium – mit Duftkerzen, weiblicher Ästhetik oder häuslicher Reinheit. Der neue *Twisted Bugle* wird seinen Platz auf dem Kaminsims neben anderen ausgewählten Dekorationsstücken finden.

Wir würden eines Tages gern ein weiteres Ballykinlar-Produkt entwickeln. Abwarten, was Anne-Marie dazu sagt. **KB**

1 Die ersten beiden Absätze stammen von **Peter Mutschler** und **Ruth Morrow**, Belfast.

B

wband "Oerterp"
"Oerterp"
eterp

B

Beetsterzwaag

Opsterland in Fryslân, NL

Population: 3,556
Languages: Frisian and Dutch

Einwohner: 3.556
Sprachen: Friesisch und Holländisch

The municipality of Opsterland has a population of approximately 30,000, spread across 16 villages. The biggest village, with over 7,000 inhabitants, is Gorredijk, the smallest is Oldeterp, with 80. The municipal offices are in Beetsterzwaag.

Every year on King's Day, a parade passes along the main street. The floats in 2016 asked for more tolerance amongst faith groups, and a group dressed as chickens drew attention to intensive livestock farming. Schoolchildren fantasized about the land of dinosaurs, and a man in a dress pretended to be a princess. The route goes past people's homes and country estates. Each float is driven down the shopping street two times and ends at the petrol station.

Beetsterzwaag is well known regionally for the rehabilitation centre and care homes which have been built on land that used to be part of country estates. Most of the woodland is still privately owned. The landed gentry who ruled the roost here amassed huge fortunes from peat extraction and land development. At the end of the 19th century the peat workers, inspired by the Dutch socialist and anarchist Ferdinand Domela Nieuwenhuis (1846–1919), also known as "our liberator", united to protest against the abysmal working conditions. That glaring inequality gap between rich and poor might seem like a thing of the past, but it is still a hot topic of debate even today. **WF**

Die Gemeinde Opsterland zählt ungefähr 30.000 Einwohner, die sich auf 16 Ortschaften verteilen. Das größte Dorf ist Gorredijk mit über 7.000 Einwohnern, das kleinste Oldeterp mit achtzig Einwohnern. Der Verwaltungssitz ist Beetsterzwaag.

In Beetsterzwaag findet jedes Jahr am Königstag ein Umzug durch die Hauptstraße statt. 2016 war das Motto der Motivwagen mehr religiöse Toleranz, und eine Gruppe in Federkostümen protestierte gegen die Massenhaltung von Hühnern, während Schulkinder die Welt der Dinosaurier nachfantasierten. Ein Mann in Frauengewändern gab vor, eine Prinzessin zu sein. Der Zug bewegt sich an den Häusern und Landsitzen entlang und geht dabei zweimal durch die Geschäftsstraße. Er endet an der Tankstelle.

Regional bekannt ist Beetsterzwaag durch sein Rehabilitationszentrum und die Pflegeheime, die auf den Ländereien der Großgrundbesitzer entstanden. Die Wälder sind zum größten Teil noch in Privatbesitz. Der mächtige Landadel hatte sich durch den Abbau von Torf und die Verpachtung und den Verkauf von Land riesige Vermögen erwirtschaftet. Gegen Ende des 19. Jahrhunderts schlossen sich die Torfstecher zusammen und protestierten gegen die katastrophalen Arbeitsbedingungen, befeuert von den Ideen des niederländischen Sozialisten und Anarchisten Ferdinand Domela Nieuwenhuis (1846–1919), auch bekannt als »unser Befreier«. Die historische Kluft zwischen Arm und Reich ist mittlerweile Geschichte in Opsterland, aber eine nach wie vor gern erzählte Geschichte, ein Beispiel von Ungleichheit, die sich in heutigen Besitzverhältnissen fortsetzt. **WF**

→ GOODS

B

illy

Brezoi

Vâlcea, RO

Population: 6,022

Einwohner: 6.022

The mountains around Brezoi are steep and forested and managed as common land. Under communism, a huge timber factory was built in the village, along with residential blocks for the newly arrived working class. After the fall of the Ceauşescu government, the factory was shut down, and in a phase of extreme food scarcity, pigs were even kept in the courtyards of the prefab housing estates.

Traditional houses have small gardens for growing one's own food, with vine trellises, fruit trees, vegetable beds and potatoes, chickens and pigs, and sometimes one or two cows or goats.

At milking time, a few cows come walking into the village, but not nearly as many as in the past, says Michaela. She is the head of the village school and the local NGO for cultural conservation and socio-economic development. Her organization is a long-term partner in the Eco Nomadic School, a European network in which local projects visit one another and local knowledge meets trans-local input and exchange. Myvillages has been involved since 2010.

For some years now, the Eco Nomadic School topic in Brezoi has been the Odai (singular: Odaja), small hill farms in the nearby mountains, often only reachable by foot, which in the past were part of the subsistence farming of individual families. An Odaja consists of a simple house with one or two bedrooms, a meadow orchard (mostly plums), grassy slopes, a barn, a fenced-in vegetable garden and high-tapering haystacks for the animals. Odai were usually farmed in the summer, but now mostly lie fallow throughout the year and are falling into ruin.

Die Berge um Brezoi sind steil und bewaldet und werden als Allmende bewirtschaftet. Im Dorf wurde während des Kommunismus eine riesige Holzfabrik gebaut, ebenso Wohnblöcke für die neu hinzugezogenen Arbeiterfamilien. Nach dem Fall der Ceauşescu-Regierung wurde die Fabrik stillgelegt, und in einer Phase extremer Lebensmittelknappheit hielt man in den Höfen der Plattenbausiedlungen Schweine.

Die traditionellen Wohnhäuser haben kleine Gärten zur Eigenversorgung, mit Weinspalieren, Obstbäumen, Gemüsebeeten und Kartoffeln, mit Hühnern und Schweinen, ein oder zwei Kühen oder Ziegen.

Zur Melkzeit kommen ein paar Kühe ins Dorf gelaufen, aber lange nicht mehr so viele wie früher, sagt Michaela. Sie leitet die Dorfschule und den örtlichen Verein zur Kulturpflege und wirtschaftlichen Entwicklung. Der Verein ist fester Partner der Eco Nomadic School, einem europäischen Netzwerk, in dem lokale Projekte gegenseitig besucht werden und lokales Wissen auf translokalen Input und Austausch trifft. Myvillages ist seit 2010 dabei.

Seit einigen Jahren geht es in Brezoi um die Odai (Singular: Odaja), kleine, oft nur zu Fuß erreichbare Höfe in den nahe gelegenen Bergen, die in der Vergangenheit Teil der Subsistenzwirtschaft einzelner Familien waren. Eine Odaja besteht aus einem einfachen Haus mit ein oder zwei Schlafräumen, Streuobstwiese (meist Pflaumen), Grashängen, einer Scheune, eingezäuntem Gemüsegarten und spitz aufragenden Heuhaufen für die mitgenommenen Tiere. Odai werden im Sommer bewirtschaftet, jetzt jedoch liegen die meisten ganzjährig brach und verfallen.

Mircea, Gigi, Maria und Alexandra Onică nutzen ihre von Mirceas Vater errichtete Odaja nach wie vor und

B

Mircea, Gigi, Maria, and Alexandra Onică continue to use the Odaja built by Mircea's father, and have recently built a second one, whose future use is put up for discussion during workshops of the Eco Nomadic School. Can their traditional farming be continued without seeming museum-like? What economic strategies make sense for the next generation? Can additional income for local families be generated through rental or touristic use, without this straining the relationship to the village?

Those familiar with the Odaja life fascinate with their skills: they know how to quickly make a fire, are able to feed large groups with ease, and to slaughter without a noise. Mircea knows exactly who produces what in his mountain valley, be it cheese, wool, or the omnipresent plum schnapps Țuică. He also knows how to build an Odaja, starting with the felling of the trees, and how the resources of the forest can be managed collectively. The colleagues from the Eco Nomadic School contribute practical and conceptual ideas: for installing compost toilets or for tourist marketing.

The new Odaja is called "Starry Sky". The common house snake lives in its foundations. **KB**

haben in den vergangenen Jahren eine zweite gebaut, deren künftige Nutzung sie in den Workshops der Eco Nomadic School zur Diskussion stellen. Lässt sich deren traditionelle Bewirtschaftung fortführen, ohne museal zu wirken? Welche ökonomischen Strategien machen auch für die nächste Generation noch Sinn? Lässt sich durch Vermietung oder touristische Nutzung ein Zusatzeinkommen für die Familien des Orts generieren, ohne dass die Beziehung zum Dorf belastet wird?

Diejenigen, die mit dem Odaja-Leben vertraut sind, begeistern mit ihren Künsten: Sie verstehen sich auf schnelles Feuermachen, versorgen mit Leichtigkeit große Gruppen und können fast lautlos schlachten. Mircea weiß genau, wer in seinem Bergtal etwas herstellt und wie er das macht, sei es Käse, Wolle oder der allgegenwärtige Pflaumenbrand Țuică. Er weiß auch, wie man eine Odaja baut, vom Fällen der Bäume an, und wie sich die Waldbestände gemeinschaftlich bewirtschaften lassen. Die Kollegen von der Eco Nomadic School steuern praktische und konzeptionelle Ideen bei: zur Anlage von Komposttoiletten oder zur touristischen Vermarktung etwa.

Die neue Odaja heißt »Sternenhimmel«. In ihrem Steinfundament wohnt die übliche Hausschlange. **KB**

B

C

Company Drinks

Company: Movements, Deals and Drinks has started in spring 2014 as an art project in the shape of a community drinks enterprise, where art and business meet and merge. Revisiting the history of east Londoners going "hop picking" to the nearby Kent countryside, Company Drinks extends the collective harvest labour further, to complete a whole cycle of production, trade, and re-investment. This time we don't only pick, but keep the crop, make the drinks, and trade them directly.

The drinks are made with fruit and plants harvested, foraged, and gleaned across the London Borough of Barking and Dagenham, where Company Drinks has its home, and from farms in nearby Kent and Essex. **KB**

Company: Movements, Deals and Drinks begann im Frühjahr 2014 als Kunstprojekt: eine gemeinschaftlich organisierte Getränkefirma, in der Kunst und Geschäft zusammenkommen. Company Drinks greift zurück auf die Geschichte der Ost-Londoner, die im Sommer im nahen Kent Hopfenpflücken gingen, und erweitert die Erfahrung der gemeinsamen Erntearbeit zu der eines Kreislaufs aus Produktion, Handel und Investition. Dieses Mal gehen wir nicht nur Pflücken, sondern behalten die Ernte, machen die Getränke und handeln mit ihnen.

Die Getränke werden aus Früchten und Pflanzen hergestellt, die in den Londoner Bezirken Barking und Dagenham, wo Company Drinks zu Hause ist, und in Betrieben in Kent und Essex geerntet, gesammelt und aufgelesen werden. **KB**

ELDERFLOWER LEMONADE
Ingredients: Carbonated Water, English Beet Sugar, Lemon, Elderflower, Citric Acid
Best before: 12/2015
The flowers used to produce this lemonade were harvested during a community picking afternoon at Eastbrookend Country Park in Dagenham in late May 2015 – including Molly the horse.

C

C

CONCEPTUAL ART

A conversation between Ronald Van de Sompel (**R**) and Wapke Feenstra (**W**)

W: What Vito Acconci did in the late 1960s was physically to probe and explore artistic space, and assign the audience a different role in the process. He called it "stretching the space", testing the boundaries. I know the performances only from collected photos, Polaroids, and black-and-white videos in exhibitions. The question asked at that time – "How do we relate to one another and our living environment?" – is still as pressing as ever. The same goes for: "Who is my audience?".

R: I get the impression that, for you, although it is not always explicit, language is also important. I'm thinking of titles such as *Company Drinks, Tekenen in Vlassenbroek, Vorratskammer* …

W: … and *International Village Shop* and *Schnapsbar*. Yes, it means we can "play shops" or run a clandestine bar anywhere we want.

R: Language can be a metaphor, but basically what you are doing is searching for a concept via words. Language becomes an image.

W: Language is important. Personally, I find the ideas of Lawrence Weiner particularly appealing because they are socialist, because they're about sharing and producing images yourself. As soon as he writes a few discerning statements on a wall, the image evoked by the language in that space belongs just as much to you as to the thousands of passers-by who read it after you.

R: But it still seems to me that the general public looks at conceptual art, in its historical form, as the product of a tight approach that keeps repeating itself. What I find interesting about your projects is that the concepts are dynamic. There is no system that takes you straight from concept to realization. You keep asking new questions on the basis of the context. That also connects with form. And because you take Weiner as your example: when you buy one of his works, you get the concept,

Ein Gespräch zwischen Ronald Van de Sompel (**R**) und Wapke Feenstra (**W**)

W: Vito Acconci hat in den späten 1960er-Jahren den Raum der Kunst physisch ausgelotet und erkundet und im Zuge dessen auch dem Publikum eine andere Rolle zugewiesen. Er nannte das »Raumdehnung«, ein an die Grenzen Gehen. Ich kenne seine Performances nur von Fotos, Polaroidbildern und Schwarzweißvideos in Ausstellungen. Aber die Frage: »Wie verhalten wir uns zueinander und zu unserer belebten Umgebung?« ist so dringlich wie eh und je. Dasselbe gilt für die Frage: »Wer ist mein Publikum?«

> **R:** Ich habe den Eindruck, dass Sprache für euch ebenso wichtig ist, auch wenn das nicht immer so deutlich zum Ausdruck kommt. Ich denke dabei an Werktitel wie *Company*, *Tekenen in Vlassenbroek*, *Vorratskammer*, ...

W: ... und *International Village Shop* und *Schnapsbar*. Ja, das heißt dann, dass wir »Einkaufsladen spielen« oder eine illegale Bar betreiben können, wo immer es uns gefällt.

> **R:** Sprache kann metaphorisch sein, aber im Grunde sucht ihr doch mit Worten nach einem Konzept. Sprache wird zum Bild.

W: Sprache ist wichtig. Ich fühle mich besonders vom Denken Lawrence Weiners angezogen, weil es sozialistisch ist, weil es darin um Teilen geht und das eigene Erzeugen von Bildern. Er schreibt ein paar genaue Beobachtungen an eine Wand, und im selben Moment gehört uns das Bild, das die Sprache in diesem Raum hervorruft, ebenso wie den Tausenden anderen Passanten, die diese Sätze nach uns lesen.

> **R:** Dennoch scheint mir, dass die allgemeine Öffentlichkeit Konzeptkunst in ihrer historischen Form als das Ergebnis einer eng gefassten, unablässig wiederholten Herangehensweise wahrnimmt. Mich interessiert nun gerade an euren Projekten, dass deren Konzepte dynamisch sind. Es gibt kein System, das euch direkt vom Konzept zur Umsetzung führt. Ausgehend vom Kontext stellt ihr immer neue Fragen, auch was die Form angeht. Und da du gerade Weiner zum Vorbild nimmst: Wenn man eine seiner Arbeiten kauft, erhält man ein Konzept, aber

C

but the execution can be totally different. You can write the text in a straight line on a wall or make the words dance. All you are required to do is use a specific font. So the unique character of the artwork is breached, making way for a certain democratization. That relationship between the actual content of conceptual art and a flexible evolution towards form is carried much further in your projects. You are much more open in the way you engage with something that definitely starts out as a concept.

W: Of course you allow space for other people's ideas. And every context brings its own facets and visions. The question of "How can this ever acquire form?" is always at the back of my mind. Sometimes I share it, but I do try to stay in control. Sometimes, all of a sudden, everything falls into place. Or the turn of events is not what I had expected, but I can easily go along with it.

R: When I introduced your work to the management team at the Architecture Department of the Flemish Government in 2012, there were a few raised eyebrows. Cooperation, community participation and suchlike... and in rural areas? No-one said: "We do not think this is a good idea." It was more like: "We're not entirely sure about this."

W: I often feel irked by these doubts and the perception of the work as "strange". I want to tell people to look at their own history. Remind them that Dadaism dates from 1916, and that a shoemaker from Drachten participated in it.

R: True, and what is more, one of the first texts to explore the political status of participation was written by Walter Benjamin, *The Author as Producer*, which dates back to 1934. It seems to me that your projects can be understood precisely from that perspective of participation, of the process; and it is this inclusive aspect that creates a kind of reversal in what people do and do not "understand". It's bound up with involvement. You invoke a paradox when you say: "We work inclusively." By adopting a certain perspective you access a much broader group, people who might never come into contact with art in a direct way; on the other hand, that group is limited to people who actively participate. And they are still much more involved than the average observer.

W: You could say that there are different layers of participation; we mount exhibitions, participate in festivals, publish books. ... but you've got a point; if you don't get involved and just stand back and watch, nothing will happen. You need to broaden your vision and step into the narrative. That sense of exclusion is something that comes at you from the art world, with associations of "them and us". But our projects are intended for "us" as well. Of course, we exchange thoughts and ideas with the participants in the various places, but the aim is also to represent elsewhere and awaken another form of participation each time.

dessen Ausführung kann jedes Mal völlig anders ausfallen. Man kann den Text in einer geraden Zeile an die Wand schreiben oder die Wörter zum Tanzen bringen. Nur eine bestimmte Schriftart ist vorgegeben. Die Einzigartigkeit des Kunstwerks wird aufgebrochen, und es kommt zu einer Art Demokratisierung. Dieses Verhältnis zwischen dem eigentlichen Inhalt einer Konzeptarbeit und ihrer flexiblen Formfindung wird bei euren Projekten viel weiter getragen. Ihr seid viel offener in eurer Auseinandersetzung mit dem, was zunächst als Konzept klar bestimmt ist.

W: Natürlich geben wir den Vorstellungen anderer Menschen ihren Raum. Außerdem bringt jeder Kontext seine eigenen Facetten und Visionen mit sich. Die Frage: »Wie kann das jemals eine Form annehmen?« habe ich dabei ständig im Hinterkopf. Manchmal beziehe ich andere mit ein, versuche dabei aber stets, die Kontrolle zu behalten. Ab und zu geschieht es, dass alles wie von selbst an seinen richtigen Platz findet. Oder es entwickelt sich in eine Richtung, die ich nie erwartet hätte, aber ich kann das geschehen lassen.

R: Als ich eure Arbeit 2012 in der Architekturabteilung der Flämischen Regierung vorstellte, reagierten einige aus dem Leitungsgremium mit Stirnrunzeln. Kooperation, partizipierende Gemeinden … schön und gut, aber auf dem Land? Niemand sagte: »Wir halten das für keine gute Idee.« Es klang eher nach: »Wir sind uns da nicht so ganz sicher …«

W: Mich irritieren solche Zweifel oft, ebenso wie die Wahrnehmung unserer Arbeit als »seltsam«. Ich will Menschen ermutigen, sich ihre eigene Geschichte anzusehen. Ich will sie daran erinnern, dass Dada 1916 entstand und dass ein Schuster aus der friesischen Kleinstadt Drachten daran mitgewirkt hat.

R: Ganz richtig. Übrigens wurde einer der ersten Texte über den politischen Stellenwert von Partizipation in der Kunst, *Der Autor als Produzent,* auch schon 1934 von Walter Benjamin geschrieben.
Mir scheint, dass sich eure Projekte von der Partizipation, vom Prozess her erschließen. Und diese Einbeziehung der Betrachter hat offenbar auch zur Folge, dass die Leute ganz anders »verstehen« oder nicht verstehen. Eure Arbeit steht und fällt damit, dass andere sich darin einbringen. Ihr erzeugt eine paradoxe Situation, indem ihr sagt: »Es ist inklusive Kunst.« Mit eurer Herangehensweise sprecht ihr einerseits ein viel breiteres Publikum an, darunter Menschen, die sonst nie in unmittelbaren Kontakt mit Kunst kommen, andererseits beschränkt sich diese Gruppe eben auf diejenigen, die einfach mitmachen. Die werden sich dann auch viel stärker einbezogen fühlen als jeder durchschnittliche Betrachter.

W: Man könnte auch sagen, dass es verschiedene Schichten und Ebenen von Partizipation gibt. Wir machen Ausstellungen, beteiligen uns an Festivals, publizieren Bücher …, aber es stimmt schon: Wer sich nicht selbst einbringt, sich einfach zurücklehnt und zusieht, wird nichts erleben. Man muss schon seinen Horizont erweitern und sich auf die Erzählung einlassen. Dieses Gefühl, nicht dazuzugehören, schleicht sich ab und an aus der Kunstwelt herüber –

R: Would it be true to say that, over the years, you have concentrated more on representation to improve accessibility? You do, after all, apply a certain aestheticism.

C

W: Of course, you never stop thinking about representation. Often, time catches up with you or sends you down a different route. The search continues. For instance, since 2007, we have been developing *Village Produce Films* to showcase newly developed local products in the shop. These are short films that trace the origin and history of the items by showing actions and processes, with a minimum of commentary. Do you know the products from our shop? Like our *Potato Sleeper*? I've got some here. Would you like one with a green or a red handle?

R: I've got one already, Wapke. We use it in the kitchen for potatoes and onions.

W: Did you remember that they come from Neuenkirchen in Lüneburger Heath?

R: No, I didn't.

W: Never mind … and are made with Kunstverein Springhornhof, where we got together and talked about heathland potatoes, the felt industry, and the annual Kartoffelfest (potato festival). This is a bestseller and a tried and tested object. The prototype was designed with a workgroup that was specially set up for this product. When free felt comes from the factory at Soltau, a new batch is made by a seamstress in the village who has a sewing machine that is able to stitch thick felt. I'll now show you another local object, a very unusual one called the *Ittinger Egg*. The workgroup at Kartause Ittingen didn't want to make something useful. The big exception. This is made from hop bark fiber from their own hop gardens. This residue is put through the mincer at the butcher's and emerges as a sort of paper mache, which Kathrin used to make this product with the workgroup. Hidden inside each egg is a unique clay object, containing a memory. You have to break the egg to find out what it is.

R: Can you buy it?

W: Yes, you can, but hardly anyone has wanted one so far. We've only sold two. Because, of course, it's not much to look at and it's really quite pricey.

R: This looks more like an artwork in the traditional sense. It has a certain aesthetic – or anti-aesthetic – appeal, and the story is intriguing; the fact that you've got a secret and create a mystery that runs parallel with the history of the Carthusian Monastery. I think that, when you look at it from the art perspective, this would be more successful for classical collectors

Myvillages macht ja »da« was mit »denen«. Aber unsere Projekte richten sich eben auch an »uns«. Klar, wir arbeiten zusammen mit den Teilnehmern an den jeweiligen Orten. Unser Ziel ist aber stets auch, die Arbeiten anderswo präsentieren zu können und dort andere Formen von Partizipation in Gang zu bringen.

C

R: Könnte man sagen, dass ihr euch im Lauf der Jahre zunehmend mit der Präsentation eurer Projekte befasst habt, um sie allgemein zugänglicher zu machen? Immerhin kommt darin eine gewisse Ästhetik zur Geltung.

W: Natürlich beschäftigt uns unablässig die Frage, wie wir unsere Arbeiten darbieten sollen. Oft holt uns die Zeit ein oder zwingt uns, andere Wege zu gehen. Auch die Suche nach Formen und Formaten setzen wir fort. Beispielsweise entwickeln wir seit 2007 *Village Produce Films*, um für neue Dorfwaren in unserem Laden zu werben. Das sind Kurzfilme über Ursprung und Geschichte der Produkte. Sie zeigen die Arbeitsschritte und Entstehungsprozesse mit einem sparsamen Kommentar. Kennst du die Produkte in unserem Laden? Zum Beispiel unseren *Kartoffelbeutel*? Ich habe welche hier. Möchtest du einen mit grüner oder einen mit roter Schlaufe?

R: Ich habe schon einen, Wapke. Wir nutzen ihn in unserer Küche für Kartoffeln und Zwiebeln.

W: Erinnerst du dich noch, dass sie aus Neuenkirchen in der Lüneburger Heide kommen?

R: Nein.

W: Sie stammen vom Kunstverein Springhornhof, wo wir uns mit den Leuten vor Ort zusammengesetzt und über die Heidekartoffeln, die Filzverarbeitung und das jährliche Kartoffelfest unterhalten haben. Der *Kartoffelbeutel* ist ein echter Renner, außerdem ein geprüftes und getestetes Produkt. Ein Prototyp wurde mit einer eigens dafür gebildeten Arbeitsgruppe entwickelt. Immer wenn aus der Filzfabrik in Soltau Ware geliefert wird, fertigt eine Näherin eine neue Charge für uns an. Sie hat eine Nähmaschine, die mit dem dicken Filz zurechtkommt. Hier zeige ich dir eine andere Dorfware – ein ziemlich ungewöhnliches Produkt namens *Ittinger Ei*. Die Arbeitsgruppe in der Kartause Ittingen wollte nichts Nützliches erzeugen. Die große Ausnahme in unserem Laden. Das *Ittinger Ei* besteht aus Hopfenresten, die in der dortigen Brauerei anfallen. Diese Fasern werden beim Fleischer durch den Wolf gedreht und kommen als eine Art Papiermaché wieder heraus, das Kathrin verwendet hat, um mit der Arbeitsgruppe dieses Produkt zu gestalten. In jedem Ei verbirgt sich eine einzigartige Tonfigur, die eine Erinnerung enthält. Um herauszufinden, was drin ist, muss man das Ei ganz zerbrechen

R: Kann man es kaufen?

W: Ja, aber bisher wollte kaum jemand eines haben. Wir haben nur zwei verkauft. Weil es natürlich nicht viel hermacht und außerdem noch einen gesalzenen Preis hat.

or museums. There's an uncanniness about it, which it gets from the anti-aesthetic aspects, and which could prompt resistance. But I could get over that. (*Both laugh.*) And, as I said, I do use the potato bag. It is a fine, aesthetic object but it's closer to Arts and Crafts design than an art object in the traditional sense. (*We look at other shop items such as the* Frogbutter Spoon *and the* Ohner Linen Book. *Ronald buys a notebook.*)

W: Will you dare to write in it?

R: Yes, that could be a problem case. (*Laughing*) It's bizarre, because I've got loads of notebooks, but this one is – between quotes – a "work of art". I think I'll probably cherish it as a unique object. In itself, it is quite interesting, because it could be an example of both artwork and design. It is a functional object with a specific design; but "design" also exists as a much more comprehensive category than is suggested by the context in which we usually apply the term. Boris Groys wrote an essay entitled "The Obligation to Self-Design", in which he analyses the history of design, or to be more precise, the aestheticization of our lives as "godless people", in the sense intended by Nietzsche when he declared at the start of the 20th century that god was dead. Groys argued that as long as god was alive, the design of the soul was more important to people than the design of the body. However, the modern subject has a new obligation – the obligation to self-design – an aesthetic presentation of itself as an ethical subject. Essentially, "design" is taking the place of religion here. Groys says that the ethically inspired polemic against design, which was launched repeatedly in the 20th century – remember the "Ornament and Crime" lecture by Adolf Loos – can only be understood from that broader historical shift and this new definition of design as "self-design". This kind of polemic would be totally incomprehensible if it were directed solely at traditional applied arts.
It might seem like a detour that detracts us from our actual subject, but this discussion shows that we can no longer sidestep questions on the techniques and practice of "self-design".
The question of whether an object such as a notebook can be classified as design rather than as an autonomous artwork is greatly relativized in that context.

W: And where do you place the shop?

R: The way the shop is able to function also depends on the context; in a museum it may seem more logical for these items to be in the shop, but you can still display them behind glass in an exhibition space, where they are presented purely as aesthetic objects. In one way or another, I even suppose that this variant is an ideal interim form, possibly accompanied by information about the local origin and history.

R: Das sieht für mich mehr nach Kunst im traditionellen Sinn aus. Es hat eine gewisse ästhetische – oder anti-ästhetische – Anmutung, und die Geschichte dahinter finde ich spannend: dass man ein Geheimnis hat, mit irgendeiner Parallele zur Geschichte des Kartäuserklosters. Mir scheint, es könnte, aus einer Kunstperspektive betrachtet, eher bei klassischen Sammlern oder Museen Erfolg haben. Es ist etwas Unheimliches daran, weil es nicht schön aussehen will und dadurch mitunter Widerstand und Ablehnung hervorruft. Aber damit könnte ich leben. (*Beide lachen.*) Und, wie gesagt, ich nutze den *Kartoffelbeutel* wirklich. Der ist ein edler, ästhetischer Gegenstand, hat aber mehr mit Arts-and-Crafts-Kunsthandwerk zu tun als mit einem Kunstgegenstand im traditionellen Sinn. (*Wir sehen uns noch andere Dorfladenwaren an, darunter den* Froschbutterlöffel *und das* Ohner Leinenbuch. *Ronald kauft eines.*)

W: Wirst du es über dich bringen, in dieses Buch zu schreiben?

R: Ja, das könnte zum Problem werden. (*Lacht.*) Es ist schon komisch: Ich besitze jede Menge Notizbücher, aber nur dieses hier ist, in Anführungszeichen, ein »Kunstwerk«. Wahrscheinlich werde ich es in seiner Einzigartigkeit hüten wie meinen Augapfel. Interessant daran ist auch, dass es als Kunst ebenso wie als Design durchgehen könnte. Es ist ein funktionaler, zweckdienlich gestalteter Gegenstand, aber »Design« oder in Deutsch »Gestaltung« kann viel mehr umfassen als das, was wir dieser Kategorie üblicherweise zuordnen. Boris Groys hat einen Aufsatz mit dem Titel »Die Pflicht zum Selbstdesign« geschrieben. Darin analysiert er die Geschichte des Designs oder genauer der Ästhetisierung unseres Lebens als »gottlose« Menschen im Sinn von Nietzsches Verkündung am Beginn des 20. Jahrhunderts, dass Gott tot sei. Nach Groys war, so lange Gott lebte, die Gestaltung der Seele für die Menschen wichtiger als die des Körpers. Doch nun habe das moderne Subjekt eine neue Pflicht, nämlich die zum Selbstdesign beziehungsweise zur ästhetischen Aufbereitung seiner selbst als ethischen Subjekts. »Design« nimmt dieser Argumentation zufolge im Wesentlichen den Platz der Religion ein. Groys meint nun, dass die in mehreren Anläufen seit Beginn des 20. Jahrhunderts aufkommende ethisch motivierte Polemik gegen äußerliche Gestaltung – beispielsweise der Aufsatz »Ornament und Verbrechen« von Adolf Loos – nur vor dem Hintergrund dieser weit reichenden historischen Verschiebung und Neubestimmung von Gestaltung zu »Selbstdesign« verständlich wird. Diese Polemik richtet sich nicht nur gegen die traditionellen angewandten Künste. Dass ich jetzt mit dir über Design rede, mag wie eine Ablenkung von unserem eigentlichen Thema erscheinen, aber die Debatte verdeutlicht auch, dass wir Fragen nach der Technik und Praxis des »Selbstdesigns« nicht länger ausweichen können. Ob nun ein Gegenstand wie ein Notizbuch als Design und nicht als autonome Kunst einzustufen ist, relativiert sich in diesem Zusammenhang ganz erheblich.

W: Und wo würdest du den Dorfladen einordnen?

W: We teach attendants and volunteers about the story behind each object whenever an exhibition is held. And, of course, we have the *Village Produce Films*, which show the maker and the surroundings, and we are thinking about staging a play. Antje has already done a try-out. We want to see how the different narrative structures can come together, and whether that creates openings for an exciting new form of expression. A travelling theatre show? Or perhaps we could challenge some institutes to experiment with a series of exhibitions.

R: There is a lot of experimentation in this field at present. You can see an interplay evolving between the curatorial and learning departments in larger, classical museum structures. The history and context of items on display can also be communicated by the museum staff.

W: Yes, that's right. In Leipzig we found out first-hand that this can work. The museum tours that are held there at the weekend always end at the *International Village Show*, where visitors hear more about the villages that feature in the exhibition. Then the shop opens and the new items are introduced. People get an opportunity to buy products and, what's more, they can get schnapps from under the counter.

Ronald Van de Sompel is an independent curator who has worked in various museums including M–Museum Leuven, Museum of Fine Arts, and S.M.A.K. in Ghent (BE), and art centres such as BALTIC Centre for Contemporary Art in Gateshead (UK). For several years he was also employed as an advisor on commissioned art by the Architecture Department of the Flemish Government in Brussels. He is currently a research and symposium associate at "Oslo Pilot" (NO), a two-year project which explores the role of art in public space. He lives in Brussels.

R: Wie der Dorfladen funktioniert, hängt auch vom Kontext ab: In einem Museum könnte sich die Frage aufdrängen, warum diese Waren nicht eher im Shop des Museums angeboten werden. Aber ihr könntet sie auch hinter Glas im Ausstellungsraum selbst zeigen, wo sie dann als rein ästhetische Objekte dastünden. Das schiene mir in mancher Hinsicht als eine ideale Zwischenform, vielleicht noch ergänzt um Informationen zur jeweiligen Geschichte und lokalen Herkunft.

W: Wir erzählen Aufsehern und Praktikanten vor jeder neuen Ausstellung die Geschichten der jeweiligen Ladenangebote. Außerdem stellen die *Village Produce Films* Erzeugerinnen und Erzeuger in ihrem Umfeld vor. Wir denken auch darüber nach, ein Theaterstück zu inszenieren. Antje hat schon einen Versuch damit gemacht. Wir wollen herausfinden, wie sich die verschiedenen Erzählstrukturen verbinden lassen und ob sich daraus Möglichkeiten für spannende neue Ausdrucksformen ergeben. Ein Wandertheater vielleicht? Oder vielleicht können wir ein paar Institutionen dazu bringen, mit einer Ausstellungsreihe zu experimentieren.

R: Auf diesem Gebiet wird zurzeit vieles ausprobiert. Es zeichnet sich auch eine engere Zusammenarbeit zwischen den kuratorischen und pädagogischen Abteilungen in größeren, klassischen Museen ab. Geschichte und Kontext von Ausstellungsobjekten können auch die Angestellten der Museen vermitteln.

W: Das stimmt. In Leipzig haben wir gesehen, dass das funktionieren kann. An Samstagen und Sonntagen enden die Führungen dort immer im Gartenhaus der *International Village Show*, wo die Besucher mehr über die in der Ausstellung vorkommenden Dörfer erfahren. Danach öffnet der Laden, und die neuen Waren werden vorgestellt. Die Besucher können Produkte kaufen, und wer möchte, kriegt unterm Ladentisch auch noch einen Schnaps.

Ronald Van de Sompel ist Kurator. Er hat unter anderem am M-Museum Leuven, am Museum voor Schone Kunsten und am Stedelijk Museum voor Actuele Kunst (S.M.A.K.) in Gent (BE) gearbeitet, außerdem für Kunsthallen wie das BALTIC Centre for Contemporary Art in Gateshead (GB). Er war mehrere Jahre Berater für Auftragswerke an der Abteilung für Architektur der Flämischen Regierung in Brüssel. Zurzeit arbeitet er als Forscher und Symposiumsberater für das zweijährige Projekt »Oslo Pilot« (NO), in dem es um die Rolle der Kunst im öffentlichen Raum geht. Er lebt in Brüssel.

C

JOSA MOTOR

C

Cuevas del Becerro

Andalucía, ES

Population: 1,847

In Madrid I got to know two men from the union of Spanish farmers and livestock breeders; I contact them when I am invited to an exhibition at the Centro Andaluz de Arte Contemporáneo in Sevilla and am on the search for Andalusian farmers. The union members might live in rough valleys, but they are well connected and send me to their Compañero Juan García in Cuevas del Becerro in the Province of Málaga. Juan introduces me to the leader of the Sinti of Málaga, and he takes me to the young men in the greenhouse, who have started cultivating vegetables in order to live in the village and not have to seek work abroad like their friends, to a mason who now breeds snails, and to the cooperative, the biggest business in the village. If someone is shy, Juan stands next to them.

Juan and his family live in a narrow house in the centre of the village. He and his brothers and sisters take turns caring for their ill mother. She mostly eats gazpacho. Juan is a beekeeper, and his daughter, Ana, and son-in-law have also bought hives: "A dignified way to earn one's living," says Juan. The bee autochthonous to Africa and southern Spain is very aggressive.

The cooperative of Cuevas del Becerro stores and sells grain for small farmers, it runs a petrol station, and above all it presses oil. As we are standing surrounded by Juan's olives at one point, the famous song "Andaluces de Jaén" is sung, with mobile phone accompaniment, and we all cry a bit. I learn that, at the end of the Second World War, when Europe was freed from Fascism, the Spanish socialists presumed and hoped in vain that Spain would also be liberated. In the evening, we watch Tele Venezuela and Juan falls asleep on the sofa. **AS**

Einwohner: 1.847

In Madrid habe ich zwei Männer von der Gewerkschaft der spanischen Landwirte und Viehzüchter kennengelernt; an sie wende ich mich, als ich zu einer Ausstellung in das Centro Andaluz de Arte Contemporáneo in Sevilla eingeladen werde und auf der Suche nach andalusischen Bauern bin. Die Gewerkschafter mögen in rauen Tälern leben, aber sie sind gut verbunden und schicken mich zu ihrem Compañero Juan García in Cuevas del Becerro in der Provinz Málaga. Juan stellt mich dem Oberhaupt der Sinti von Málaga vor, er nimmt mich mit zu den jungen Männern im Gewächshaus, die mit dem Anbau von Gemüse begonnen haben, um nicht im Ausland nach Arbeit suchen zu müssen wie ihre Freunde, zu einem Maurer, der jetzt Schnecken züchtet, und zur Kooperative, dem größten Unternehmen des Dorfes. Wenn jemand schüchtern ist, stellt Juan sich neben ihn.

Juan und seine Familie wohnen in einem schmalen Haus mitten im Dorf. Mit seinen Brüdern und Schwestern wechselt er sich ab bei der Pflege der kranken Mutter. Meistens isst sie Gazpacho. Juan ist Imker, und auch seine Tochter Ana und die Schwiegersöhne haben Bienenstöcke gekauft: »Eine würdige Art, sich das Leben zu verdienen«, sagt Juan. Die afrikanisch-südspanische Biene ist sehr aggressiv.

Die Kooperative von Cuevas del Becerro lagert und verkauft Getreide für die Kleinbauern, sie betreibt eine Tankstelle und vor allem presst sie das Öl. Als wir einmal in Juans Oliven stehen, wird das berühmte Lied »Andaluces de Jaén« gesungen, mit Handybegleitung, und wir alle weinen ein bisschen. Ich lerne, dass die spanischen Sozialisten am Ende des Zweiten Weltkriegs, als Europa vom Faschismus befreit wurde, vergeblich vermutet und gehofft hatten, auch Spanien würde befreit werden. Am Abend gucken wir Tele Venezuela und Juan schläft auf dem Sofa ein. **AS**

→ ICH BIN GERNE BAUER

Dedemsvaart

Overijssel, NL

Population: 12,360

Einwohner: 12.360

People who live in Dedemsvaart work, for example, in poultry farming, door production, or the transport sector, or commute to Zwolle.

The place where Dedemsvaart is located was uninhabited until the end of the 18th century. A large moor: impassable and unliveable. There were only a few spots at which a route to the north was possible.

The landscape that we see today formed after the land was drained and the peat excavated; it lies one and a half metres below its previous level. Some people got rich with peat excavation; their splendid houses stand along Moerheimstraat. The ground that remained was quite suitable for professional gardening. The owner of one such gardening business was the father of Mien Ruys, a renowned landscape and garden architect; the garden behind her parents' house in Dedemsvaart served her as a field of experimentation throughout her life, and is now a national garden monument, tended and kept alive by gardeners and volunteers. With Gerrit Rietveld, Mien Ruys shared the desire to make good design accessible for many. She developed the Confectie Borders, small standard gardens as inspiration for people who did not have much experience or the money for a landscape architect. She used railway sleepers in garden design and invented the washed concrete slab. She was not interested in drawing from plentiful resources, but rather in experimentation: a shade garden, a yellow garden, gardens in which the strongest plants survive or those best adaptable to the soil. **AS**

Wer in Dedemsvaart lebt, arbeitet zum Beispiel in der Geflügelproduktion, der Türenproduktion oder in der Transportbranche, oder er pendelt nach Zwolle.

Dort, wo Dedemsvaart liegt, lebten bis zum Ende des 18. Jahrhunderts keine Menschen. Ein großes Moor, unpassierbar und unbewohnbar. Wenige Stellen nur gab es, an denen der Weg in den Norden möglich war.

Die Landschaft, die wir heute sehen, hat sich gebildet, nachdem das Land entwässert und der Torf abgebaut waren; sie liegt eineinhalb Meter unter dem früheren Niveau. Einige Menschen sind reich geworden mit dem Torfabbau; ihre prächtigen Häuser stehen entlang der Moerheimstraat. Der Boden, der übrig blieb, war gut geeignet für den professionellen Gartenbau. Der Besitzer eines solchen Gartenbauunternehmens war der Vater von Mien Ruys, einer berühmten Landschafts- und Gartenarchitektin; der Garten hinter dem Haus ihrer Eltern in Dedemsvaart diente ihr ein Leben lang als Experimentierfeld und ist jetzt ein nationales Gartendenkmal, betreut und am Leben gehalten von Gärtnern und Freiwilligen. Mien Ruys teilte mit Gerrit Rietveld den Wunsch, gute Gestaltung für viele zugänglich zu machen. Sie entwickelte die Confectie Borders, kleine Standardgärten als Anregung für Menschen, die nicht viel Erfahrung und nicht das Geld für einen Landschaftsarchitekten hatten. Sie nutzte Bahnschwellen in der Gartengestaltung und erfand die Waschbetonplatte. Sie war nicht daran interessiert, aus dem Vollen zu schöpfen, sondern am Experiment: ein Schattengarten, ein gelber Garten, Gärten, in denen die Pflanzen wachsen, die sich durchsetzen oder die dem Boden am besten angepasst sind. **AS**

→ GOODS

CHARLEY BIGGS'
CHICKEN n' SAUCE!
"KICKIN' IT UP"
THR
BYERS
GEN
BYERS
303-822-5325
SIGN UP TODAY!
Byers General Store Customer Rewards
www.byersgeneral.com
The card that rewards you when you shop!
Rewards Card
Welcom

FTWAY
ERAL
STORE
ace Fans
isit
ew
vice
li
Garden Center
Propane
Fire Wood
912·XVK

The I-70 Scout
Strasburg, CO
Phone: (303)622-9796

D

Deer Trail

D

Arapahoe County, Colorado, US

Population: 600

Every day, dozens of grain-filled wagons trundle across the rails, heading for Denver or the south. With petrol pumps, saloons, a high school, and sports facilities, the little town of Deer Trail plays an important role in the region.

The rodeo has been a tradition here since 1869, and Deer Trail claims to be the very first place ever to have organized one on US soil. A rattlesnake has just been run over on the rodeo terrain. The snake is venomous, so its head gets chopped off and is buried deeper than the body. Cowboys and cowgirls enter the ring and rope cattle. They are followed by a green rodeo clown and winners and losers.

On a windy day, we boarded a four-wheel drive truck and headed for Jolly Ranch. We drove across prairies and the last stretch of road is just a dirt track. We were still in Deer Trail when we reached our destination. The ranch continues to Highway 36, which cuts through a ghost town called Last Chance. In the distance, on the horizon, is a large reservoir that supplies the ranch with water. While the horses were being saddled, Cara Jolly explained that her family rides among the cattle every other day. They have many quarter-horses and more than 400 head of stock, and they want to avoid problems at all costs, so they observe the animals gently and monitor them for diseases, injuries, and weight gain. Occasionally they quickly rope a steer or drive some cattle towards the ranch. Cara practices her rodeo techniques in the farmyard, on barrels, dummies, and young calves. She's pretty good at it, too; she won the junior championship not that long ago. **WF**

Einwohner: 600

Jeden Tag rumpeln Dutzende Waggons voller Getreide über die Gleise nach Süden oder in Richtung Denver. Mit Tankstellen, Saloons, einer High School und Sporteinrichtungen spielt das Dorf Deer Trail eine wichtige Rolle in der Gegend.

Die Tradition des Rodeo-Reitens reicht bis ins Jahr 1869 zurück, und Deer Trail erhebt den Anspruch, das allererste Rodeo auf dem Boden der Vereinigten Staaten veranstaltet zu haben. In der Rodeo-Arena wurde soeben eine Klapperschlange überfahren. Da die Schlange giftig ist, wird ihr Kopf abgeschlagen und tiefer vergraben als der Körper. Cowboys und Cowgirls reiten auf den Platz und fangen Kälber mit Lassos ein, gefolgt von einem grünen Rodeo-Clown und sämtlichen Verlierern und Gewinnern.

Am nächsten Tag steigen wir in einen Geländewagen und fahren zur Jolly-Ranch. Der Weg führt durch die Prärie, und der letzte Teil der Straße ist nur noch ein Feldweg. Als wir unser Ziel erreichen, sind wir immer noch im Dorf Deer Trail. Das Land der Ranch reicht bis zum Highway Nr. 36, der mitten durch ein Geisterdorf namens Last Chance führt. In der Ferne, am Horizont, sehen wir ein großes Auffangbecken, das die Ranch mit Wasser versorgt. Während die Pferde gesattelt werden, erklärt Cara Jolly, dass sie und ihre Eltern jeden zweiten Tag mit den Tieren in die Prärie reiten. Sie besitzen etliche Quarter Horses und mehr als 400 Rinder, und sie wollen unter allen Umständen Problemen vorbeugen. Daher beobachten sie die Herde sorgsam und achten auf erste Anzeichen von Krankheiten, Verletzungen oder Gewichtszunahme. Ab und zu fangen sie einen Stier flugs mit dem Lasso ein oder treiben ein paar Rinder zur Ranch. Auf dem Hof übt Cara ihre Rodeo-Technik mit Fässern, einer Dummy-Kuh und kleinen Kälbern. Sie kann das schon ziemlich gut. Vor einiger Zeit hat sie das Jugendturnier gewonnen. **WF**

→ FARMERS & RANCHERS

D

E

Ekumfi Ekrawfo Central Region, GH

Population: ca. 20,000 across three villages

Einwohner: etwa 20.000 in drei Dörfern

An important road leads from Accra westwards, along the coast, but without providing a view of the sea, in the direction of Ivory Coast. People driving to Ekumfi Ekrawfo take one of the first turnings into the interior of the country; a road that ultimately extends as far as Kumasi and over which the vehicles of presidential candidates travel when there is an election campaign. The large villages that belong to Ekrawfo begin behind the small river, and here is Everlove the Queen Mother, Nana Esi Nisin VIII.

The hierarchy of the dignitaries and bearers of responsibility in the villages is broad, with functions that we could translate as chiefs, chieftains, and elders; the Queen Mother is powerful, and revered far beyond her village. When Everlove is in Ekrawfo, she is not permitted to go shopping; the things she needs must be brought to her. When protocol is supposed to be followed, she sits on a special chair and her feet stand in wide, leather sandals on an animal hide. Dignitaries never speak in public themselves; they have a linguist and speak and listen through their linguists, even if everyone is standing close to one another: Individuals who would like to say something say it to the linguist; the linguist says it to the Queen Mother, chieftains, and elders, and he passes their answer back. When the linguist addresses the chiefs, he exposes his shoulder. Guests bring schnapps with them, and this schnapps is poured onto the ground. It does not matter that we are not aware of this and have therefore forgotten the schnapps; the protocol is well thought through, but pragmatic, and it is rich in individuals. Razak, who came with us, is quickly sent to fetch some from the shop. **AS**

Eine wichtige Straße führt von Accra westwärts, der Küste entlang, doch ohne dass man das Meer sehen könnte, in Richtung Elfenbeinküste. Wer nach Ekumfi Ekrawfo fährt, nimmt einen der ersten Abzweige ins Landesinnere; eine Straße, die am Ende bis Kumasi reicht und über die die Wagen der Präsidentschaftskandidaten fahren, wenn Wahlkampf ist. Hinter dem kleinen Fluss beginnen die großen Dörfer, die zu Ekrawfo gehören, und hier ist Everlove die Queenmother, Nana Esi Nisin VIII.

Die Hierarchie der Würden- und Verantwortungsträger in den Dörfern ist breit angelegt, mit Ämtern, die wir als Chiefs, Häuptlinge und Älteste übersetzen könnten; die Queenmother ist mächtig und angesehen weit über ihr Dorf hinaus. Wenn Everlove in Ekrawfo ist, darf sie nicht einkaufen gehen; das, was sie braucht, muss ihr gebracht werden. Wenn dem Protokoll gefolgt werden soll, sitzt sie auf einem besonderen Stuhl und ihre Füße stehen in ledernen breiten Sandalen auf einem Fell. Würdenträger sprechen in der Öffentlichkeit nicht selbst, sie haben einen Linguisten und sprechen und hören durch ihren Linguisten, auch wenn alle nahe beieinander stehen: Wer etwas sagen möchte, sagt es dem Linguisten; der Linguist sagt es der Queenmother, den Häuptlingen und Ältesten, und er gibt ihre Entgegnung zurück. Wenn der Linguist sich an die Chiefs wendet, entblößt er die Schulter.

Gäste bringen Schnaps mit, und dieser Schnaps wird auf den Boden gegossen. Es macht nichts, dass wir das nicht wissen und also den Schnaps vergessen haben; das Protokoll ist durchdacht, aber pragmatisch, und es ist reich an Personen. Razak, der mit uns gekommen ist, wird schnell zum Einkaufen ins Geschäft geschickt. **AS**

→ GOODS

SCHNAPPS

ELSE-WHERE

Launches, events, and exhibitions that took place in parallel to the *International Village Show* in Leipzig. / Präsentationen und Ausstellungen, die gleichzeitig mit der *International Village Show* in Leipzig stattfanden.

2014

Las bienvenidas están in todas partes / Greeting is everywhere, solo Antje Schiffers, CAAC, Sevilla (ES), curator / Kurator: Manuel Olveira.

Trade Show, at / bei Agrocité, R-Urban by / von atelier d'architecture autogérée, Colombes (FR), curators / Kuratoren: Kathrin Böhm, Gavin Wade.

Umeå Skafferi / Umeå Pantry, Survival Kit Festival, European Cultural City 2014, curators / Kuratoren: Cecilia Andersson, Sujy Lee, Bildmuseet Umeå (SE).

Odaja Workshop, Brezoi (RO), as part of / im Rahmen von Eco Nomadic School.

Farmers & Ranchers, The Feed Store, M12 Studio, Byers, Colorado (US), curator / Kurator: Kirsten Stoltz.

Company Drinks Bar, Frieze Art Fair, London (GB), with / mit Create London.

Farmers & Ranchers, solo Wapke Feenstra, Fries Museum, Leeuwarden (NL), curator / Kurator: Saskia Bak.

2015

Farmers & Ranchers: Growing Up in Changing Landscapes, television broadcast / Fernsehausstrahlung, Fryslân DOK (NL).

Sector Primario, MUSAC, León (ES), curator / Kurator: Manuel Olveira.

A–Z The Marzona Collection / A–Z Sammlung Marzona; Q–Questions and (various) Answers, Formen des Festlegens, Hamburger Bahnhof, Berlin (DE), curators / Kuratoren: Daniela Bystron, Lisa Marei Schmidt.

Grow It Yourself, Parco Arte Vivente (PAV), Torino (IT), curator / Kurator: Marco Scotini.

Made in Zvizzchi – Meschdunarodnij Celski Magasin, Archstoyanie Festival 2015, Ugra Parc (RU).

Höfer Spitze, launch and shop, community hall / Warenvorstellung im Dorfgemeindehaus, Höfen (DE).

A Schelde Riverscape, book launch / Buchvorstellung, Scheepvaartmuseum Baasrode, Dendermonde (BE), curator / Kurator: Ronald Van de Sompel.

Fufu Bowls, product launch with / Warenvorstellung mit Nana Esi Nisin VIII, Ekumfi Ekrawfo and / und Accra Open Stock Market (GH), curator / Kurator: Susanne Altmann.

Company Drinks Bar, Frieze Art Fair, London (GB).

Company Drinks, Transformation Marathon, Serpentine Galleries, London (GB).

Made in Zvizzchi – Meschdunarodnij Celski Magasin, 6. Moscow Biennale of Contemporary Art, Bogorodskoe Exhibition Hall (RU), curator / Kurator: Georgy Nikich.

2016

Myvillages & Company Drinks, book launch and bar / Buchvorstellung und Bar, Culture Now series, Institute of Contemporary Art (ICA), London (GB).

International Village Shop, Kunsthuis SYB, Beetsterzwaag (NL).

Frieze Art Fair, London

Ekumfi Ekrawfo

Club, Zvizzchi

E

International Village Shop, with / mit La Libera Scuola del Giardino, Parco Arte Vivente (PAV), Torino (IT), curators / Kuratoren: Orietta Brombin, Marco Scotini.

Hopping Afternoon, with / mit Company Drinks, Hoppers Hospital, Five Oak Green, Kent (GB).

Foreign Pickers, film launch / Filmvorstellung, Delfina Foundation, Politics of Food Programme, London (GB).

Foreign Pickers, film screening / Filmvorführung, Art in Romney Marshes, Kent (GB).

Twisted Bugle Launch, Community Centre, Ballykinlar / Ballykinler (GB).

Company Drinks Bar, Frieze Art Fair, London (GB).

Foodscape, Arts Maebashi, Maebashi (JP), curator / Kurator: Fumihiko Sumitomo.

Confectie Boxes Launch, Tuinen Mien Ruys, Dedemsvaart (NL).

Company Drinks, presentation, tasting, and apple picking / Vorstellung, Verkostung und Apfelpflücken, with / mit Kathrin Böhm, Kunst- und Kulturverein Alte Schule Baruth (DE).

MUSAC, Léon

Fries Museum, Leeuwarden

PAV, Torino

CAAC, Sevilla

Dorfgemeindehaus, Höfen

Bogorodskoe Exhibition Hall, Moscow

EVERYDAY ART SPACE

This text was written in response to Lane Relyea's book *Your Everyday Art World.* (Boston: MIT Press, 2013).

Our work sometimes looks dangerously close to the everyday. We make sauerkraut. We dig clay. We paint a shop sign.

Lane Relyea (p. 73):

What the everyday provides is a realm not reducible either to institutional codes on the one hand or to purely private experience on the other; the everyday is neither as over-socialized as proponents of institutional critique make the museum out to be nor as under-socialized as aesthetic theory describes the encounters with artwork. Indeed when it comes to the question of art's transcendence, the everyday context allows one to elude both the Scylla of too much belief and the Charybdis of too much scepticism.

As a place for artistic practice, the everyday has no art production infrastructure as such. There is no gallery manager, no exhibition schedule, no reception desk, no press release, and no white walls, but there is undoubtedly plenty of production, public space, specialisms, social rituals, annual calendars, and modes of communication. Working within the everyday realm means being moored, making connections, gaining a certain trust, opening up spaces, linking, and networking. Myvillages are proud of the many connections we have made, maintained, and extended over the years, our understanding of and artistic response to the local everyday as a starting point, our fairly confident, critically discursive minds, and our stories from travelling the rural.

Lane Relyea's sharp critique of the current global cultural networking phenomenon is at first unnerving, as it accuses cultural practitioners of having become caught up in a self-perpetuating networking mechanism that results in exclusivity for those who are hypermobile and well-connected, rather than facilitating horizontal accessibility. Relyea reminds readers of the more political motivations that led to the establishment of peer-led networks, collaborative and decentralized working structures, and self-organized frameworks. He describes this hyper-connectivity as a new status quo within the arts – the domain of the well-connected, constantly mobile, discursively up-to-date, and at

E

Der Text entstand als Stellungnahme zu Lane Relyeas Buch, *Your Everyday Art World*, MIT Press 2013.

Unsere Arbeit sieht dem Alltäglichen manchmal gefährlich ähnlich. Wir machen Sauerkraut. Wir graben nach Lehm. Wir malen ein Ladenschild.

Lane Relyea (S. 73):

»Mit dem Alltag haben wir einen Lebensbereich zur Verfügung, der sich nicht auf institutionelle Codes einerseits und rein privates Erleben andererseits reduzieren lässt. Der Alltag ist weder so übersozialisiert, wie die Wortführer der Institutionenkritik das Museum darstellen, noch so untersozialisiert, wie die ästhetische Theorie die Begegnung mit Kunstwerken beschreibt. Wenn es um die Frage der Transzendenz von Kunst geht, ermöglicht uns der alltägliche Kontext sogar, der Scylla von zu viel Glauben und der Charybdis von zu viel Skepsis zu entgehen.«

Als Ort für das künstlerische Schaffen bietet der Alltag der Kunstproduktion keine Infrastruktur im engeren Sinn. Es gibt darin keinen Galeristen, keinen Ausstellungskalender, keinen Empfangstresen, keine Pressemitteilung und wenig weiße Wände. Aber es gibt unzweifelhaft jede Menge Produktion, Spezialistentum, öffentlichen Raum, gesellschaftliche Rituale, Jahreskalender und Kommunikationsformen. Im Bereich des Alltags zu arbeiten heißt ankern, Verbindungen knüpfen, ein gewisses Maß an Vertrauen gewinnen, Räume erschließen, sich verbinden und vernetzen. Myvillages ist stolz auf die vielen Kontakte, die wir über die Jahre geknüpft, aufrechterhalten und erweitert haben; stolz auf unser Verständnis von und unseren künstlerischen Umgang mit dem Alltag als Ausgangspunkt; stolz auf unsere einigermaßen selbstbewussten, kritischen, diskursiven Geister; stolz auf unsere Geschichten von den Reisen über Land.

Daher irritiert uns Lane Relyeas scharfe Kritik des gegenwärtigen Phänomens globaler kultureller Vernetzung im ersten Moment, denn er wirft den Kulturschaffenden vor, dass sie in einem Netzwerkmechanismus gefangen sind, der zum reinen Selbstläufer geworden ist und sich ausschließlich an die hypermobilen und gut vernetzten Zeitgenossen unter uns wendet, statt horizontale Zugänglichkeit anzustreben. Relyea erinnert uns daran, dass die Gründung von Netzwerken unter Gleichgesinnten, die kooperativen und dezentralisierten Arbeitsweisen und die selbst organisierten Strukturen ursprünglich politischen Anliegen entsprachen. Er beschreibt die Hyper-Konnektivität als einen neuen Status quo in den Künsten – einen Herrschaftsbereich der gut vernetzten, immer mobilen, zugleich

the same time locally engaged artist or curator. He calls for networked cultural practice to remain critical and politically engaged, and not be swallowed up by what has become a general global, sociocultural phenomenon as a result of the dynamics of digitalization and globalization, where everyone becomes an ever-more-spread-out and decentred actor – or "omnivore", as he puts it.

E

A networked society in which everyone can adapt supposedly active relations to production and the imposed concept of the "pro-sumer" (marketer-speak for professional or "producerly" consumers) dilutes any self-driven collectivity. Relyea warns that the current networking craze might be too embedded in purely social flows and therefore shift away from the architectonic and the spatial, which are crucial in achieving and practising collectivity.

For Myvillages, the everyday has always had a place and a particular public, and the way we work from within this place is concrete and collective. New networks emerge locally through the set-up of projects as collaborative productions, and different local projects start to connect to one another over time as a result of how we work. The network has different depths and frequencies, and the current *International Village Show* is its two-year-long visual, social, and spatial centre in a Myvillages-style attempt to action the everyday as artists – whether that everyday is located rurally or in the art world. It is where sauerkraut meets painting, clay digging meets conceptual art, and artists meet farmers, and everybody can decide how long they want to stay. **KB**

Lane Relyea is an associate professor and chair of the Department of Art Theory and Practice at Northwestern University, and the editor-in-chief of *Art Journal*.

aber vor Ort engagierten Künstlerinnen und Kuratoren, die diskursiv immer auf dem neuesten Stand sind. Relyea fordert ein vernetztes Kulturschaffen, das sein kritisches Bewusstsein und sein politisches Engagement wahrt – das sich nicht von einem inzwischen globalen soziokulturellen Phänomen im Gefolge der Digitalisierung und Globalisierung verschlucken lässt, das uns zu immer breiter aufgestellten und immer weiter dezentrierten Akteuren macht: zu »Allesfressern«, wie er es ausdrückt.

Eine vernetzte Gesellschaft, in der jeder ein vermeintlich aktives Verhältnis zur Produktion entwickeln kann und in der uns das Konzept des »Prosumenten« (Marketing-Sprache für berufsmäßige, produzentenaffine Konsumenten) aufgezwungen wird, verwässert jegliche selbst gesteuerte Form von Gemeinschaft. Relyea warnt uns, dass auch die gegenwärtige Vernetzungshysterie bald in einen rein geselligen Verkehr eingebettet sein könnte und sich vom Architektonischen und Räumlichen abkoppelt, die für das Schaffen und Arbeiten in Gemeinschaft beide unerlässlich sind.

Für Myvillages hatte der Alltag immer einen Ort und eine spezifische Öffentlichkeit, und unsere Arbeitsweise von diesem Ort aus ist konkret und kollektiv. Neue Netzwerke entstehen vor Ort durch die Art, in der Projekte als Gemeinschaftsproduktionen auf den Weg gebracht werden, und mit der Zeit verknüpfen sich durch unser Vorgehen einzelne lokale Projekte untereinander. Das Netzwerk hat verschiedene Tiefen und Frequenzen, und die *International Village Show* ist sein auf zwei Jahre angelegtes visuelles, soziales und räumliches Zentrum. Sie ist unser Versuch, nach Myvillages-Art den Alltag als Künstlerinnen in Bewegung zu bringen, ob dieser Alltag nun auf dem Land oder in der Kunstwelt stattfindet. Die *International Village Show* ist der Ort, an dem Sauerkraut und Malerei, Tongrube und Konzeptkunst, Künstlerinnen und Bauern einander begegnen, und es bleibt allen überlassen, wie lange sie dabei sein wollen. **KB**

Lane Relyea ist Associate Professor und Leiter des Department of Art Theory and Practice an der Northwestern University in Evanston, Illinois, außerdem Chefredakteur des *Art Journal*.

Farmers & Ranchers

F

We stop off at a bison farm on the plains of Colorado. Standing at a rusty fence, I catch sight of brown dots in the distance. Seldom have I seen such wide expanses of parched and arid land and still heard people talk about food production. Bison are again being bred on the prairies, now for the menus of classy restaurants.

The Rocky Mountains in the distance look familiar, reminding me of the scenic backgrounds in the Westerns and TV series of my youth. A Dutch immigrant, a butcher from the village of Simla, tells me that real arrows, bullets and buckles from army uniforms are found on this land. He has been running a butcher's business with his wife and son for 20 years. They are still something of a novelty here. Europeans started arriving 200 years ago, all the way from the Balkans to Ireland – but not the Netherlands. This place is not like Wisconsin, the Promised Land for the famous Frisian dairy cow; it is Angus and Hereford that thrive here. The mixed breed with the white face is popular; then there are the pale and haughty Longhorns with their random markings. The ranches claim that beef from their cattle makes the best hamburgers in the United States. They prove it with a barbecue. The landscape around the ranch is associated worldwide with the excitement of rodeo scenes from movies. Yet, the younger generation in this part of the United States do not consider a career in agriculture "cool".

Wir halten bei einer Bisonfarm auf den High Plains in Colorado. An einem rostigen Zaun stehend, bemerke ich in der Ferne braune Punkte. Selten zuvor habe ich so endlose Weiten verdorrten, trockenen Landes gesehen, und doch höre ich, dass Menschen hier Nahrung produzieren. Für die Speisekarten hochpreisiger Restaurants werden in der Prärie wieder Bisons gezüchtet.

Die Rocky Mountains in der Ferne kommen mir bekannt vor. Sie erinnern mich an die Schauplätze der Western und der Fernsehserien meiner Jugend. Ein niederländischer Einwanderer, ein Metzger aus dem Dorf Simla, erzählt mir, dass man auf diesem Land noch echte Pfeile, Gewehrkugeln und Gürtelschnallen von Armeeuniformen finden kann. Er betreibt mit seiner Frau und seinem Sohn seit zwanzig Jahren eine Metzgerei. Sie sind immer noch eine Art Kuriosität. Vor 200 Jahren kamen die ersten Europäer hierher. Sie stammten aus allen möglichen Gegenden von Irland bis zum Balkan, aber nicht aus den Niederlanden. Denn wir sind nicht in Wisconsin, dem gelobten Land für die berühmte friesische Milchkuh. Hier gedeihen Angus- und Hereford-Rinder. Die Kreuzung mit dem weißen Gesicht ist beliebt, außerdem gibt es die blassen und hochmütigen Langhörner mit ihrem zufälligen Fleckenmuster. Die hiesigen Viehzüchter behaupten, das Fleisch ihrer Rinder ergebe die besten Hamburger Amerikas. Beim Grillen beweisen sie es. Die Landschaft rund um diese Ranch verbindet man in aller Welt mit den spannenden Rodeo-Szenen aus dem Kino. Dennoch gilt Landwirtschaft als Beruf in diesem Teil Amerikas unter der jüngeren Generation nicht als »cool«.

F

Our ranch visits have been organized by the Future Farmers of America group in Deer Trail and the M12 Collective from Byers. I've met teenagers who want to follow in the farming footsteps of their parents. First, they quiz me on farming in Friesland, and are fascinated when they hear that excess rainwater is pumped into the sea. There are also a few raised eyebrows when I say that you can't drive a car at the age of 16, but that you can drink alcohol at the age of 18. The interest intensifies when they see photos of horses being milked as well as cattle.

Since the spring of 2013, 12 young Frisians have been involved in the project. Teenagers with agricultural ambitions live in both parts of the world, no matter how different the landscape. I am reminded of my cousin Lysbeth who, like these kids in Colorado, is 16 years old and lives on a farm. Growing up and helping out on the family farm is a familiar experience, one that I recognize from my own youth. This group wants to continue down this route, so they are all studying agriculture at high school level.

Farmers & Ranchers starts with an online platform where they can come together. They make slide shows about their work on the land and with the animals. Visits on both sides of the Atlantic are organized. Fragile visions of the future are shared through films and stories. The teenagers meet on farms run by their parents or grandparents. The contrasting landscapes accentuate scarcity and water management.

Unsere Besuche auf Ranches wurden von der Gruppe Future Farmers of America in Deer Trail und der Künstlergruppe M12 organisiert. Ich lerne Jugendliche kennen, die in die landwirtschaftlichen Fußstapfen ihrer Eltern treten wollen. Als Erstes wollen sie wissen, wie das Bauernleben in Friesland sei, und sie können kaum glauben, dass bei uns überschüssiges Regenwasser ins Meer gepumpt wird. Es gibt auch einiges Stirnrunzeln, als ich sage, dass man in Friesland mit 16 noch nicht Auto fahren, aber mit 18 Jahren schon Alkohol trinken darf. So richtig interessant wird es für die Jugendlichen, als sie Fotos von Stuten sehen, die wie Kühe gemolken werden.

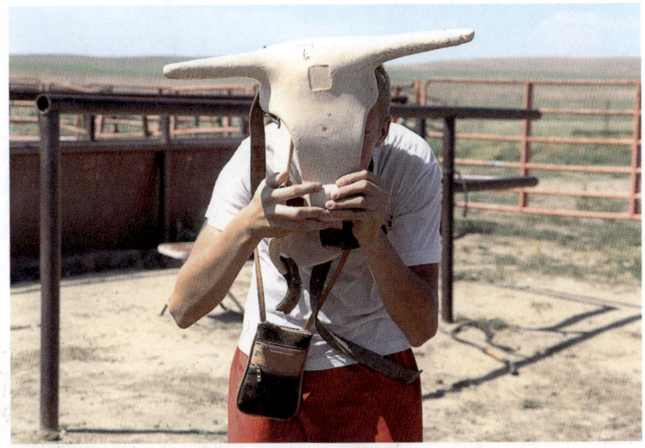

Seit dem Frühjahr 2013 engagieren sich auch zwölf junge Friesinnen und Friesen in dem Projekt. Jugendliche mit landwirtschaftlichen Ambitionen gibt es auf beiden Erdteilen, wie verschieden die Landschaften auch sein mögen. Ich muss an meine Kusine Lysbeth denken, die wie diese Jugendlichen in

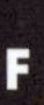

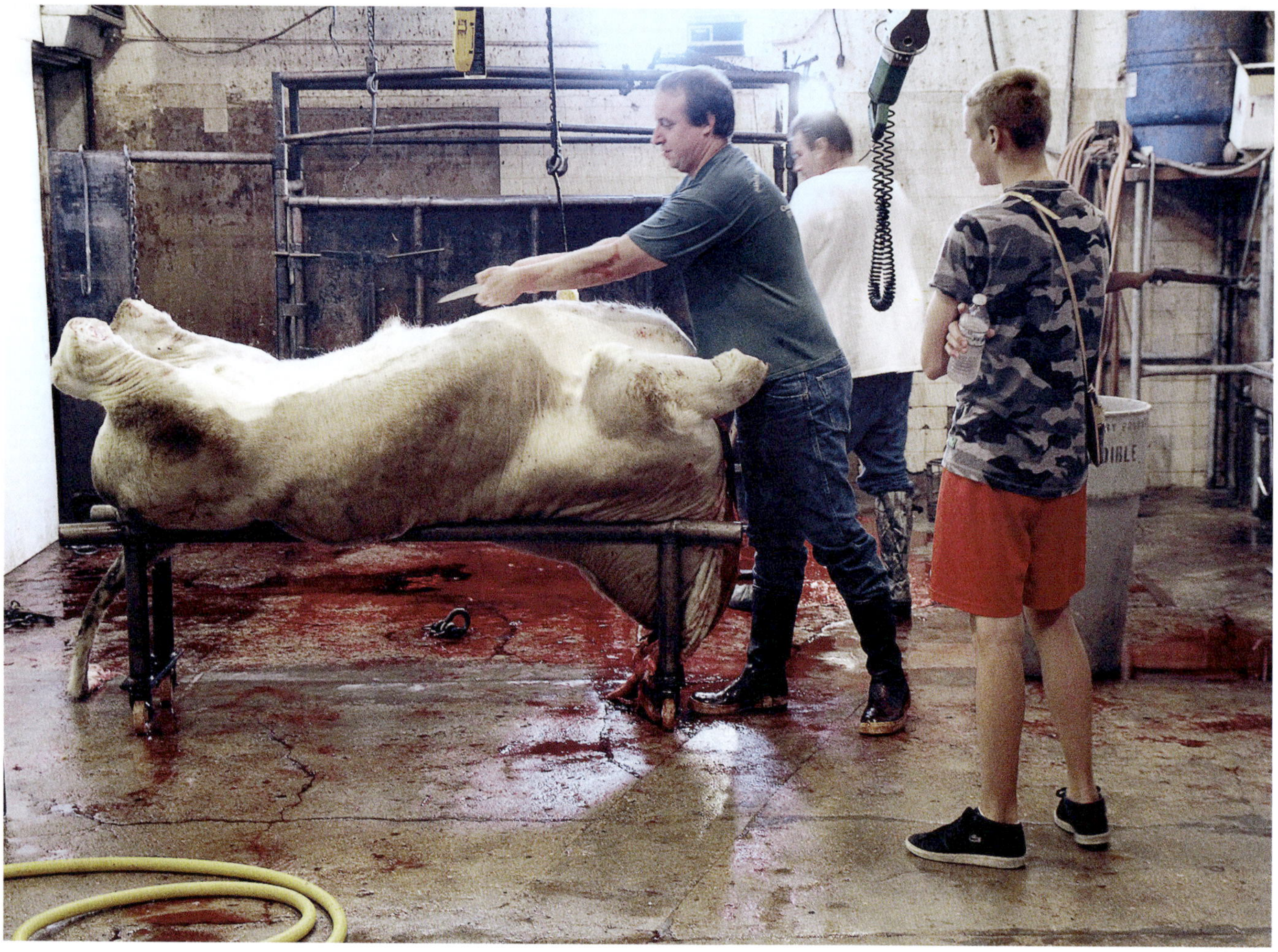

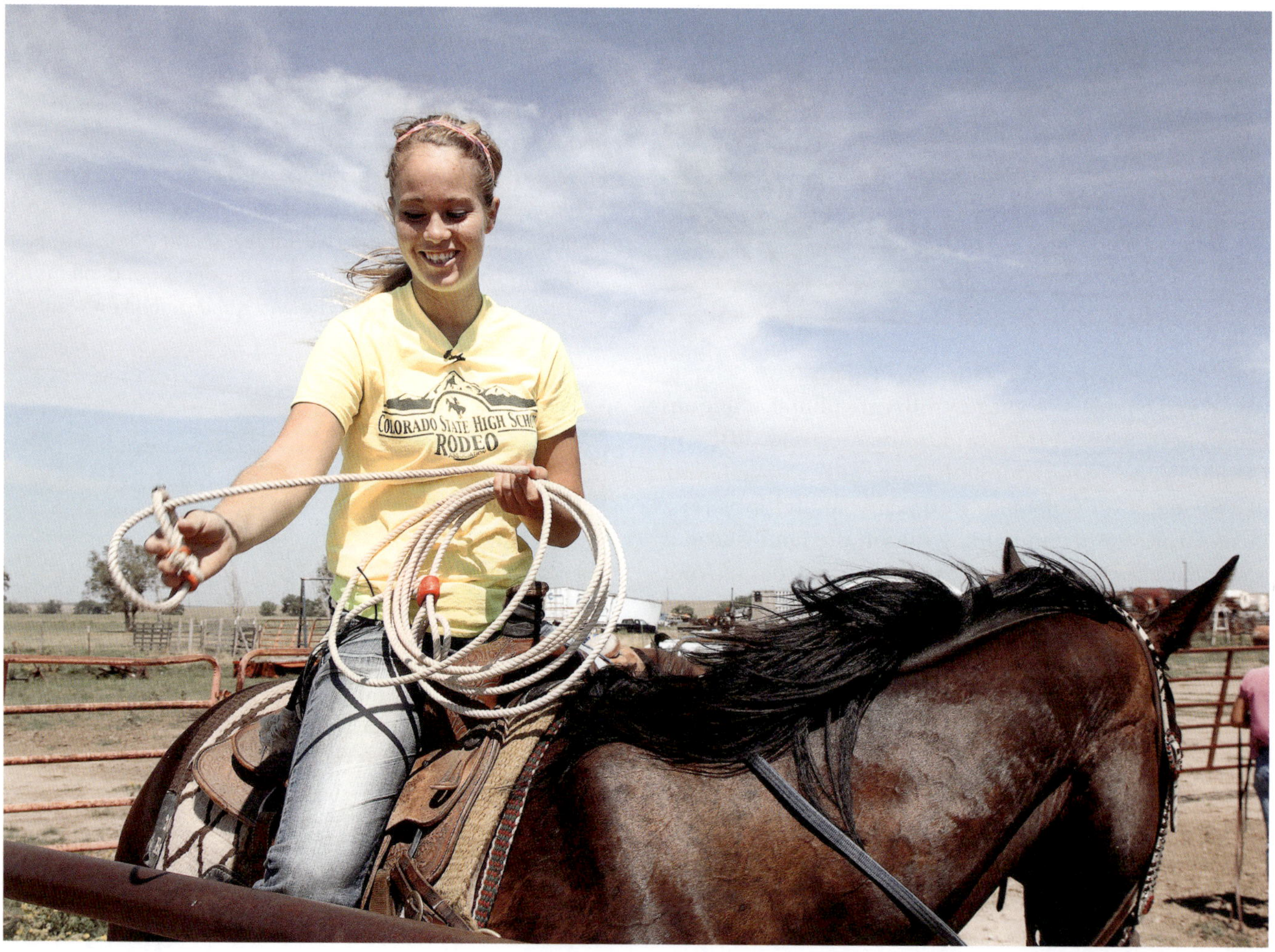
COLORADO STATE HIGH SCHO
RODEO

Farmers & Ranchers sketches a picture of young people in transition, moving from the parental home to an independent life. They have clearly had to shoulder responsibility from an early age, working with costly machinery and large animals, helping maintain an economically viable business. They take us to Friesland and Colorado, and grow up in two stereotyped images of farming life: the dairy cow in the field and the cowboy on the prairie. **WF**

Colorado 16 Jahre alt ist und auf einem Bauernhof lebt. In einem Familienbetrieb aufzuwachsen und mit anzupacken ist eine Erfahrung, die mir vertraut ist. Diese Jugendlichen wollen den Weg weiter gehen und nehmen deshalb auf High-School-Niveau Unterricht in Landwirtschaft.

Farmers & Ranchers beginnt mit einer Online-Plattform, über die die Beteiligten zueinander finden. Auf beiden Seiten des Atlantiks werden Austauschbesuche organisiert. Vorsichtige Visionen der Zukunft gehen in Filmen und Erzählungen reihum. Die Jugendlichen treffen einander auf Höfen, die von ihren Eltern oder Großeltern geführt werden. Die gegensätzlichen Landschaften schärfen das Bewusstsein für knappe Ressourcen und den sorgsamen Umgang mit Wasser.

Farmers & Ranchers entwirft ein Bild von Jugendlichen im Übergang vom Elternhaus zum selbstständigen Leben. Alle mussten erkennbar von Kindheit an Verantwortung übernehmen, haben mit teuren Maschinen und großen Tieren gearbeitet und mitgeholfen, den Betrieb wirtschaftlich über Wasser zu halten. Sie nehmen uns mit nach Friesland und Colorado, wo sie inmitten zweier Klischeebilder der Landwirtschaft aufgewachsen sind: Milchkühe auf der Weide und Cowboys in der Prärie. **WF**

Farmers & Ranchers: Growing Up in Changing Landscapes, 2015, 28:20 min

F

FOREIGN PICKERS

F

Company Drinks is rooted in the history of east Londoners "going picking" in large numbers to the nearby Kent countryside. Kent – like many agricultural areas – has always relied on seasonal migrant labour to come for the picking season. From around 1850 until the 1950s, up to 100,000 pickers – mainly women and children from the East End – would come each year for the hops harvest, make a bit of money, live in rows of hoppers huts, and get some fresh air for their children. Some people in Kent called them "the foreigners".

In 2016 we went back to Kent to find out who is picking today. We filmed a get together of former hop-pickers and the pickers of today, organized a "Hopping Afternoon" at the Hoppers Hospital in Five Oak Green, and went picking together to make a new Pickers Soda and Pickers Cider for Company Drinks.

Gill Harper who works for Mid Kent Growers, a commercial fruit growers' co-operative in Kent, explains how picking works today.

How many pickers are there?
Oh thousands, some of the farms have 500 to 600 pickers, the big farms like Mansfields, they're like villages, really. Others only have a handful of pickers.

How long does the season last?
Now until October, really. A lot of them come to pick the strawberries, then they stay on for the soft fruit (cherries and plums), and then move on to the apples.

What do people do after?
Some of them go to other places, to pick other things: tomatoes on the Isle of Wight, sprouts, veg, even strawberries late on in Scotland. On the bigger farms, they often stay as long as they can. On the smaller farms they are just there for the summer harvest, and then go home.

Where do they come from?
All the new Eastern European states. Latvia, Lithuania, Poland, Romania, Bulgaria. Previously, with the permit scheme [1], we had Ukrainians as well, and they had to go home at the end of their visa. They often used to be students, and would have been signed out from their universities for the summer. But now, as EU citizens, they don't need a visa, so they don't have to go home afterwards. This is part of the reason immigration difficulties have increased.

Who comes?
Used to be students, but more and more older people, too. People will ask, "Can I bring my dad, my aunt?". Family groups do come over a lot,

F

Company Drinks ist eng mit der Geschichte der Ost-Londoner verbunden, die früher in das nahe gelegene ländliche Kent zum »Pflücken« strömten. Wie in vielen landwirtschaftlichen Regionen verließ man sich auch in Kent auf Saisonarbeiter, um die Ernte einzubringen. Zwischen 1850 und 1950 kamen jährlich bis zu 100.000 Pflücker – meistens Frauen und Kinder aus dem Londoner East End – zur Hopfenernte nach Kent, wo sie für geringen Lohn arbeiteten, die Hopper Huts bevölkerten und ihren Kindern frische Landluft verschaffen konnten. Für die Leute in Kent waren sie »Fremde«.

Wir sind 2016 nach Kent gefahren, um uns die heutige Situation anzuschauen. Wir filmten ein Treffen von ehemaligen Pflückern und ihren heutigen Kollegen, organisierten einen »Hopfen-Nachmittag« im Hoppers Hospital in Five Oak Green und pflückten gemeinsam, um für Company Drinks Gleaning Cider und Thinning Soda zu machen.

Gill Harper von Mid Kent Growers, einer Kooperative von Obstbauern, erklärt, wie heutzutage gepflückt wird.

Wie viele Pflücker gibt es hier?
Oh, Tausende, auf manche Farmen arbeiten 500 bis 600 Pflücker. Große Farmen wie Mansfields sind richtige Dörfer, andere haben gerade mal eine Handvoll Helfer.

Wie lange geht die Saison?
Eigentlich bis Oktober. Viele kommen zur Erdbeerernte und bleiben, bis das Beerenobst (Kirschen und Pflaumen) so weit ist, anschließend geht's dann in die Äpfel.

Und was machen die Leute danach?
Manche ziehen weiter und ernten andere Dinge, Tomaten auf der Isle of Wight, Sprossen, Gemüse und sogar späte Himbeeren in Schottland. Auf den großen Farmen bleiben sie meistens, so lange sie können, auf den kleineren helfen sie nur im Sommer und gehen dann wieder nach Hause.

Woher kommen sie?
Aus den neuen osteuropäischen EU-Ländern. Lettland, Litauen, Polen, Rumänien, Bulgarien. Als noch die früheren Regelungen für eine Arbeitserlaubnis galten, [1] kamen auch Ukrainer. Damals konnten alle nur so lange bleiben, wie ihr Visum gültig war. Meistens waren das Studenten, die sich für den Sommer bei ihrer Universität abgemeldet hatten. Aber als EU-Bürger brauchen sie jetzt kein Visum mehr und müssen anschließend auch nicht in ihr Land zurück, was dazu beiträgt, dass die Einwanderungsproblematik an Bedeutung gewonnen hat.

Wer kommt?
Anfangs waren es vor allem Studenten, inzwischen kommen aber auch Ältere. Die Leute fragen: »Kann ich meine Tante, meinen Vater mitbringen?« Häufig

Foreign Pickers, 2016, 23 min

F

like the original pickers. But it's quite hard work, particularly if you want to make money: pickers need speed, accuracy, and care.

Where do they live?
Accommodation is supplied by the farm in the vast majority of cases. Caravans, huts, bunkhouses. Those who are going to live here all the time might rent local houses. But 80 per cent live in that sort of accommodation.

F

How do they get here?
Buses mainly. Some fly, but it's mainly by bus.

What's the pay?
The living wage, £7.20 an hour. Sometimes there are bonuses and overtime. They have all the workers' rights of the EU, really.

What hours do they work?
They generally work up to a 48-hour week, eight hours a day, six days a week.

Why do they come?
Money is definitely the biggest driver. Sending money home buys a lot more: some people have parents who are doctors at home, but they earn more money picking fruit.

What's the attitude of local people?
Generally fine. Remember, this isn't something that English people are queuing up to do. The pickers are vital.

What about Brexit?
It will be interesting, if it happens[2]. Perhaps they'll have to reintroduce the visa schemes. We wouldn't have the industry without the pickers.

1 Seasonal Agricultural Workers Scheme (SAWS)
2 The interview took place in May 2016, before the UK voted to leave the EU.

kommen auch ganze Familien, wie das früher bei den Hopfenpflückern üblich war. Die Arbeit ist aber ziemlich hart, vor allem, wenn man Geld machen will: Gefragt sind Schnelligkeit, Genauigkeit, Sorgfalt.

Wie werden sie untergebracht?
Für die Unterkünfte sorgt meistens der Farmer: Wohnwagen, Hütten, Schlafbaracken. Für solche, die ständig hier sind, mieten sie bei den Einheimischen auch Wohnungen an. Aber 80 Prozent wohnen in Behelfsunterkünften.

F

Wie kommen sie hierher?
Meistens mit Bussen. Manche fliegen auch, aber die meisten nehmen den Bus.

Wie werden sie bezahlt?
Sie kriegen den Mindestlohn von £ 7,20 die Stunde. Manchmal gibt es auch Prämien, Überstundenzuschläge. Eigentlich werden alle nach dem europäischen Arbeitsrecht bezahlt.

Wie viele Stunden arbeiten sie?
Gewöhnlich arbeiten sie 48 Stunden in der Woche, acht Stunden am Tag, sechs Tage in der Woche.

Warum kommen sie?
Geld ist definitiv der größte Anreiz. Wenn sie Geld nach Hause schicken, bekommen sie viel mehr dafür: Manche haben Eltern, die zu Hause als Ärzte arbeiten, sie verdienen aber weniger als ein Obstpflücker.

Welche Haltung legen die Einheimischen ihnen gegenüber an den Tag?
Im Allgemeinen sind sie freundlich. Schließlich ist das keine Arbeit, für die ein Engländer Schlange stehen würde. Ohne Erntehelfer ginge hier gar nichts.

Welche Folgen hätte der Brexit?[2]
Gute Frage, falls es dazu kommt. Vielleicht brauchen sie dann wieder ein Visum. Wir brauchen jedenfalls die Pflücker.

1 Seasonal Agricultural Workers Scheme (SAWS): Gesetzliche Regelungen Saisonarbeiter betreffend
2 Das Interview fand im Mai 2016 statt, bevor sich die Mehrheit der Briten am 23. Juni 2016 für einen Austritt aus der EU entschied.

STOP

Franschhoek Valley

Western Cape, ZA

F

The wine estates are located side-by-side behind their gates and the tree-lined avenues running from the main road to the mountains. Farm workers wait on the R 45, walk along the road, ride on bakkies or in minibuses. Wedding parties and local and international tourists visit the wine estates. Picnic tables stand in front of a water lily pond. In the bright forest, we look for trails to the river. One can also drive ahead to the wine tasting and on to the restaurant. There is a lot of competition amongst good restaurants in the Franschhoek Valley.

Wine is cultivated on 30 of the 70 hectares at Solms-Delta. In the cellar, tubes lie calmly in the dark, water runs, and the running of water is unusual, now, in the drought and with the scarcity of water at the end of the summer.

The grape pulp is drying behind the halls with a heavy smell. Here the palms stand in the wind.

After the harvest, there is a celebration for all the farm workers in the valley, a feast with hundreds of tables, and concerts from the morning to night. Dancing on the straw begins quite early, it is not possible to be too swanky for this day; the young girls and the men, paying guests and older women with drunken, wasted faces all dance.

Solms-Delta belongs to Mark, the neurologist, Richard, his friend, and the Farm Workers Trust. A grape grower who has no winery, Hagen says, also cannot buy one. He will not make enough money with the wine so as to pay it off. He can cultivate and sell his grapes to a winery. The sun slowly crawls across the north towards dusk. The children of the workers play cricket on the lawn between the oaks. **AS**

Seite an Seite liegen die Weingüter hinter ihren Toren und Alleen. Alleen laufen von der Landstraße den Bergen zu. Landarbeiter warten an der R 45, sie gehen die Straße entlang, sie fahren auf Bakkies mit oder in Kleinbussen. Hochzeitsgesellschaften, einheimische und internationale Urlauber besuchen die Weingüter. Vor dem Seerosenteich stehen die Picknicktische. Im hellen Wald suchen wir Trampelpfade zum Fluss. Man kann mit dem Auto zur Weinprobe vorfahren und weiter zum Restaurant. Die Konkurrenz ist groß unter den guten Restaurants im Franschhoek Valley.

Auf 30 der 70 Hektar wird in Solms-Delta Wein angebaut. In der Kellerei liegen Schläuche ruhig im Dunkel, Wasser läuft, und das Laufen von Wasser ist ungewohnt, jetzt, in der Trockenheit und bei dem Wassermangel zum Ende des Sommers.

Der Trester trocknet hinter den Hallen mit seinem schweren Geruch. Hier stehen die Palmen im Wind.

Nach der Ernte wird ein Fest gegeben für alle Farmarbeiter im Tal, ein Fest mit Hunderten von Tischen und Konzerten vom Morgen bis in die Dunkelheit. Schon früh beginnt der Tanz auf dem Stroh, man kann nicht zu schick sein für diesen Tag, es tanzen die jungen Mädchen und die Männer, zahlende Gäste und alte Frauen mit betrunkenen, wüsten Gesichtern.

Solms-Delta gehört Mark, dem Neurologen, Richard, seinem Freund, und dem Farm Workers Trust. Ein Weinbauer, der keine Kellerei hat, sagt Hagen, der kann auch keine kaufen. Er wird mit dem Wein nicht genug Geld verdienen, um sie abzuzahlen. Er kann anbauen und seine Trauben an eine Kellerei verkaufen. Die Sonne wandert über den Norden der Abenddämmerung entgegen. Die Kinder der Arbeiter spielen Cricket auf dem Rasen zwischen den Eichen. **AS**

→ ICH BIN GERNE BAUER

F

FREMD

F

Alien, are things relating to your own image that you do not want to accept. Alien, are things that are not negotiable within one's own cultural system. You use the alien to handle topics which you don't want to have too close to yourself. The alien is not codified; it shifts as a result of interaction. In contact with the alien, your own potentialities are able to expand and your own categories are able to open up.

All people are alike – this is true on a particular level of abstraction, but in order to think further I have to be able to express difference. I am able to accept and come to terms with otherness.

A binary worldview is static; starting from more dynamic conditions makes sense. Nevertheless, dynamism alone as a conceptual model also does not bring us any further. I require poles so as to think. Complete relativization takes away my ability to express myself.

“Everything is relative” is an indicator of not thinking.

In the last few years, I have been working in Ghana and South Africa quite frequently. In both countries, a social order in which the many seem to depend on a few clever, capable, or responsible individuals is alien to me. I think that the burdens on the latter are too great; the whole thing infuriates me. One time, I was flying from Accra to Johannesburg, a night flight; on my right a ten-year-old boy who was flying alone, to my right a man who first began his late dinner when I said to him beamingly: You're invited. The boy pulled the blanket over his head and leaned against me as he slept. He turned to me when he wanted water.

I live with my husband and son in Cape Town. My assistant, Ziphozhake, lives with her sister and her children in a small house in Kayelitsha Township. When I returned from Ghana, I was dissatisfied with her work and her lack of concentration. But on that return flight, something in me had softened – instead of putting pressure on her and demanding reasonable work for what I pay her, as suggested itself to me, I invited Zipho to live with us, in the children's room, even though one of us therefore has to sleep on the floor. No idea, but the work is once again handled with ease. **AS**

Written based on a conversation with **Bernd Scherer,** philosopher and Director of the Haus der Kulturen der Welt, Berlin.

F

Fremd ist das, was du von deinem eigenen Bild nicht wahrhaben willst. Fremd ist das, was in deinem eigenen Kultursystem nicht verhandelbar ist. Am Fremden behandelst du Themen, die du näher bei dir nicht behandeln möchtest. Das Fremde ist nicht festgeschrieben, es verschiebt sich in der Interaktion. Im Kontakt mit dem Fremden kann sich die eigene Potenzialität erweitern und die eigenen Kategorien können sich öffnen.

Alle Menschen sind gleich – das stimmt auf einem bestimmten Abstraktionsniveau, aber um weiterzudenken, muss ich Differenz artikulieren können. Ich kann Andersheit akzeptieren und verhandeln.

Ein duales Weltbild ist statisch; es ist sinnvoll, von dynamischeren Verhältnissen auszugehen. Dynamik allein bringt uns als Vorstellungsmodell aber auch nicht weiter. Ich brauche Pole, um zu denken. Vollständige Relativierung nimmt mir die Möglichkeit zur Artikulation.

»Alles ist relativ« ist ein Indikator für Nicht-Denken.

In den letzten Jahren habe ich häufiger in Ghana und Südafrika gearbeitet. In beiden Ländern befremdet mich eine soziale Ordnung, in der viele sich an wenige besonders Kluge, Tüchtige oder Verantwortungsbewusste zu hängen scheinen. Ich denke, die Lasten für die Letzteren sind zu hoch; die Sache macht mich ärgerlich. Einmal fliege ich von Accra nach Johannesburg, ein Nachtflug; zu meiner Rechten sitzt ein zehnjähriger Junge, der allein fliegt, zu meiner Linken ein Mann, der sein spätes Abendessen erst beginnt, als ich ihm strahlend sage: You're invited. Der Junge zieht die Decke über den Kopf und lehnt im Schlaf an mir. Er wendet sich an mich, wenn er Wasser möchte.

Ich wohne mit Mann und Sohn in Kapstadt. Meine Assistentin, Ziphozhake, lebt mit ihrer Schwester und deren Kindern in einem kleinen Haus im Township Kayelitsha. Als ich aus Ghana zurückkomme, bin ich unzufrieden mit ihrer Arbeit und ihrem Mangel an Konzentration. Aber etwas hat mich weichgekocht bei diesem Rückflug – anstatt sie unter Druck zu setzen und angemessene Leistung für ihre Bezahlung zu fordern, wie es mir nahe liegt, lade ich Zipho ein, bei uns zu wohnen, im Kinderzimmer, auch wenn einer von uns deshalb auf dem Boden schlafen muss. Keine Ahnung, aber die Arbeit geht wieder leicht von der Hand. **AS**

Geschrieben nach einem Gespräch mit **Bernd Scherer,** Philosoph und Intendant des Hauses der Kulturen der Welt, Berlin.

GARTENH

G

The GfZK has one old building, one new building, and a former coach house in a large, tree-filled garden near the centre of Leipzig. We set up our "Gartenhaus" (garden house) in one part of this coach house.

The Gartenhaus was given a display window and a wide, roof-covered bench. If a film is running in the Gartenhaus, people can watch it through the window and hear the sound, which is also transmitted outside. In the evening and winter, the Gartenhaus is like a television into villages of the world. The vending machine is ready to trade day and night. In the summer, we open the window to serve drinks. Inside, there is a counter, shelves for products, and a corner bench.

The *International Village Show* includes a Frisian shell path leading through the bushes and a bed with wild strawberries and grapes from Franconia. One time, we supplemented the exhibition with a caravan. A platform was converted into a meeting place for village youth. We use the garden for catering, for grilling and cooking, for pit fires, and for bonfires in winter.

The GfZK has a café in the new building, designed by Céline Condorelli; hotel rooms designed by Jun Yang and Christine Hill, and a labyrinth by Olaf Nicolai in the garden. For a few summers, Jun Yang used the Gartenhaus as the "Hei Di" kiosk.

The villages and landscapes in which we work are hundreds, sometimes thousands of kilometres away from each other. The Gartenhaus creates a space for all these locations and the local participants. It gives us the opportunity to try out forms of representation for the villages, forms of polyphony in this representation, as well as to include hospitality, nonchalance, the seasons of the year, and coming together as elements of an artistic language.

The "Gartenhaus" is a new exhibition space typology where Myvillages meet one another and with guests from the distant villages; residents of Leipzig, exhibition visitors, colleagues, and official representatives of sponsors and partners come here. The doors of the Gartenhaus are open during the opening hours of the gallery and for special events. **KB**

AUS

G

Die GfZK verfügt über einen Altbau, einen Neubau und ein ehemaliges Kutscherhaus in einem großen, baumbestandenen Garten nahe dem Leipziger Zentrum. In einem Teil dieses Kutscherhauses richten wir unser Gartenhaus ein.

Das Gartenhaus bekommt ein Schaufenster und eine breite, überdachte Bank. Läuft im Gartenhaus ein Film, kann man ihn durchs Fenster sehen und bekommt den Ton nach draußen übertragen. Am Abend und im Winter ist das Gartenhaus wie ein Fernseher in die Dörfer der Welt. Der Verkaufsautomat ist Tag und Nacht bereit. Im Sommer öffnen wir zum Ausschank die Fenster. Im Inneren gibt es eine Theke, Ladenregale und eine Eckbank.

Zur *International Village Show* gehören ein friesischer Muschelweg, der durch die Büsche führt, und ein Beet mit Walderdbeeren und Wein aus Franken. Einmal ergänzen wir die Ausstellung durch einen Wohnwagen. Eine Plattform wird zum Treffpunkt der Dorfjugend umgestaltet. Wir nutzen den Garten für die Bewirtung, zum Grillen und Kochen, für Grubenbrände und Lagerfeuer im Winter.

Zur GfZK gehören ein Café im Neubau, 2015–2017 gestaltet von Céline Condorelli; Hotelzimmer, gestaltet von Jun Yang und Christine Hill, und ein Labyrinth von Olaf Nicolai im Garten. Jun Yang hatte den Ort unseres Gartenhauses für einige Sommer als Kiosk »Hei Di« ausgestattet.

Die Dörfer und Landschaften, in denen wir arbeiten, sind Hunderte, manchmal Tausende von Kilometern voneinander entfernt. Das Gartenhaus schafft einen Raum für all diese Orte und die vor Ort Beteiligten. Es gibt uns die Möglichkeit, Formen der Repräsentation der Dörfer auszuprobieren, Formen der Mehrstimmigkeit in dieser Repräsentation, sowie Gastfreundschaft, Lässigkeit, Jahreszeiten, Zusammentreffen als Elemente künstlerischer Sprache aufzunehmen.

Das Gartenhaus ist ein neuer Typus Ausstellungsraum, hier trifft sich Myvillages untereinander und mit Gästen aus den entfernten Dörfern, hierher kommen Leipziger, Ausstellungsbesucher, Kollegen und offizielle Vertreter der Förderer und Partner. Das Gartenhaus ist zu den Öffnungszeiten der Galerie geöffnet und zu speziellen Veranstaltungen. **KB**

EKRAWFO
EKUMFI

GEOLOGIE

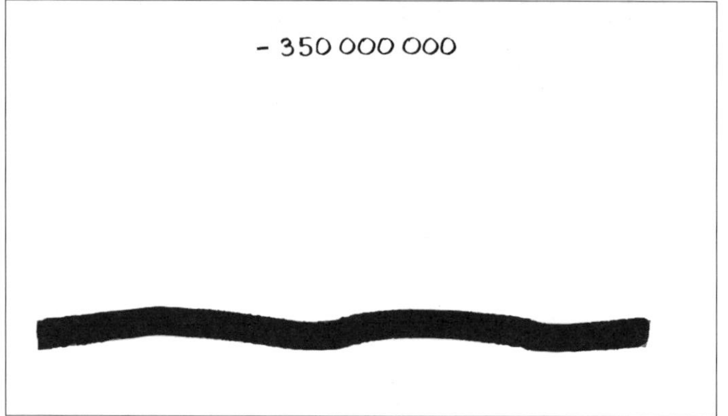

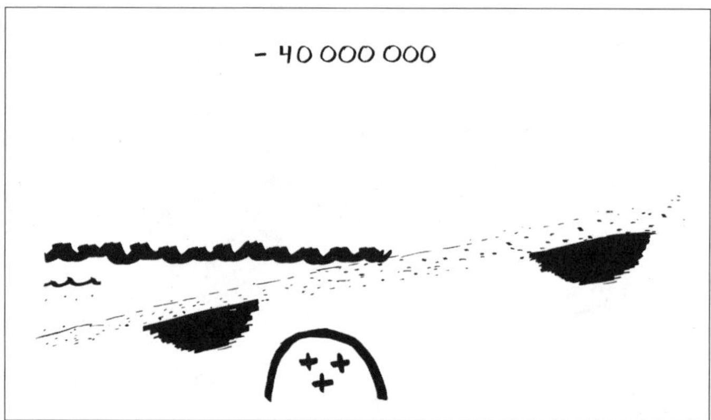

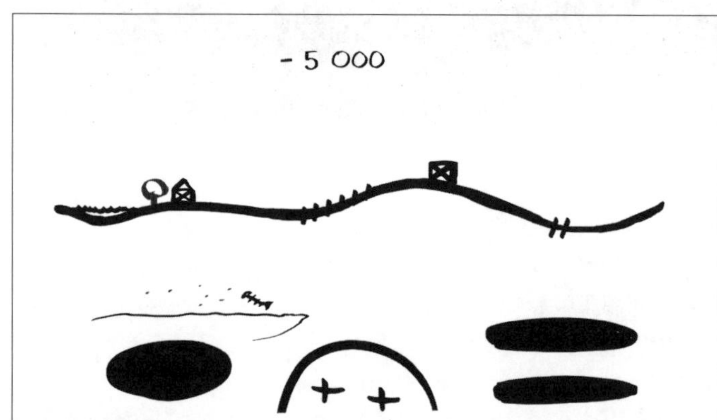

Geologische Animation Leipzig, 2015, 4:36 min

- 260 000 000

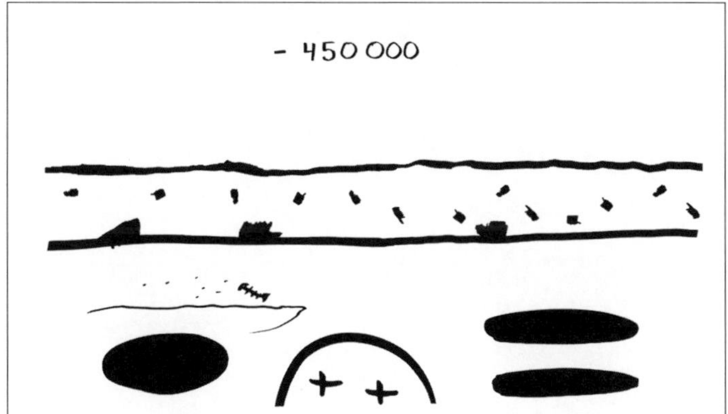
- 450 000
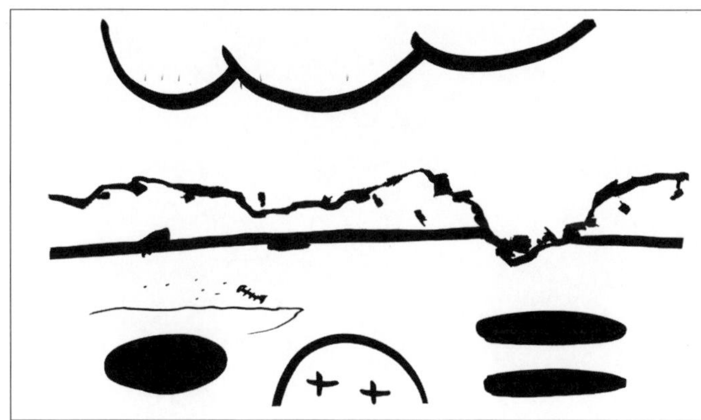

G

GO
OD
S

G

Caravan Pot

Lehm in Dosen

Fanas Arrow

Farmers' Chinaware

Twisted Bugle

Leinölkühltürme

Banki

Fufu Bowls

Seville Orange Marmalade

Automatentiere

»Es gibt was da ist«

Ittinger Ei

Höfer Spitze

Kornkombi

Leinenbuch

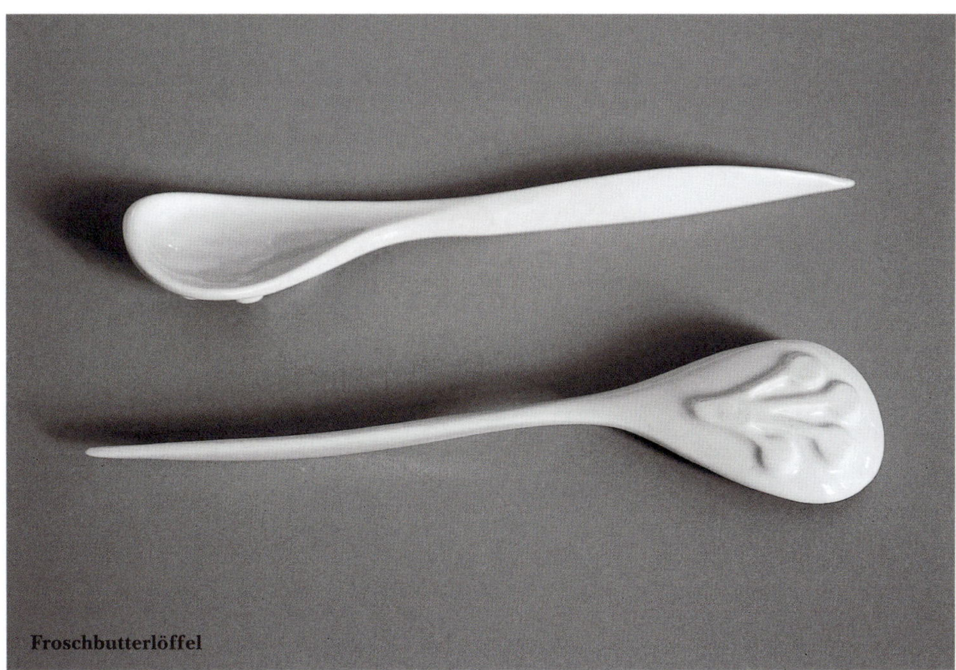

Froschbutterlöffel

Kartoffeljanker

Farmers' Chinaware

Potato Sleepers

Weidejacke

Word Search Poster

Esch F6

Company Drinks

Paardenmelk Zeep

Confectie Box

Beestachtige Schat

Banki

Caravan Pots, 2011
To finally get their local community centre, Anne-Marie Dillon and the "Forever Young Pensioners" group in Ballykinlar in Northern Ireland simply organised a caravan, decorated it and plonked it in the middle of the village. The Caravan Pot *commemorates this act.*

Flowerpot
Terracotta, cast and glazed, transfers
15 × 15 × 30 cm
Edition: 20
(new edition 2013: 15 / 2016: 12)
Ballykinlar / Ballykinler (GB)

Caravan Pots, 2011
Als sie den langen Kampf um ein Gemeinschaftshaus satthatten, stellten Anne-Marie Dillon und die »Forever Young Pensioners« in Ballykinlar in Nordirland einfach einen Wohnwagen auf, schmückten und nutzten ihn. Der Caravan Pot, ein Blumenübertopf, erinnert an diesen Akt.

Blumenübertopf
Terrakotta, gegossen und glasiert, Abziehbilder
15 × 15 × 30 cm
Auflage: 20
(Neuauflage 2013: 15 / 2016: 12)
Ballykinlar / Ballykinler (GB)

Farmers' Chinaware, 2014
The Centro Andaluz de Arte Contemporáneo (CAAC) in Seville is located in the large former Cartuja (charterhouse) monastery on an island in the Guadalquivir River, from where ships of discoverers and conquistadors set off for the Americas. Columbus lived at this monastery for a time. In the 19th and 20th century, the Cartuja de Sevilla produced porcelain here, a well-known porcelain, the good china in many Spanish families. Today, the factory is located in a suburb of Seville. For Antje's exhibition at the CAAC, it produced plates and small bowls according to her specifications, with decorative orders of barley, oats, wheat, and combine harvesters.

Porcelain dishes, printed (underglaze)
Large plate: ø 25.8 cm
Small plate: ø 20.5 cm
Small bowl: 7.5 × ø 10.5 cm
Edition: each 40 pieces
Seville (ES)

Farmers' Chinaware, 2014
Das Centro Andaluz de Arte Contemporáneo (CAAC) in Sevilla befindet sich in einem großen ehemaligen Kartäuserkloster auf einer Insel im Fluss Guadalquivir, von dem aus die Schiffe der Entdecker und Konquistadoren nach Amerika aufgebrochen sind. Kolumbus hat zeitweise in diesem Kloster gelebt. Im 19. und 20. Jahrhundert produzierte hier die Cartuja de Sevilla Porzellan, ein berühmtes Porzellan, das gute Geschirr vieler spanischer Familien. Heute befindet sich die Fabrik in einem Vorort von Sevilla. Sie haben für Antjes Ausstellung im CAAC nach ihren Vorlagen ein Bauernporzellan produziert, Teller und Schälchen mit einem Dekor aus Gersten-, Hafer-, Weizen- und Mähdrescherborte.

Porzellangeschirr, bedruckt (Unterglasur)
Großer Teller: ø 25,8 cm
Kleiner Teller: ø 20,5 cm
Schälchen: 7,5 × ø 10,5 cm
Auflage: je 40 Stück
Sevilla (ES)

Linen Book, 2014
Ohne is a village with 650 inhabitants on the Vechte River in the south of County of Bentheim. "If they could do it in the past, we'll probably also manage," the "Committee to Identify Goods for Ohne" said to itself and then planted flax for the production of Ohner linen on three mornings – somehow with the awareness that it would be a lot of work, but undaunted.

Book, hand-bound
Linen, hand-woven, card, paper (blank)
18.6 – 18.8 × 10.7 cm, 48 pages
Edition: 160
Ohne (DE)

Leinenbuch, 2014
Ohne ist ein Dorf mit 650 Einwohnern an der Vechte im Süden der Grafschaft Bentheim. »Wenn die das früher konnten, werden wir das wohl auch hinkriegen«, sagte sich das »Komitee zur Findung einer Ohner Ware« und baute auf drei Morgen Flachs an für die Produktion von Ohner Leinen. Irgendwie mit dem Bewusstsein, dass es viel Arbeit werden würde, aber furchtlos.

Buch, handgebunden
Leinen, handgewebt, Pappe, Papier (blanko)
18,6 – 18,8 × 10,7 cm, 48 Seiten
Auflage: 160
Ohne (DE)

Seville Orange Marmalade, 2014
The nuns of the Santa Paula Convent live a cloistered life. They made 180 jars of orange marmalade for us from the oranges that grow in the large garden of the Centro Andaluz de Arte Contemporáneo, the erstwhile charterhouse, in Seville, and are not otherwise utilized.

Orange marmalade
Jar, each 300 g
Edition: 180
Seville (ES)

Seville Orange Marmalade, 2014
Die Nonnen des Klosters Santa Paula leben in Klausur. Sie haben für uns 180 Gläser Orangenmarmelade gekocht von den Orangen, die im großen Garten der Cartuja in Sevilla wachsen und nicht genutzt werden.

Orangenmarmelade
Glas à 300 g
Auflage: 180
Sevilla (ES)

Fufu Bowls, 2014/15

Everlove wanted to provide work in the village, above all for young women; we wanted a new product for the International Village Shop. We jointly considered abilities and resources and got stuck with bamboo, bamboo, which grows cathedral-like behind the fields of the village.

From bamboo, it is possible to make houses and fences, lamps and armchairs, bicycles and bowls. The committee of Ekumfi Ekrawfo wanted bowls: bowls to eat fufu. They were supposed to be dark brown or black, just like the ceramic bowls known up to now, which break quite easily; dark brown or black, these are the colours that whet the appetite for fufu. We sat with the committee in the courtyard of the palace where Everlove lives with some of her relatives, and found instruction videos on the Internet that taught us the Asian technique of coiling a bowl.

Bowls
Bamboo, oil mixture
3 – 5 × ø 17 – 19.5 cm
Edition: 21 pieces
Ekumfi Ekrawfo (GH)

Fufu Bowls, 2014/15

Everlove wünscht sich Arbeit im Dorf, vor allem für junge Frauen; wir wünschen uns ein neues Produkt für den International Village Shop. Wir erkunden gemeinsam Ressourcen und Fertigkeiten und bleiben beim Bambus hängen, Bambus, der hinter den Feldern des Dorfes kathedralengleich wächst.

Aus Bambus kann man Häuser machen und Zäune, Lampen und Sessel, Fahrräder und Schüsseln. Das Komitee von Ekumfi Ekrawfo wünscht sich Schüsseln: Schüsseln, aus denen man Fufu essen kann. Dunkelbraun oder schwarz sollen sie sein, ganz so wie die Keramikschüsseln, die bisher bekannt sind, aber leicht kaputtgehen, Dunkelbraun oder Schwarz, das seien die Farben, die Appetit auf Fufu machen. Wir sitzen mit dem Komitee im Hof des Palastes, in dem Everlove mit einigen ihrer Verwandten wohnt. Wir finden Instruktionsvideos im Internet, die uns die asiatische Technik des Schüsselwickelns beibringen.

Schüsseln
Bambus, Ölmischung
3 – 5 × ø 17 – 19,5 cm
Auflage: 21 Stück
Ekumfi Ekrawfo (GH)

Fufu Bowls, 2015, 14 min

Höfer Lace, 2015
"Fostering community life" is one of the worldly wisdoms that the women of Höfen would like to pass on. The design for a new Höfer lace, woven in the Hofer lace-weaving mill in Rattelsdorf, is based on it.

Synthetic lace, white and champagne-coloured
7000 × 50 or 70 cm
By the metre
Höfen (DE)

G

Höfer Spitze, 2015
»Gemeinschaftsleben pflegen« gehört zu den Lebensweisheiten, die die Höfer Frauen weitergeben möchten. Auf ihnen basiert die Gestaltung für eine neue Höfer Spitze, gewebt in der Spitzenweberei Hofer in Rattelsdorf.

Synthetikspitze, weiß und champagnerfarben
7000 × 50 bzw. 70 cm
Meterware
Höfen (DE)

Höfer Spitze, 2015, 4:56 min

Banki / Jars, 2015, and Animal Figures, 2016

There is clay in Zvizzchi, good-quality clay suitable for moulding and firing. Some residents knew about it; a geologist who Wapke invited in 2013 also pointed it out. It was supposed to become the raw material for ceramics from Zvizzchi. We tested the characteristics of the clay: the red crumbled two weeks after being fired, the grey turned light pink when fired, and the yellow red. We dried, soaked, and sieved the grey and yellow clay, and built a simple wood-firing oven with Vadim's help. Two ceramists were invited to work with this clay and with men, women, and children from Zvizzchi: Alexandra Bikmatova from Moscow and Chajim Grosser, who travelled with us from Berlin.

Jars
Clay, fired (Raku-fired)
4.5 – 18 × ø 6 – 13 cm
Alexandra Bikmatova
Edition: 22
Zvizzchi (RU)

Animal Figures
Clay, fired (pit-fired)
4 – 4.5 × 2 – 2.5 cm
Chajim Grosser
Edition: 35
Zvizzchi (RU), Berlin (DE), Leipzig (DE)

Banki / Dosen, 2015, und Tierfiguren, 2016

In Zvizzchi gibt es Ton, einen guten Ton, der sich zum Formen und Brennen eignet. Davon wussten einige Bewohner, darauf hat auch die Geologin hingewiesen, die Wapke 2013 eingeladen hat. Er sollte das Grundmaterial für Keramik aus Zvizzchi sein. Wir haben den Ton auf seine Eigenschaften geprüft: Der rote zerbröselte zwei Wochen nach dem Brand, der graue brannte blassrosa, der gelbe rot. Wir haben grauen und gelben Ton getrocknet, gewässert und gesiebt und mit Vadims Hilfe einen einfachen Holzbrandofen gebaut. Zwei Keramiker waren eingeladen, mit diesem Ton und mit Männern, Frauen und Kindern aus Zvizzchi zu arbeiten: Alexandra Bikmatova aus Moskau und Chajim Grosser, der aus Berlin mit uns gereist ist.

Dosen
Ton, gebrannt (Raku-Brand)
4,5 – 18 × ø 6 – 13 cm
Alexandra Bikmatova
Auflage: 22
Zvizzchi (RU)

Tierfiguren
Ton, gebrannt (Grubenbrand)
4 – 4,5 × 2 – 2,5 cm
Chajim Grosser
Auflage: 35
Zvizzchi (RU), Berlin (DE), Leipzig (DE)

Glina is Zvizzchi (Clay from Zvizzchi / Ton aus Zvizzchi), 2015, 16:49 min

G

"Esch" F6, 2015/16

"Pastorenesch", "Eilerings Esch", "Übbings Esch" – in County of Bentheim, many parcels of land are called "Esch", as well as many of the roads that lead along these parcels of land. The "Plaggenesch" was created using "plaggen" manuring, therefore anthropogenic soil. A top layer of grass or heath "plaggen" was removed, used as bedding in the stall, and then spread on the fields as fertilizer along with manure, ash, wood charcoal, and kitchen waste, thus improving the soil. Inspired by contemporary research on Terra Preta, a black earth from the Amazon region that is also anthropogenic, along with the Fachbereich 6 (Department 6), the municipal works depot of the City of Nordhorn, we developed "Esch F6", a black earth consisting of buffalo manure from the Nordhorn Animal Park, wood charcoal charred from wood remnants from the works depot, and compost from the green waste composting at the Gildehaus, fermented anaerobically.

Anthropogenic black earth
Wood charcoal, bison manure, compost, composite foil and label
30 × 50 cm
Edition: 200
Nordhorn (DE)

Esch F6, 2015/16

Pastorenesch, Eilerings Esch, Übbings Esch – in der Grafschaft Bentheim heißen viele Flurstücke Esch und manche Straßen, die auf diese Flurstücke hinführen. Der Plaggenesch ist entstanden durch Plaggendüngung und damit ein anthropogener Boden. Gras- oder Heideplaggen wurden abgestochen, im Stall ein Jahr lang als Einstreu benutzt und dann zusammen mit dem Mist, mit Asche, Holzkohle und Küchenabfällen als Dünger auf die Felder gebracht, die damit dauerhaft verbessert wurden. Angeregt durch die zeitgenössische Forschung zu Terra preta, einer ebenfalls anthropogenen Schwarzerde aus dem Amazonasgebiet, entwickeln wir gemeinsam mit dem Fachbereich 6, dem Baubetriebshof der Stadt Nordhorn, den Esch F6, eine Schwarzerde aus Büffelmist vom Tierpark Nordhorn, Holzkohle, geköhlert aus Restholz des Baubetriebshofs, und Kompost von der Grünschnittkompostierung in Gildehaus, anaerob fermentiert.

Anthropogene Schwarzerde
Holzkohle, Bisonmist, Kompost, Verbundfolie und Aufkleber
30 × 50 cm
Auflage: 200
Nordhorn (DE)

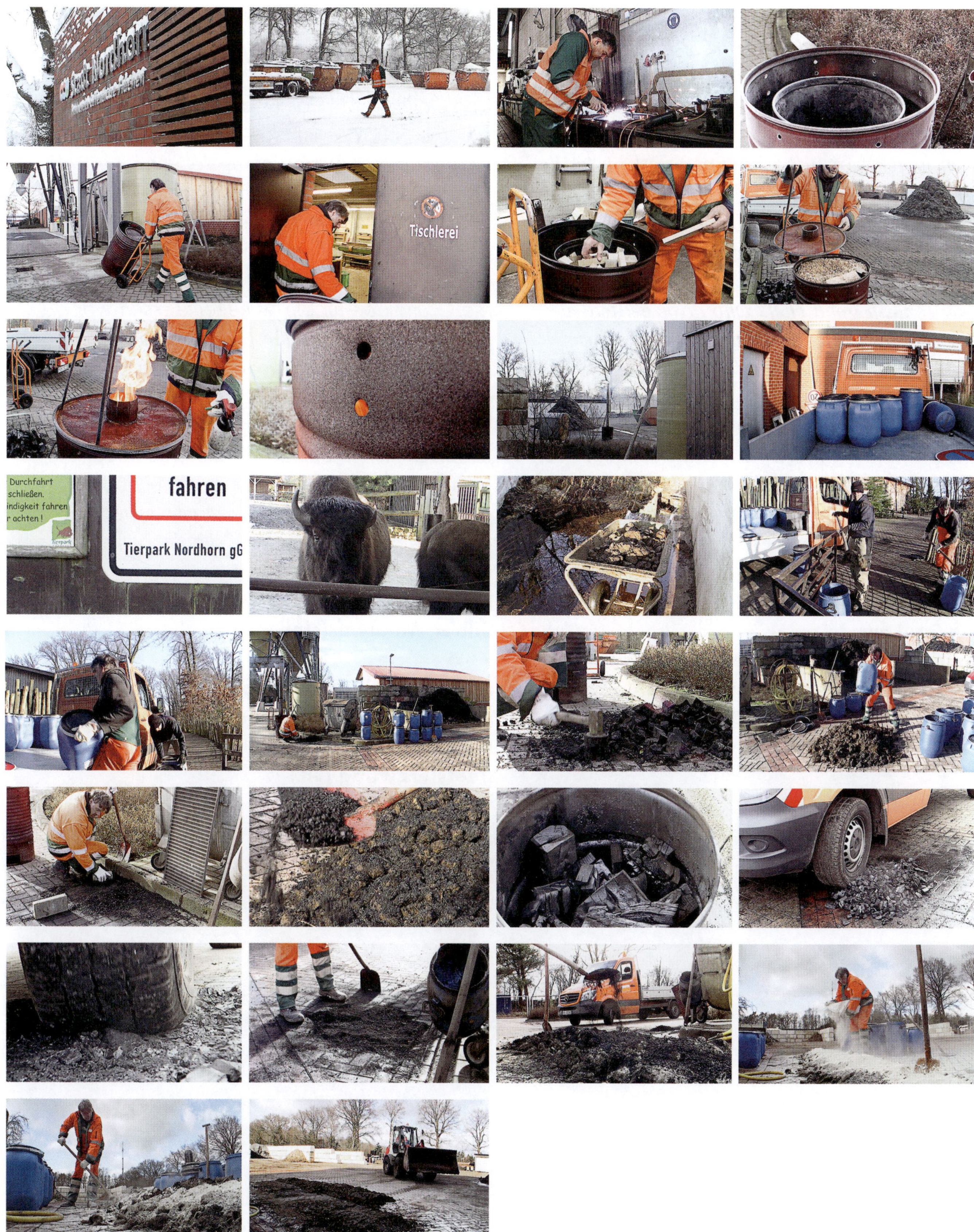

G

Esch F6, 2016, 7:43 min

G

Beestachtige Schat / Wild Treasure, 2016

In many details, the product of Beetsterzwaag reflects the great economic inequality that shaped the village. A pocket-sized silver case holds the beginning of a love letter, which can be read in full by means of a link to the group that came up with the product. The case has the shape of a bean, based on a local type of bean that was a food staple for poor people, but which is now very en vogue with good chefs who have dedicated themselves to regional cuisine. The silver can be processed locally: the craft of the silversmith has a long tradition here since products made from it were demanded and commissioned by large landowners. Moleskin, the fur of the poor, protects the case.

Case
Silver, moleskin
7 × 5 × 4 cm
Edition: Can be delivered as long as there are silversmiths and moles can still be trapped in Opsterland.
Beetsterzwaag (NL)

Beestachtige Schat / Tierischer Schatz, 2016

In vielen Details spiegelt das Produkt von Beetsterzwaag die große ökonomische Ungleichheit, die das Dorf geprägt hat. Eine silberne Schatulle im Hosentaschenformat beinhaltet den Anfang eines Liebesbriefes, ganz zu lesen durch einen Link zu der Gruppe, die das Produkt erdacht hat. Die Schatulle hat die Form einer Bohne, einer einheimischen Bohnensorte folgend, die die Grundlage für ein Arme-Leute-Essen war, jetzt aber bei den guten Köchen, die sich der regionalen Küche verschrieben haben, sehr en vogue ist. Das Silber kann vor Ort verarbeitet werden: Das Handwerk des Silberschmieds hat hier Tradition, denn es gab Nachfrage und Aufträge vonseiten der Großgrundbesitzer. Ein Maulwurfsfell, der Pelz der Armen, schützt die Schatulle.

Schatulle
Silber, Maulwurfsfell
7 × 5 × 4 cm
Auflage: Solange es Silberschmiede gibt und Maulwürfe gefangen werden in Opsterland, kann geliefert werden.
Beetsterzwaag (NL)

Beestachtige Schat, 2016, 8:10 min

Confectie Boxes, 2016

In the landmarked garden of Mien Ruys in Dedemsvaart, the concepts of design that apply are "simple forms and exuberant vegetation" and "do not try to manipulate the soil, but instead adapt your choice of plants to the soil". In the 1960s, Mien Ruys developed the Confectie Borders, instructions for designing small, urban gardens for everyone. In keeping with this idea, the committee of employees and volunteers of Tuinen Mien Ruys produce the Confectie Boxes, *combinations of seeds for particular conditions.*

Seed Boxes
(Sunny Box, Shadow Box, Acid Box, Chalky Box, Bee Box)
Box, seeds, plastic labels
5 × 11 × 18 cm
Edition: each 80
Dedemsvaart (NL)

Confectie Boxes, 2016

Im denkmalgeschützten Garten von Mien Ruys in Dedemsvaart gelten als Konzepte der Gestaltung »einfache Formen und überbordende Vegetation« sowie »Versuche nicht, den Boden zu manipulieren, sondern passe deine Pflanzen dem Boden an«.
In den Sechzigerjahren entwickelte Mien Ruys die Confectie Borders, Anleitungen zur Gestaltung kleiner städtischer Gärten für alle. In Anlehnung daran erfindet und produziert das Komitee von Mitarbeitern und Mitarbeiterinnen des Tuinen Mien Ruys die Confectie Boxes, *Zusammenstellungen von Saatgut für besondere Gegebenheiten.*

Saatgutkisten
(Sunny Box, Shadow Box, Acid Box, Chalky Box, Bee Box)
Karton, Saatgut, Kunststoffschilder
5 × 11 × 18 cm
Auflage: je 80
Dedemsvaart (NL)

Confectie Boxes, 2016, 7:47 min

G

Twisted Bugle, 2016

The British Army moved out of their barracks in Ballykinlar in Northern Ireland, and with the soldiers their families as well. Together with the "Ballykinlar Army Wives" Kathrin has developed a product that recalls everyday life in the barracks. Without having a military need or use, something that looks good on an every mantelpiece. A horn signal was blown every day at the Abercorn Barracks. For the new product Paddy Bloomer, a local artist, twists and transforms a bugle into a candlesnuffer, along with a candle, produced by the Army Wives.

Candlesnuffer with candle
Brass and stearin
40 × 12 × 27 cm
Edition: 10
Ballykinlar / Ballykinler (GB)

AS

Twisted Bugle, 2016

Die britische Armee zieht ab aus ihrer Siedlung im nordirischen Ballykinlar, und mit den Soldaten auch ihre Familien. Mit den »Ballykinlar Army Wives« hat Kathrin ein Produkt entwickelt, das an das Leben in der Siedlung erinnern soll, ohne einen militärischen Gebrauch oder Nutzen zu haben, etwas, das gut aussieht auf jedem Kaminsims. Täglich wurde in den Abercorn Barracks ein Hornsignal geblasen. Das Horn, der Bugle, wird für das neue Produkt von Paddy Bloomer verdreht und umgeformt und damit zu einem glänzenden Kerzenlöscher, komplett mit einer Kerze, gegossen von den Army Wives.

Kerzenlöscher mit Kerze
Messing und Stearin
40 × 12 × 27 cm
Auflage: 10
Ballykinlar / Ballykinler (GB)

AS

Twisted Bugle, 2016, 5:42 min

Classics from our Shop:

Horsemilk Soap, since 2003
Horsemilk Creme, since 2003
Mare milk, vegetable oils, wax, and fat, essential oils
Soap: transparent bioplastic with label, 6 × 11 cm
Edition: unlimited
Wjelsryp, Fryslân (NL)

G

Frogbutter Spoon, 2006
Porcelain
4 × 22 cm
Edition: 100
Höfen, Upper Franconia (DE)

Potato Sleeper, 2009
Felt, webbing
30 × 30 cm
Edition: 60 (new editions 2012 and 2015: each 60)
Neuenkirchen, Lüneburger Heide (DE)

Linseed Oil Cooling Tower, 2009
Glass, cork
12–14 × ø 7.8–8 cm
Edition: 63 (new edition 2012: 40)
Boxberg, Oberlausitz (DE)

Fanas Arrow, 2010
Instructions for producing an arrow that flies a long distance
Wood, paper
Piece of wood ca. 2 × 3 × 50 cm
Instructions 8.75 × 41.11 cm
Edition: unlimited
Fanas, Graubünden (CH)

Tinned Clay, 2011
Clay, tin
7 × ø 10 cm
Edition: 50
Höfen (DE)

Klassiker aus unserem Laden:

Paardenmelk Zeep, seit 2003
Paardenmelk Creme, seit 2003
Stutenmilch, pflanzliche Öle, Wachse und Fette, ätherische Öle
Seife: transparentes Bioplastik mit Aufkleber, 6 × 11 cm
Auflage: unbegrenzt
Wjelsryp, Fryslân (NL)

Froschbutterlöffel, 2006
Porzellan
4 × 22 cm
Auflage: 100
Höfen, Oberfranken (DE)

Kartoffelbeutel, 2009
Filz, Gurtband
30 × 30 cm
Auflage: 60 (Neuauflagen 2012 und 2015: je 60)
Neuenkirchen, Lüneburger Heide (DE)

Leinölkühlturm, 2009
Glas, Kork
12–14 × ø 7,8–8 cm
Auflage: 63 (Neuauflage 2012: 40)
Boxberg, Oberlausitz (DE)

Fanas Arrow, 2010
Anleitung zur Herstellung eines weit fliegenden Pfeils
Holz, Papier
Holzscheit ca. 2 × 3 × 50 cm
Anleitung 8,75 × 41,11 cm
Auflage: unbegrenzt
Fanas, Graubünden (CH)

Lehm in Dosen, 2011
Lehm, Weißblech
7 × ø 10 cm
Auflage: 50
Höfen (DE)

"Es gibt was da ist"
(What you see is what you get)
Tablecloth, 2011
Organic cotton, red and white
jacquard fabric
In total 5500×165 cm
From this, each:
1×825×165 cm
2×660×165 cm
6×495×165 cm
5×85×85 cm
Woven at the Textiel Museum, Tilburg (NL)

Embroidered Workware, 2012
Corn combo, sizes 44–50
Grain combo, sizes 44–52
Potato-beetle-child combo, sizes 92–116
Potato cardigan, sizes 44–52
Willow jacket, sizes 44–50
Edition in total: 69
Schüttdorf (DE)

Ittinger Egg – also called the
"Functionless Egg 'Secret'", 2013
Hops fibres, pressed, clay
12×5×5 cm
Edition: 67
Ittingen (CH)

Word Search Poster, 2013
Poster, four-colour
84.1×59.4 cm (DIN A1)
Edition: 1,000
Birmingham (GB)

Tischdecke »Es gibt was da ist«, 2011
Jacquardgewebe, rot-weiß,
aus organischer Baumwolle
insgesamt 5500×165 cm
davon je:
1×825×165 cm
2×660×165 cm
6×495×165 cm
5×85×85 cm
Gewebt im Textiel Museum, Tilburg (NL)

Bestickte Arbeitskleidung, 2012
Maiskombi, Größe 44–50
Kornkombi, Größe 44–52
Kartoffelkäferkinderkombi, Größe 92–116
Kartoffeljanker, Größe 44–52
Weidejacke, Größe 44–50
Auflage insgesamt: 69
Schüttdorf (DE)

Ittinger Ei – auch genannt
»Funktionsloses Ei ›Geheimnis‹«, 2013
Hopfenfaser, gepresst, Ton
12×5×5 cm
Auflage: 67
Ittingen (CH)

Word Search Poster, 2013
Plakat, vierfarbig
84,1×59,4 cm (DIN A1)
Auflage: 1.000
Birmingham (GB)

G

Großbardau

Saxony / Sachsen, DE

Population: 1,780

Einwohner: 1.780

G

Roads seem to be important. There are roads in the drawings of all the students[1] from Grossbardau. Village roads, federal roads, dirt roads.

The street on which the Museum of Contemporary Art Leipzig is located, is named after Carl Christian Philipp Tauchnitz, the son of the book printer Carl Christoph Traugott Tauchnitz, who was born in Grossbardau in 1761.

A broad and well-tarmacked road runs through Grossbardau itself. There is no village centre as such. We are told the best meeting place is the bus stop or the kiosk. Most of the students at the school in Grossbardau come from other villages. During the school run the meeting point for parents is the car park next to the school. It is 30 kilometres to Leipzig. One would go there quite often, especially on weekends

The number plate is MTL – which is not that cool.
KB

1 The drawings were created within the framework of a six-month-long project with Year Nine students at the school centre in Grossbardau and Myvillages. The project addressed the question of what young people actually do in the countryside today. Where do they meet? What is important? What is a hangout? The observations and results of various exercises and workshops were translated into ideas for a new meeting point, which was opened on the platform in the GfZK garden in July 2015.

Die Straßen seien wichtig. Auf allen Zeichnungen der Schülerinnen und Schüler[1] aus Großbardau sind Straßen. Dorfverbindungsstraßen, Bundesstraßen, Feldwege.

Die Straße, an der die Galerie für Zeitgenössische Kunst in Leipzig liegt, ist nach dem Sohn des 1761 in Großbardau geborenen Buchdruckers Carl Christoph Traugott Tauchnitz, Carl Christian Philipp Tauchnitz, benannt.

Durch Großbardau selbst führt eine der gut ausgebauten Dorfverbindungsstraßen im Muldentalkreis. Eine Dorfmitte als solche gäbe es nicht. Man würde sich an der Bushaltestelle treffen, oder beim Imbiss. Die Schülerinnen des Evangelischen Schulzentrums kommen fast alle aus anderen Dörfern. Treffpunkt der Eltern ist der Parkplatz neben der Schule, am Morgen und beim Abholen. Es sind 30 Kilometer bis in die Stadt. Man führe da schon öfter hin, vor allem am Wochenende.

Das Autokennzeichen ist MTL – das sei weniger cool.
KB

1 Die Zeichnungen sind im Rahmen eines mehrmonatigen Projekts mit Schülerinnen und Schülern der Jahrgangsstufe 9 und 10 des Evangelischen Schulzentrums in Großbardau und Myvillages entstanden. Es ging um die Frage, was Jugendliche heute auf dem Land eigentlich so machen. Wo trifft man sich? Was ist wichtig? Wie sieht der ideale Treffpunkt aus? Die Beobachtungen und Ergebnisse aus unterschiedlichen Übungen und Workshops wurden in Ideen für einen neuen Treffpunkt übersetzt, der im Juli 2015 auf der Plattform im Garten der GfZK eröffnet wurde.

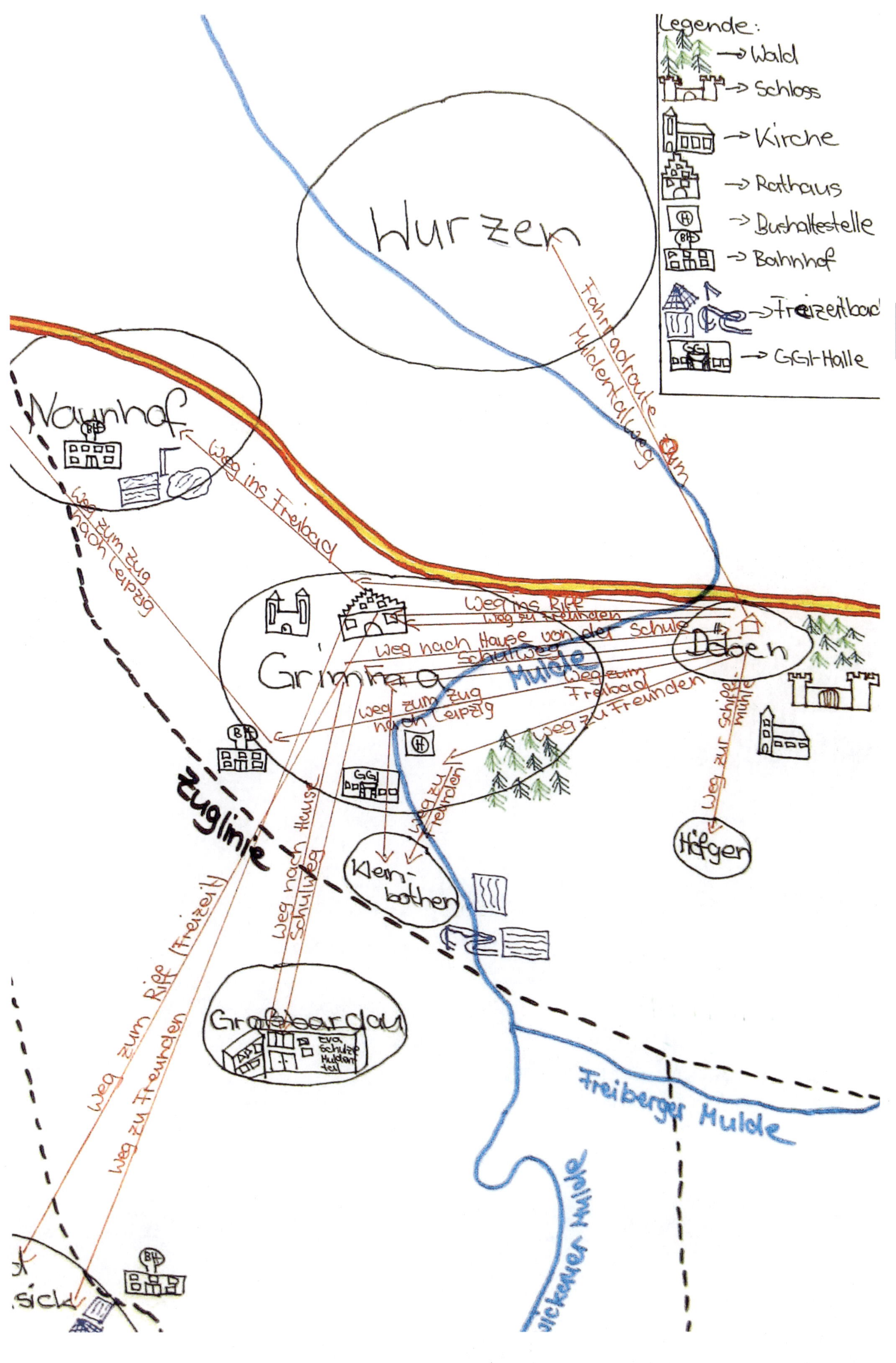
Legende:
Wald
Schloss
Kirche
Rathaus
Bushaltestelle
Bahnhof
Freizeitbad
GGI-Halle
Wurzen
Naunhof
Grimma
Döben
Höfgen
Kleinbothen
Großbardau
Mulde
Freiberger Mulde
Zuglinie
Fahrradroute zum Muldentalweg
Weg ins Freibad
Weg zum Zug nach Leipzig
Weg ins Riff
Weg zu Freunden
Weg nach Hause von der Schule
Schulweg
Weg zum Freibad
Weg zur Schiffsmühle
Weg zu Freunden
Weg nach Hause Schulweg
Weg zum Riff (Freizeit)
Weg zu Freunden
Eva Schulze Muldental

H

Hinojosa del Valle

Extremadura, ES

Population: 514

Einwohner: 514

Hinojosa del Valle is located in the Extremadura, not far from Almendralejo, in the region with the fertile, red, loamy soil. We drive for a long time through grapes, for a long time through olives. The rosary beads on the rear-view mirror sway. A great deal of food is produced here. It's the end of September and still very hot. The men who harvest the grapes rest fatigued in the shade on the side of the road in front of the cooperative. Already harvesting at two or three a.m. in the light of headlamps and unloading the first cart at six has become established practice.

I am staying with Laureano, with Tere, his wife, and Isabel, one of his daughters. Laureano looks after the business of the Yñiguez-Ovando family. The Yñiguez-Ovandos live in Seville. The property has belonged to their family for many generations. The operations comprise 1200 hectares of land on which primarily grain is grown. Laureano shares the work with Ramón; they only hire temporary employees in the planting season. Laureano has lived on the land his entire life. Estates that are no longer needed lie white between the fields of Extremadura. We live in the village, in an old house built by the Yñiguez-Ovandos for four nuns, a house with beautiful tiles, stone floors, and a portrait of Franco in the room of the Patrón. I take siestas on the sofa there. Animals are slaughtered in February. Two of the eight pigs that live in a pen near the old hacienda, near the holm oaks, where I painted the picture, bite the dust. It has to be cold to slaughter; the slaughter is a festive occasion. Everyone works from early until late in the night. Chorizo is made and Salchichones, fat bacon is salted, and ham, the world-famous Jamón ibérico de bellota. After the slaughter, I sometimes receive a packet in Berlin. **AS**

Hinojosa del Valle liegt in der Extremadura, nicht weit von Almendralejo, im Gebiet der roten fruchtbaren Lehmböden. Lange fahren wir durch Wein, lange durch Oliven. Der Rosenkranz am Rückspiegel schaukelt. Hier wird produziert. Es ist Ende September und immer noch sehr heiß. Müde lagern die Männer, die in der Weinlese arbeiten, im Schatten am Straßenrand vor der Kooperative und warten am Mittag, bis ihre Fuhre an der Reihe ist zum Wiegen und Abladen. Es hat sich etabliert, schon um zwei oder drei Uhr im Licht von Kopflampen zu ernten und um sechs das erste Fuder abzuladen.

Ich wohne bei Laureano, bei Tere, seiner Frau, und Isabel, einer seiner Töchter. Laureano ist Verwalter des Betriebs der Familie Yñiguez-Ovando. Die Yñiguez-Ovando leben in Sevilla. Ihnen gehört das Land seit vielen Generationen. Es umfasst 1.200 Hektar, auf denen vor allem allem Getreide angebaut wird. Die Arbeit teilt sich Laureano mit Ramón, nur zur Zeit der Aussaat beschäftigen sie Aushilfen. Laureano hat sein ganzes Leben auf der Finca gelebt. Wir wohnen im Dorf, in einem alten Haus, gebaut von den Yñiguez-Ovando für vier Ordensschwestern, einem Haus mit schönen Kacheln, steinernen Fußböden und einem Porträt Francos im Zimmer des Patrón. Dort auf dem Sofa halte ich Siesta.

Im Februar wird geschlachtet. Zwei der acht Schweine, die im Pferch bei der alten Hacienda leben, bei den Steineichen, wo ich das Bild gemalt habe, müssen dran glauben. Es muss kalt sein zum Schlachten; das Schlachten ist ein Fest. Alle arbeiten von früh bis tief in die Nacht. Chorizo wird gemacht und Salchichones, fetter Speck wird eingesalzen und der Schinken, der weltberühmte Jamón Ibérico de Bellota. Manchmal bekomme ich in Berlin nach dem Schlachten ein Paket. **AS**

H

Höfen

Oberfranken, DE

Population: 250
Landscape: rolling hills
Breweries: one
Shops: none
Most popular drinks: beer and apple spritzer
Most common means of transport: car
Full-time farmers: none
Part-time farmers: two

Einwohner: 250
Landschaft: leicht hügelig
Brauereien: eine
Läden: keine
Beliebteste Getränke: Bier und Apfelschorle
Häufigstes Transportmittel: Auto
Vollerwerbslandwirte: keine
Nebenerwerbslandwirte: zwei

Höfen is a one-road village. The road ascends gently from the lower marshes of the Itz Valley, takes two turns, and then falls away sharply towards Höfenneusig. When you bicycle into the village at night, you notice a temperature difference of two degrees.

A new residential area was built a few years ago, and therefore a second road, which has not yet been given a name. The house numbers are no longer sequential, but chronological.

> The road is swept before holidays.
> For special occasions, the local fried dough specialties, "Ausgezogene Krapfen" and "Geschnittene Hasen", stack up in the living room.
> When everyone washes their windows at the same time, it is either Easter or the village fair.
> Drinking coffee together always takes place on the last Friday of the month.

Until the 1970s, the houses were "typically Franconian", mostly sandstone foundations and timber-frame construction for the rest. The farmyards still open up to the street in a U-form, but nearly all the houses have been replaced with new, solid two-storey buildings with enough space for two to three flats.

The farms themselves have always been relatively small, round only 20 hectares in size. The soil is clay-rich and fertile, and the landscape between the village and forest was characterized by fruit fields, primarily cherries and apples, as well as

Höfen ist ein Straßendorf. Die Straße steigt sanft aus dem Itzgrund auf, macht zwei Kurven und fällt dann steil Richtung Höfenneusig ab. Wenn man mit dem Fahrrad nachts ins Dorf hineinfährt, merkt man den Temperaturunterschied von zwei Grad.

Seit ein paar Jahren gibt es ein Neubaugebiet, und somit auch eine Art zweiter Straße, die jedoch keinen Namen bekommen hat. Die Hausnummern ergeben sich nicht mehr der Reihe nach, sondern in Abfolge der Neubauten.

> Die Straße wird vorm Feiertag gekehrt.
> Zu besonderen Anlässen stapeln sich »Ausgezogene Krapfen« und »Geschnittene Hasen« im Wohnzimmer.
> Wenn alle ihre Fenster gleichzeitig putzen, ist entweder Ostern oder Kirchweih.
> Gemeinsames Kaffeetrinken ist immer am letzten Freitag im Monat.

Die Häuser waren bis in die Siebziger »typisch fränkisch«, also zumeist Sandstein im Erdgeschossbereich und Fachwerk für den Giebel. Die Hofanlagen öffnen sich immer noch U-förmig zur Straße hin, fast alle Häuser sind jedoch durch massive zweistöckige Neubauten mit genug Platz für zwei bis drei Wohnungen ersetzt worden.

Die Höfe selbst waren immer relativ klein, nur um die 20 Hektar groß. Der Boden ist lehmig und fruchtbar und die Landschaft zwischen Dorf und Wald war von Obstäckern geprägt, vorwiegend Kirschen und Äpfel, sowie von Kartoffeln oder Getreide. Zwischen Dorf

→ GOODS

H

potatoes or grain. The land between the village and the river is a floodplain and used for haymaking. There is one part-time farmer who runs a brewery with a beer garden and restaurant. There are still two cows in the village, as a hobby and for the milk.

At about 5:15 a.m., quite a few people drive off to the early morning shift at Bosch or other car supply industries in the region. The bell in the chapel rings at seven, twelve, and six p.m.

In 2005, I suggested to the women that we could invent a product to be presented and sold at the annual village fair. Why? was the question that came as the answer. Because there are local stories, knowledge, and ideas that are worth thinking about collectively. Because it would be nice to see the women of Höfen relating to terms such as innovation and product development. Because something new for the fair would bring back the sales stand, which is missed by many, and it would mean another public space that invites a visit, in addition to the church service and a stop at the pub.

The *Frogbutter Spoon* was created for the fair in 2006, together with a frog wine cork and a frog skeleton cape for Halloween. In 2007, there were *Surplus Doily Bags* and jar lamps. We have made *Village Produce Films*, fruit baked in a shell of clay with noses, *Tinned Clay*, postcards, and, in 2015, the new *Höfer Lace*. **KB**

und Fluss ist das Land Überschwemmungsgebiet und wird zum Heumachen genutzt. Einer der beiden Landwirte betreibt eigentlich eine Brauerei mit Biergarten und Wirtschaft. Kühe gibt es zwei im ganzen Dorf, zum Hobby und für die eigene Milch.

Um 5.15 Uhr morgens fahren etliche zur Frühschicht, bei Bosch oder in einen der Zulieferbetriebe in der Gegend. Um sieben, zwölf und 18 Uhr läutet die Glocke in der Kapelle.

2005 schlug ich den Höfer Frauen vor, gemeinsam ein neues Produkt zu erfinden, das man bei der Kirchweih vorstellen und verkaufen könne. Warum? war die Frage, die als Antwort kam. Weil es lokale Geschichten, Wissen und Ideen gibt, über die es sich lohnt, gemeinsam nachzudenken. Weil es schön wäre, die Höfer Frauen mit Begriffen wie Innovation und Produktentwicklung in Verbindung gebracht zu wissen. Weil eine neue Ware zur Kirchweih den von vielen vermissten Verkaufsstand wieder ins Leben brächte und man neben der Messfeier und dem Wirtshausbesuch einen weiteren öffentlichen Raum hätte, der zum Besuch einlädt.

Zur Kirchweih 2006 entstanden der *Froschbutterlöffel*, ein Froschweinkorken und ein Froschskelettcape für Halloween. 2007 gab es *Häkeldeckchentaschen* und Weckglaslampen. Es gab *Village Produce Films*, in Lehm gebackenes Obst mit Nasen, *Lehm in Dosen*, Postkarten und 2015 die *Höfer Spitze*. **KB**

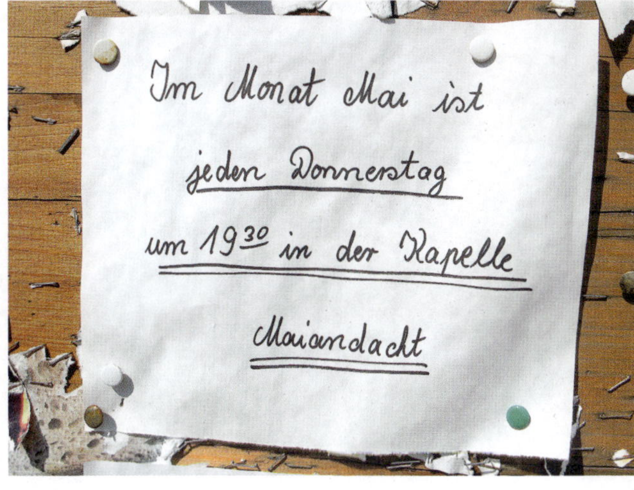
Im Monat Mai ist
jeden Donnerstag
um 19^{30} in der Kapelle
Maiandacht

Ich bin gerne Bauer und möchte es auch gerne bleiben

I offer farmers a barter transaction: a painting of their farm for a film in which they, the farmers, present their business and their work. My aunt had such a painting of her parents' farm, done in 1947, at a time when artists made few sales and farmers were popular exchange partners.

I like being a farmer and I would like to stay one was begun in 2000, first in my hometown, Heiligendorf, and its surroundings. Since 2007, I have been working on this project in cooperation with Thomas Sprenger.

While I stand with my easel on the farm, like a plein air painter of the 19th century, the farmers film themselves and comment on their film. We generally need one week for this. Whenever possible, Thomas edits the films along with the farmers.

The paintings remain at the farmsteads. Our archive contains more than 30 films about agriculture, from Macedonia, Romania and Switzerland, from Austria, England and Wales, from the Netherlands, Germany and Spain. The most recent films come from Andalusia, Extremadura, León, and South Africa.

I like being a farmer and I would like to stay one is the final sentence in the first film in our archive. Many farmers could have said the same.

The Cartuja de Sevilla produced a porcelain plate with this sentence. **AS**

Ich biete Bauern ein Tauschgeschäft an: ein Gemälde von ihrem Hof gegen einen Film, in dem sie, die Bauern, ihren Betrieb und ihre Arbeit darstellen. Meine Tante hatte ein solches Gemälde vom Hof ihrer Eltern, gemalt 1947, zu einer Zeit, als Künstler wenig Absatz hatten und die Bauern beliebte Tauschpartner waren.

Ich bin gerne Bauer und möchte es auch gerne bleiben wurde im Jahr 2000 begonnen, zunächst in meinem Heimatort Heiligendorf und in dessen Umgebung. Seit 2007 arbeite ich an diesem Projekt gemeinsam mit Thomas Sprenger.

Während ich mit meiner Staffelei auf dem Hof stehe wie eine Plein-Air-Malerin aus dem 19. Jahrhundert, filmen die Bauern sich selbst und kommentieren ihren Film. Meistens brauchen wir dafür eine Woche. Wann immer es geht, schneidet Thomas die Filme gemeinsam mit den Bauern.

Die Bilder bleiben auf den Höfen. Unser Archiv enthält mehr als 30 Filme über die Landwirtschaft aus Mazedonien, Rumänien und der Schweiz, aus Österreich, England und Wales, aus den Niederlanden, Deutschland und Spanien. Die neuesten kommen aus Andalusien, der Extremadura, León und Südafrika.

Ich bin gerne Bauer und möchte es auch gerne bleiben ist der letzte Satz im ersten Film unseres Archivs. Viele Bauern hätten ihn so sagen können.

Die Cartuja de Sevilla hat einen Porzellanteller mit diesem Satz produziert. **AS**

Cuevas del Becerro, Andalusía, ES

This year was a good year, and we got 47 barrels, which is 14 thousand kilos of honey, and, for me, that's a lot.

Almost all the honey that's produced in Spain is exported to the European Union. That's a pity, since the Spanish population feeds itself honey imported from third countries, although it would be able to supply itself. We export some 30 million kilos of honey, and the consumption is just a high.

I have orange blossom honey, also two barrels, 600 kilos, honey of tomillo, thyme. There are some kinds of honey I don't like the taste of, chestnut honey, for example, but the Germans and Arabs really like it.

The bee species that we work with throughout the region is an autochthone species of bee from North Africa and the south of Spain, from Andalusia, Morocco, and Tunisia. It's an aggressive bee, that's its character, but a bee that is well-suited to the Mediterranean climate, with long dry periods, and resistant to many diseases.

My parents were small farmers. Our farm was not big enough to feed all the children, and so we went to work outside. I worked for 15 years as a tractor driver, goatherd, and cheese-maker.

The entire time that I was working for other people, I longed for independence, to produce for myself and be personally responsible. For me, the way to do so was beekeeping.

The future of our village is in agriculture. There are many people who went to work in construction on the coast, but there's no work there anymore. Fortunately, we did not sell our land here in the village, as people in

Dieses Jahr war ein gutes Jahr und wir haben 47 Fässer bekommen, das sind 14.000 Kilo Honig, und für mich ist das eine Menge.

Fast der gesamte Honig, der in Spanien produziert wird, wird in die Europäische Union exportiert. Das ist schade, denn die spanische Bevölkerung ernährt sich von Honig, der aus Drittländern importiert wird, obwohl sie sich selbst versorgen könnte. Wir exportieren etwa 30 Millionen Kilo Honig, und genauso groß ist der Verbrauch.

Ich habe Orangenblütenhonig und auch Thymianhonig, zwei Fässer, 600 Kilo. Es gibt einige Honigsorten, die mir selbst nicht schmecken, Kastanienhonig zum Beispiel, aber die Deutschen und die Araber mögen ihn gern.

Die Biene, mit der wir in der ganzen Region arbeiten, ist eine autochthone Bienenart aus dem Norden Afrikas und Süden Spaniens, aus Andalusien, Marokko und Tunesien. Es ist eine aggressive Biene, so ist ihr Charakter, aber eine Biene, die dem mediterranen Klima mit langen Trockenzeiten gut angepasst ist und resistent gegen viele Krankheiten.

Meine Eltern waren Kleinbauern. Unser Hof war nicht groß genug, um alle Kinder zu ernähren, und so sind wir außerhalb arbeiten gegangen. 15 Jahre lang habe ich als Traktorist, als Ziegenhirte und als Käser gearbeitet.

Die ganze Zeit, in der ich für andere gearbeitet habe, habe ich mich nach der Unabhängigkeit dessen gesehnt, der selbst und in eigener Verantwortung produziert. Der Weg dahin war für mich die Imkerei.

Die Zukunft unseres Dorfes liegt in der Landwirtschaft. Es gab viele Menschen, die an der Küste im Baugewerbe gearbeitet haben, aber dort gibt es keine Arbeit mehr. Glücklicherweise

Untitled / ohne Titel (Cuevas del Becerro), 2014, oil on wood / Öl auf Holz, 45 x 64 cm

villages located closer to the coast did; so, many people are now able to use their land again, to grow something, to earn a little money, and to be active.

Fortunately, we are able to sell our olive oil really well. The olives that we grow produce an oil whose taste clients like.

I joined the union in Malaga. I was made the person responsible for beekeeping in the region, and the Provincial Secretary of COAG – the Spanish union of farmers and livestock breeders.

As a result, I have gotten to know many people from all over Spain, also comrades from La Vía Campesina and other associations. I have learned a lot from them and they have very much enriched my life.

"The low price for milk and the general crisis in the dairy sector in our region have resulted in the closing of many businesses …"

This is a report about one of the campaigns that we organized along with COAG. The milk producers not only did not earn anything each month, they even lost money; the whole family was occupied with the 500 goats, every day, four workers, and, at the end of the month, they didn't have enough money for food.

For example, we are also fighting so that the subsidies from the European Union – the money that all of us contribute as taxpayers – does not primarily go to the large landowners, but is instead distributed more fairly. In addition, it's the small businesses that create workplaces, which is what we need most!

When I once again dedicate myself exclusively to my own business, other compañeros will continue the work of COAG and advance our cause.

As farmers and livestock breeders, as village residents, we have to take a position and shape our society actively and in a community of solidarity with others.

haben wir hier im Dorf unser Land nicht verkauft, anders als die Dörfer, die näher an der Küste liegen; so können jetzt viele ihr Land wieder nutzen, um etwas anzubauen, ein kleines Einkommen zu erwirtschaften und aktiv zu sein.

Glücklicherweise können wir unser Olivenöl gut verkaufen. Die Oliven, die wir kultivieren, geben ein Öl, dessen Geschmack den Kunden gefällt.

Ich habe mich der Gewerkschaft in Málaga angeschlossen. Ich wurde zum Verantwortlichen der Region für Imkerei ernannt, und dann zum Provinzsekretär der COAG – der spanischen Gewerkschaft der Landwirte und Viehzüchter.

Ich habe dadurch viele Menschen kennengelernt, in ganz Spanien, auch Genossen von La Vía Campesina und anderen Verbänden. Ich habe viel von ihnen gelernt und sie haben mein Leben sehr bereichert.

»Der niedrige Milchpreis und die generelle Krise der Milchwirtschaft in unserer Region haben dazu geführt, dass mehrere Betriebe schließen mussten …«

Dies ist ein Bericht über eine der Kampagnen, die wir mit der COAG organisiert haben. Die Milchproduzenten haben jeden Monat nicht nur nichts verdient, sondern Geld verloren, die ganze Familie war mit den 500 Ziegen beschäftigt, jeden Tag, vier Arbeitskräfte, und am Ende des Monats hatten sie nicht genug Geld fürs Essen.

Zum Beispiel kämpfen wir auch dafür, dass die Subventionen der Europäischen Union, das Geld, das wir alle als Steuerzahler beitragen, nicht vor allem an die Großgrundbesitzer geht, sondern gerechter verteilt wird. Zudem sind es die kleinen Betriebe, die für Arbeitsplätze sorgen, das, was wir am meisten brauchen!

Wenn ich mich wieder ausschließlich meinem eigenen Betrieb widme, werden andere Compañeros die Arbeit der COAG weiterführen und unsere Anliegen voranbringen.

Als Landwirte und Viehzüchter, als Dorfbewohner müssen wir Position beziehen und aktiv und in solidarischer Gemeinschaft mit anderen die Gesellschaft gestalten.

Juan García, Cuevas del Becerro, 2014, 24 min

Hinojosa del Valle, Extremadura, ES

My name is Fernando Yñiguez-Ovando. I am one of seven brothers, and together we have two agricultural holdings in Extremadura. My father runs them; he is 91 years old, but he is the person responsible.

I'm Laureano Rosario. I've worked at the Finca Yñiguez-Ovando my whole life. I began at the age of 14. Now, I look after the business.

The property has belonged to my family for many generations. Over time, the areas have become smaller and smaller, that's the natural distribution of the estate to heirs; but my father is still able to live entirely from his property.

Here's a piece of land that belongs to me, my sons, and has nothing to do with the finca. Here we have olives, young olive trees of about three years of age.

My sons Laure and José work our own land and help on the finca in the season.

Mein Name ist Fernando Yñiguez-Ovando. Ich bin einer von sieben Brüdern, und zusammen haben wir zwei landwirtschaftliche Betriebe in der Extremadura. Mein Vater führt sie; er ist 91 Jahre alt, aber er ist der Verantwortliche.

Ich bin Laureano Rosario. Mein ganzes Leben habe ich auf der Finca Yñiguez-Ovando gearbeitet. Mit 14 Jahren habe ich begonnen. Jetzt bin ich Verwalter.

Der Besitz gehört meiner Familie seit vielen Generationen. Mit der Zeit sind die Flächen immer kleiner geworden, das ist die natürliche Erbteilung; aber mein Vater kann noch vollständig von seinem Grundbesitz leben.

Hier ist ein Stück Land, das mir gehört, meinen Söhnen, und das nichts mit der Finca zu tun hat. Hier haben wir Oliven, junge Olivenbäume von etwa drei Jahren.

Meine Söhne Laure und José bearbeiten unser eigenes Land und helfen in der Saison auf der Finca.

We also have an organic olive grove, over here. Naturally, in organic production, it's not possible to fight against things, and production is therefore quite a bit lower. You can't fertilize, you can't treat diseases, and production is therefore halved. That's why organic olive oil has to be expensive.

The biggest problem in the case of organic production is the olive fly. This fly settles in the olives, making the olives grow incorrectly and fall to the ground. In the end, you find 40 per cent on the ground and have to throw them away. That hurts.

There's a subsidy for organic production, and with the subsidy, the cultivation is worthwhile, since it compensates for the loss.

Here in the storage space, everything is full after the slaughter, the whole attic is full: the sausages, the chorizo, the blood sausage, the salchichones, the lomo would hang there; in January there's sometimes heavy frost and it freezes at night in the attic. The heat of the day is not strong enough to thaw out the attic, and we make a fire on the ground so that the frost of the night goes away during the day. Everything in the attic then ages well.

Wir haben auch einen ökologischen Olivenhain, hier drüben. Klar, in der ökologischen Produktion lässt sich nichts bekämpfen, und so fällt die Produktion bedeutend geringer aus. Man kann nicht düngen, man kann Krankheiten nicht behandeln, und so halbiert sich die Produktion. Darum muss das ökologische Olivenöl teurer sein.

Das größte Problem bei der ökologischen Produktion ist die Olivenfliege. Diese Fliegen setzen sich in die Oliven, die Oliven wachsen nicht richtig und fallen zu Boden. 40 Prozent findet man am Ende auf dem Boden und muss sie wegwerfen. Das tut weh.

Es gibt eine Subvention für ökologische Produktion, und mit der Subvention lohnt sich der Anbau, sie kompensiert den Verlust.

Hier in der Vorratskammer füllt sich alles nach dem Schlachten, das ganze Dach füllt sich: Da hängen die Würste, der Chorizo, die Blutwurst, die Salchichones, der Lomo; im Januar dann gibt es manchmal starken Frost und in der Nacht friert es im Dachboden. Die Wärme des Tages ist nicht stark genug, um den Dachboden aufzutauen, und dann machen wir ein Feuer auf dem Boden, damit der Frost der Nacht am Tag verschwindet. So reift alles auf dem Dachboden gut.

Untitled / ohne Titel (Hinojosa del Valle), 2014, oil on wood / Öl auf Holz, 42 × 70 cm

I

Finca Yñiguez-Ovando, Laureano Rosario, Hinojosa del Valle, 2014, 24 min

Solms-Delta, Western Cape, ZA

My name is Hagen Viljoen. I'm the winemaker and general manager at Solms-Delta. We are basically a wine farm situated in Franschhoek in the Franschhoek wine valley.

Our farm adheres to a third ownership model, owned jointly by the farm workers', Richard Astor, and Mark Solms. The workers' side is managed by a workers' trust, which provides them with better eductaion, better housing, better medical care. [1]

Solms-Delta as a wine farm and brand is basically 70 hectares of property, with 30 hectares under wine, of which 60 per cent is red wine and over 40 per cent is white wine. We are in the lower lying, more river alluvial soil area of the Franschhoek Valley, so the soils are quite sandy and deep, which gives very nice fruity expression to the wines. We use this specifically in our lifestyle range. And then for our premium wines, our blended range, we actually source different vineyard parcels throughout the Western Cape and try to get the best grapes we can get our hands on from different sites, including some of our own farm sites.

Through Solms-Delta, we employ about 100 people in different capacities – obviously we have the cellar which is the main production hub of the farm, the vineyards, the vineyard team; we also have a restaurant on the farm.

When Mark bought the farm, the first thing he did was actually explore its past with an archaeological dig on the farm. And what they found was quite interesting: Below the old homestead they found a Kooi settlement which dates to 2000 or 3000 years ago. One of the farm workers told Mark: "You see, Sir, our people were here before your people."

We are a wine business and through wine production, vineyard, viticulture production, and our various wine brands we ultimately need to sell the wine to be able to sustain the whole business enterprise. When you are trying to transform people's lives you can't say, "In ten years from now, when we are a profitable business, we will give you benefits." So the challenge has always been – as we are striving to increase our business and make it sustainable – to offer those benefits already. Which has put a lot of cash flow pressure on the business.

Some markets are very sympathetic to our story and what we are trying to do and other markets are more focused on price point. One would have thought there would be more sympathy and support for the story than we do actually find. We've found that our brand is very much a hand-sell, you need to tell the story and get the support behind it. Which works for premium wine, but

Mein Name ist Hagen Viljoen. Ich bin der Kellermeister und Geschäftsführer bei Solms-Delta. Solms-Delta ist ein Weinbaubetrieb in Franschhoek im Weinanbaugebiet Franschhoek Valley.

Das Eigentum an unserem Betrieb ist nach einem Third-Ownership-Modell dreigeteilt: Ein Drittel gehört den Arbeitern, je ein Drittel gehört Richard Astor bzw. Mark Solms. Die Arbeiterseite ist in einem Trust organisiert, was bessere Ausbildung, bessere Unterbringung, bessere Gesundheitsversorgung für sie gewährleistet. [1]

Solms-Delta ist etwa 70 Hektar groß, davon steht auf etwa 30 Hektar Wein, davon wiederum sind 60 Prozent Rot- und 40 Prozent Weißweine. Unser Land befindet sich in den tiefer gelegenen Schwemmgebieten des Franschhoek Valley, dadurch sind die Böden ziemlich sandig und tiefgründig, was den Weinen eine feine Fruchtnote verleiht. Diese bringen wir besonders bei unseren Lifestyle-Produkten zur Geltung. Für unsere höherwertigen Weine, unsere Cuvées, verwenden wir Trauben aus verschiedenen Lagen des westlichen Capes, wir versuchen die besten Trauben aus den verschiedenen Anbauflächen zu bekommen, davon stammen einige auch aus eigenem Anbau. Diese Weine vermarkten wir unter einem separaten Label.

Solms-Delta beschäftigt in den verschiedenen Bereichen rund 100 Personen: Hier auf der Farm gibt es die Kellerei, den Hauptproduktionsort, die Rebflächen sowie das Weinbauteam; außerdem haben wir ein Restaurant.

Das Erste, was Marc tat, nachdem er die Farm gekauft hatte, war, die Vergangenheit archäologisch zu untersuchen. Dabei fanden sie etwas Interessantes: Unter dem alten Gehöft, wo sie mit der Ausgrabung begonnen hatten, fanden sie eine Siedlung und Artefakte der Kooi, die 2000 bis 3000 Jahre alt sind. Einer der Farmarbeiter, der an den Grabungen beteiligt war, meinte daraufhin zu Mark: »Sehen Sie, unsere Leute waren vor Ihren Leuten hier.«

Am Ende sind wir ein Unternehmen, und mit der Weinherstellung, den Rebflächen, den verschiedenen Produkten und Weinmarken müssen wir wirtschaftlich arbeiten und schließlich ausreichend verkaufen, um bestehen zu können. Will man das Leben von Menschen verändern, kann man nicht einfach sagen: »Wenn wir in zehn Jahren ein gewinnbringender Betrieb geworden sind, werdet ihr davon profitieren.« Die Herausforderung war stets, diese Zusatzleistungen und Vorteile schon gleich anbieten zu können – noch während wir versuchen, das Geschäft zu erweitern und zu stabilisieren. Das hat einen enormen Liquiditätsdruck mit sich gebracht.

Einige Märkte reagieren sehr wohlwollend auf unsere Geschichte und unsere Ideen, andere Märkte dagegen sind

Solms-Delta (Franschhoek Valley), oil on wood / Öl auf Holz, 39 × 65 cm

for the lower price points, where you want volume, you don't always have that connection with your customer. And that's a very challenging point for us in our business strategy.

1 Politics in South Africa are trying to redistribute the ownership of land and means of production through the Black Economic Empowerment Program, among others. Mark Solms, a neuroscientist by profession, took over custodianship of Solms-Delta a few years after the end of apartheid. He is trying to transform the farm and make it into an example of economic viability combined with social and cultural development, for instance, by promoting employee co-ownership.

stärker preisorientiert. Insgesamt würde man erwarten, dass es mehr Sympathie und Unterstützung geben müsste, als wir tatsächlich erfahren. Wir haben gemerkt, dass unsere Marke im persönlichen Verkauf sehr gut ankommt, man muss die Geschichte erzählen und bekommt dann auch Unterstützung. Bei den Premium-Weinen funktioniert das gut, weniger bei den günstigeren, absatzorientierten Produkten, wo man diese Verbindung zum Kunden meist nicht hat. Für unsere Strategie ist das immer eine Herausforderung.

1 Südafrikas Politik versucht, das Eigentum an Land und Produktionsmitteln umzuverteilen, unter anderem durch das Black Economic Empowerment Program. Solms-Delta wurde einige Jahre nach dem Ende der Apartheid von Mark Solms, eigentlich Neurowissenschaftler, zurückgekauft. Er bemüht sich, die Farm zu transformieren und zu einem Beispiel für ökonomische Tragfähigkeit verbunden mit sozialer und kultureller Entwicklung zu machen, unter anderem durch die Teilhabe der Mitarbeiter am Eigentum.

Solms-Delta, Franschhoek Valley, 2016, 23 min

LAND OWNERS

County of Bentheim (DE)
For tax reasons, one enterprise is often assessed as several enterprises; a business then consists of several tax enterprises. Last year, 1544 enterprises filed land-use applications for 60,838 hectares of land in County of Bentheim – the average enterprise size would accordingly be 39.4 hectares. In reality, the average size of an enterprise in County of Bentheim is presumably round 50 hectares. Traditionally, enterprises are comparatively small and animals are kept on principal – it is not possible to live from an enterprise of such a size with pure crop cultivation. Such an enterprise occupies an average of two workers.

In the Province of Hannover, there are commercial farms with crop cultivation of round 200 hectares, in East Germany of 300, 400, or 500 hectares. In Southern Germany the average enterprise size is even smaller than in County of Bentheim, with round 20 hectares.

Franschhoek Valley, Western Cape (ZA)
In the Franschhoek Valley, wine grapes are cultivated, with a cultivation area of 30 to 70 hectares per enterprise. One enterprise employs some 100 workers.

Cuevas del Becerro, Andalusia (ES)
The village of Cuevas del Becerro includes 1,600 hectares of land used for cultivation. The farms are small, with an average area of two hectares. The most important thing is olive cultivation, from which 400,000 kilos of olive oil of very high quality are obtained. Grains, anise, chickpeas, beans, and vegetables are also cultivated. Livestock farming includes four enterprises with sheep, two with goats and two with pigs, one with cows and one with horses, and 19 beekeepers.

Byers and Deer Trail, Colorado (US)
A mid-size ranch has an area of 12,000 acres, therefore nearly 5,000 hectares, used as grazing land and for grain farming on large fields. One such enterprise is managed by a father with two sons; they have also bought larger ranches in Nebraska and Kansas. From them comes the hay that is waiting in stacks to be fed to the cows in the winter. The neighbour has nearly 30,000 acres; it is not possible to see all of it at one time, even when the weather is clear.

Grafschaft Bentheim (DE)
Aus steuerlichen Gründen wird ein Betrieb häufig als mehrere Betriebe veranlagt; ein Unternehmen besteht dann aus mehreren steuerlichen Betrieben. Für 60.838 Hektar Land wurden in der Grafschaft Bentheim im letzten Jahr von 1.544 Betrieben Flächennutzungsanträge gestellt – demnach wäre die durchschnittliche Betriebsgröße 39,4 Hektar. Real liegt die durchschnittliche Betriebsgröße in der Grafschaft Bentheim vermutlich bei 50 Hektar. Traditionell sind die Betriebe vergleichsweise klein, und grundsätzlich werden Tiere gehalten – mit reinem Ackerbau kann man von dieser Betriebsgröße nicht leben. Ein solcher Betrieb beschäftigt im Schnitt zwei Arbeitskräfte.

Im Hannoverschen gibt es Haupterwerbsbetriebe im Ackerbau von etwa 200 Hektar, in Ostdeutschland von 300, 400 oder 500 Hektar. In Süddeutschland ist die durchschnittliche Betriebsgröße noch geringer als in der Grafschaft, mit etwa 20 Hektar.

Franschhoek Valley, Western Cape (ZA)
Im Franschhoek Valley wird Weinbau betrieben, mit einer Anbaufläche von 30 bis 70 Hektar je Betrieb. Ein Betrieb beschäftigt etwa 100 Arbeitskräfte.

Cuevas del Becerro, Andalusien (ES)
Zum Dorf Cuevas del Becerro gehören 1.600 Hektar zum Anbau genutztes Land. Die landwirtschaftlichen Betriebe sind mit einer Durchschnittsfläche von 2 Hektar klein. Am wichtigsten ist der Anbau von Oliven, aus denen 400.000 Kilo Olivenöl von sehr guter Qualität gewonnen werden. Auch Getreide, Anis, Kichererbsen, Bohnen und Gemüse werden kultiviert. Zur Viehhaltung zählen vier Betriebe mit Schafen, je zwei mit Ziegen und Schweinen, je einer mit Kühen und Pferden sowie 19 Imker.

Byers und Deer Trail, Colorado (US)
Eine mittelgroße Ranch hat eine Fläche von 12.000 Acres, also beinahe 5.000 Hektar, genutzt als Weide und für den Getreideanbau auf großen Feldern. Einen solchen Betrieb bewirtschaftet hier zum Beispiel ein Vater mit zwei Söhnen, und sie haben zusätzlich in Nebraska und Kansas größere Ranches gekauft. Von dort kommt das Heu, das in Stapeln wartet, um im Winter an die Rinder verfüttert zu werden. Der Nachbar hat beinahe 30.000 Acres, das ist auch bei klarem Wetter nicht zu überblicken.

Beetsterzwaag, Friesland (NL)

In Beetsterzwaag, farmers lease their land from various land-owning families or foundations connected with these families. Ownership of land is based on wealth that was acquired through peat extraction and trade. The same families own the publically accessible forest and recreation areas. All areas that are not used for agriculture can only be entered from sunrise to sunset, and then also only for hiking on specified paths.

In other parts of Friesland, in Greidhoeke, for instance, farmers own the land they work; some people lease land from the Protestant church, as well.

Kent (GB)

Ninety-six per cent of all holdings in England are owned by a "sole holder". Of these 96 per cent sole holders, 84 per cent are men, 16 per cent are women.

Sixty-two per cent of farm holders are over 55. Around 32 per cent of these holders are over 65 years old. Only 12 per cent are run by someone under 44.

The average income of UK farms in 2014–15 was £39,600. The average for horticulture farms was £31,500.

Fifty-five per cent of Kent horticulture is top fruit (orchards), compared to nine per cent nationally. 11.6 per cent is small fruit (berries), compared to 3.4 per cent nationally.

In 1925, Kent had 21,790 hectares of orchards, in 1965 26,665 hectares, and in 2013 only 7281 hectares.

Nationally, 476,000 people work on farms, of which 66,000 are seasonal workers. In Kent, casual/seasonal workers makes up 40 per cent of the workforce, in contrast to 14 per cent nationally.

Ten per cent of farms in Kent are smaller than five hectares, 34 per cent have between five and 20 hectares, 21 per cent between 20 and 50, 12 per cent between 50 and 100, and 23 per cent of farms are bigger than 100 hectares.

Total fruit production across the UK in 2014 was 427,000 tonnes, with a value of £622 million. 104,000 tonnes of strawberries were grown, with a value of £244 million.

Beetsterzwaag, Friesland (NL)

In Beetsterzwaag pachten die Bauern ihr Land von einigen grundbesitzenden Familien oder Stiftungen, die in Zusammenhang mit diesen Familien stehen. Der Grundbesitz beruht auf Vermögen, die mit dem Torfabbau und -handel erworben wurden. Die öffentlich zugänglichen Wald- und Erholungsflächen sind im Besitz derselben Familien. Sämtliche Flächen, die nicht der Landwirtschaft dienen, dürfen nur von Sonnenaufgang bis Sonnenuntergang betreten werden, und auch dann nur zum Wandern auf vorgegebenen Wegen.

In anderen Gegenden Frieslands, Greidhoeke zum Beispiel, besitzen die Bauern das Land, auf dem sie arbeiten; manche pachten Flächen von der protestantischen Kirche dazu.

Kent (GB)

96 Prozent aller landwirtschaftlichen Güter in England gehören einem »sole holder« oder Alleinbesitzer. Von diesen 96 Prozent sind 84 Prozent Männer, 16 Prozent Frauen.

62 Prozent aller Landwirte sind älter als 55 Jahre, etwa 32 Prozent älter als 65 Jahre. Nur 12 Prozent der Betriebe werden von einer Person geleitet, die jünger als 44 Jahre ist.

Das Durchschnittseinkommen einer Landwirtschaft im Vereinigten Königreich betrug 2014/15 39.600 Pfund, das Einkommen eines durchschnittlichen Gartenbaubetriebs 31.500 Pfund.

55 Prozent des Erwerbsgartenbaus in Kent entfallen auf Obstgärten, gegenüber 9 Prozent im Landesdurchschnitt. 11,6 Prozent machen Kleinfrüchte (Beeren) aus, gegenüber 3,4 Prozent im Landesdurchschnitt.

1925 gab es in Kent 21.790 Hektar Obstbau, 1955 waren es 26.665 Hektar, 2013 nur noch 7.281 Hektar.

Im ganzen Land arbeiten 476.000 Menschen in der Landwirtschaft, davon 66.000 Saisonarbeiter. In Kent macht die Gelegenheits- bzw. Saisonarbeit 40 Prozent des Arbeitskräfteaufkommens aus, gegenüber 14 Prozent im Landesdurchschnitt.

10 Prozent der Höfe sind kleiner als 5 Hektar, 34 Prozent besitzen zwischen 5 und 20 Hektar, 21 Prozent zwischen 20 und 50 Hektar und 12 Prozent zwischen 50 und 100 Hektar. 23 Prozent der Landwirtschaften sind größer als 100 Hektar.

Die Gesamtproduktion an Früchten betrug 2014 im Vereinigten Königreich 427.000 Tonnen, mit einem Gesamtwert von 622 Millionen Pfund. Es wurden allein 104.000 Tonnen Erdbeeren mit einem Wert von 244 Millionen Pfund angebaut.

LANDSCAPE

The windows on intercity trains don't open. The landscape flashes past, the exact same landscape that supplies us with minerals and agricultural produce. The passengers are online and in good spirits. You can see at a glance that our modern-day schedules are no longer dictated by the harvest.

The same is true for me, but having grown up on a farm in Friesland, I have first-hand experience of the stress of harvest time and the relentless rhythms of keeping livestock. I was reminded of all this in 2014, when we were filming at dairy farms, and I saw that the timetable was still dominated by the daily feeding and milking regimes. Together we worked our way through the script and each day ended with shots of the milking robot.

The etymology of the word "agriculture" tells us that working the land is a cultural activity. The relevance of contemplating and representing landscape is underlined by a process that unfolded in the 16th and 17th century, in which landscape was transformed, little by little, into an artistic genre, through shedding its religious and mythological trappings. Over the centuries, landscape has shown itself to be a genre that can channel indefinable feelings and narrate our relationship with our environment. What does our view of landscape say about the time in which we live? What do our landscapes say about our culture? These are sweeping questions that I explored with the aid of *Filosofie van het Landschap* by the Dutch author Ton Lemaire (1970).[1]

"Landscape can be viewed from two main perspectives: the natural science perspective derived from a rational and objective relationship with the earth, which makes its subjugation possible, and the emotional and aesthetic perspective, which complements and compensates for the one-sidedness of the natural science perspective. Accordingly, landscape perfectly embodies the ambivalence of progress and reminds us of our own existential contradictions. It serves as a mirror, reflecting the tensions in our culture by objectivizing the riches and anomalies of our way of life and our history."

From the very start, the interpretation and representation of landscape have invited us to review and rethink our living environment. In 1994 I published a critique on the "framing of all things rural": "You talk to me about the farming life. You draw a picture of the world I grew up in. I let you talk, not because I am interested in your story, but because I am

Die Fenster im Intercity lassen sich nicht öffnen. Die Landschaft rast vorbei – dieselbe Landschaft, die uns mit Bodenschätzen und landwirtschaftlichen Erzeugnissen versorgt. Die Zugreisenden sind online und man sieht ihnen auf den ersten Blick an, dass unsere heutige Terminplanung von keiner Ernte mehr bestimmt ist.

Da ich aber auf einem Bauernhof in Friesland aufgewachsen bin, kenne ich den Stress der Erntesaison und den unerbittlichen Rhythmus der Viehhaltung aus eigener Erfahrung. All das fiel mir wieder ein, als wir 2014 auf Milchhöfen filmten und mir klar wurde, dass der Tagesablauf dort immer noch vom täglichen Regime des Fütterns und Melkens bestimmt ist.

Das Wort »Agrikultur« verrät uns im Gegensatz zur deutschen »Landwirtschaft«, dass die Bebauung des Landes ein kulturelles Handeln ist. Welche große Rolle das Betrachten und Abbilden von Landschaft dabei spielt, ergibt sich aus einem Prozess, der seit dem 16. Jahrhundert die Landschaft ganz allmählich in eine Kunstgattung verwandelt hat, während diese zugleich ihr religiöses und mythologisches Beiwerk ablegte. Über die Jahrhunderte hat sich die Landschaft als ein Genre erwiesen, das undefinierbare Gefühle übermitteln und von unserem Verhältnis zur Umwelt erzählen kann. Was sagt unsere Sicht der Landschaft über die Zeit aus, in der wir leben? Was verraten unsere Landschaften über unsere Kultur? Diesen weit ausholenden Fragen bin ich mithilfe des 1970 von Ton Lemaire[1] verfassten Buchs *Filosofie van het Landschap* (Philosophie der Landschaft) nachgegangen:

»Landschaft kann man von zwei Gesichtspunkten aus betrachten: einem naturwissenschaftlichen, der sich von einem rationalen und objektiven Umgang mit der Erde leiten lässt und ihre Unterwerfung begünstigt, sowie einem emotionalen und ästhetischen, der die Einseitigkeit der naturwissenschaftlichen Sicht ergänzt und kompensiert. Dementsprechend veranschaulicht Landschaft in vollkommener Weise die Ambivalenz des Fortschritts und erinnert an unsere eigenen existenziellen Widersprüche. Sie dient uns als Spiegel, der den Reichtum und die Anomalien unserer Lebensweise und Geschichte vergegenständlicht und so auch die inneren Spannungen unserer Kultur reflektiert.«

Interpretationen und Darstellungen von Landschaft boten von jeher die Gelegenheit, unsere belebte Umwelt anders zu sehen und anders zu denken. 1994 kritisierte ich die »Inszenierung des Landlebens«: »Ihr erzählt mir vom Leben auf dem Bauernhof. Ihr malt Bilder von der Welt, in der ich aufgewachsen bin. Ich lasse euch reden, nicht weil mich eure Geschichte interessiert, sondern

fascinated by your faith in its accuracy. How dare you not doubt yourself! How dare you turn my youth into a stereotype!" [2] Given the relentless pressure on our natural resources, the need, in the 21st century, to question rural landscapes is more urgent than ever. Myvillages organizes geological excursions and fruit-picking events, and visits modern farmers and ranchers for weeks on end. The interdisciplinary approach is, in itself, a cultural event, which delivers, for example, a piece of rock, a bottle of beer, a documentary film or a drawing.

Working in a group involves accessing the lives of other people. It is an inspiring and illuminative experience, but it is coupled with the fear of being obstructed in what we do or with the risk of being plucked out of our comfort zone. Mutual trust forms the bedrock of these complex dynamics, and the joy of celebrating the harvest together is second to none. Every village will testify to that.

The history of the appreciation of rural landscape and the purchase and sale of landscapes is chequered, to say the least. I talk to art dealer Marius Sterrenburg, who has been selling traditional and early-modern Dutch paintings for 25 years. He tells me that, during periods of economic crisis, there is a greater demand for a lighter palette. He cites the recent crisis, between 2007 and 2015, as an example, and explains that – because of their darker palette – landscapes by the Hague School dropped in value by 50 per cent. The market for 17th-century landscapes has been more stable in recent decades; they have, after all, sustained their value for hundreds of years, so they are not really objects of speculation. And in contrast with the time in which they were produced, landscapes are now much more popular than religious representations from the Golden Age. Today's buyer sees landscapes as neutral.
The same goes for still lifes, although it has to be said that, as in the 17th century, people do prefer flowers to dead animals.

When I sketch a landscape for an exhibition that shares the experience of rural life, I assume that the viewer understands immediately that this is not a a figment of the imagination. It is very important to me that it comes across as real. We were physically present there, and although our presentations are guided by what we see and perceive, the visions of the local residents are, for the most part, directly observed in the way the landscape looks. Is the representation of rural life shared by Myvillages different from the contrived landscapes that Jacob van Ruisdael painted in his studio in Haarlem? Or are we closer to the 19th century, when artists headed outdoors to pursue and capture the intrinsic nature of the rural environment?

Art dealers can prove that works by the latter group are authentic by identifying traces of earth and flora in samples of paint. Looks as if our audience will just have to trust us to disembark from the train now and then. **WF**

1 **Ton Lemaire**, *Filosofie van het Landschap* (Ambo: Amsterdam, 2002), 7th ed., p. 248.
2 Annual catalogue (Apert Gallery: Amsterdam, 1994).

weil mich euer eigener Glaube an deren Realitätsnähe fasziniert. Was fällt euch eigentlich ein, ohne jegliche Selbstzweifel aus meiner Jugend ein Klischee zu machen?«[2] Angesichts der schonungslosen Ausbeutung unserer natürlichen Ressourcen ist es im 21. Jahrhundert dringlicher denn je, Landschaft kritisch zu betrachten. Myvillages organisiert geologische Exkursionen und Obsternten und besucht moderne Landwirte über mehrere Wochen. Der interdisziplinäre Ansatz ist schon für sich genommen ein kulturelles Ereignis, aus dem dann zum Beispiel ein Gesteinsbrocken, eine Flasche Bier, ein Dokumentarfilm oder auch eine Zeichnung hervorgeht.

In einer Gruppe zu arbeiten heißt auch, einen Zugang zum Leben anderer Menschen zu suchen. Es ist eine anregende und erhellende Erfahrung, aber stets auch verbunden mit der Sorge, auf Hindernisse zu stoßen oder aus unserer Komfortzone vertrieben zu werden. Gegenseitiges Vertrauen ist der feste Untergrund dieser komplexen Dynamik, und es gibt keine größere Freude, als gemeinsam eine Ernte zu feiern. Jedes Dorf kann das bezeugen.

Die Geschichte der Wertschätzung, aber auch des Kaufens und Verkaufens von Landschaft ist kontrastreich. Ich habe mich darüber mit dem Kunsthändler Marius Sterrenburg unterhalten, der seit 25 Jahren traditionelle und frühe moderne niederländische Malerei verkauft. Er erzählte mir, dass in wirtschaftlich schwierigen Zeiten die Nachfrage nach einer helleren Farbpalette zunimmt. Als Beispiel nannte er die letzte Krise von 2007 bis 2015: Die Landschaften der Haager Schule verloren in dieser Zeit aufgrund ihrer dunkleren Farbtöne die Hälfte ihres Werts. Der Markt für Landschaftsmalerei aus dem 17. Jahrhundert war in den vergangenen Jahrzehnten eher stabil. Schließlich haben diese Bilder ihren Wert über Jahrhunderte bewahrt und sind keine Spekulationsobjekte im eigentlichen Sinn mehr. Und anders als in der Zeit, als sie entstanden, sind Landschaften heute sehr viel beliebter als religiöse Motive aus dem Goldenen Zeitalter. In den Augen heutiger Käufer ist die Landschaft ein neutrales Sujet. Dasselbe gilt für Stillleben, obwohl man auch sagen muss, dass die Leute damals wie heute den toten Tieren Blumen vorziehen.

Wenn ich für eine Ausstellung eine Landschaft zeichne, gehe ich davon aus, dass die Betrachter unmittelbar erkennen, dass es sich nicht um ein Fantasiegebilde handelt. Es ist mir sehr wichtig, die Landschaft als eine reale erscheinen zu lassen. Wir waren dort körperlich anwesend, und was wir dort sehen und wahrnehmen, ist meist direkt in die Erscheinungsweise eingegangen. Unterscheidet sich die Darstellung des Landlebens, wie Myvillages sie unternimmt, von den gekünstelten Landschaften, die ein Jacob van Ruisdael in seinem Haarlemer Atelier malte? Oder sind wir dem 19. Jahrhundert näher, in der sich Künstler aufmachten, der inneren Natur der ländlichen Umgebung auf die Spur zu kommen?

Indem sie Spuren von Erde und Pflanzen in den Farben nachweisen, können Kunsthändler heute beweisen, dass die Arbeiten Letzterer authentisch sind. Unser Publikum wird uns wohl oder übel glauben müssen, dass wir hin und wieder aus dem Zug steigen. **WF**

1 **Ton Lemaire**, *Filosofie van het Landschap* (Ambo: Amsterdam, 2002), 7. Ausgabe, S. 248.
2 Annual catalogue (Apert Gallery: Amsterdam, 1994).

МЕЖДУНАР СЕЛСКИ МА

ОДНЫЙ
ГАЗИН

International Village Shop
Tienda International del Pueblo
Internationaler Dorfladen
Internationale Dorpswinkel

M

International Village Shop,
Höfer Village Fair, Höfen (DE)
The International Village Shop *opens its doors in the village hall in Höfen on the first weekend of October for the annual fair: small exhibitions, goods from our product range, new innovations from Höfen, and sweets – since 2006. Some of the classics in the* International Village Shop *come from Höfen, such as* Frogbutter Spoons, Surplus Doily Bags *and* Tinned Clay.

When Kathrin's grandparents ran the village shop in Höfen, they had a stall the length of the building out in the street for the fair. The children were allowed to sell sweets to other children – as it is the case today.

Internationaler Dorfladen,
Höfer Kirchweih, Höfen (DE)
Jedes Jahr zur Kirchweih am ersten Wochenende im Oktober öffnet der Internationale Dorfladen *in Höfen im Dorfgemeinschaftshaus. Kleine Ausstellungen, Waren aus unserem Sortiment, Höfer Neuentwicklungen und Süßigkeiten – seit 2006. Aus Höfen kommen einige der Klassiker im* International Village Shop, Froschbutterlöffel *etwa,* Häkeldeckentaschen *und* Lehm in Dosen.

Als Kathrins Großeltern in Höfen einen Gemischtwarenladen führten, gab es zur Kirchweih einen großen Stand auf der Straße am Haus entlang. Die Kinder durften den Kindern Süßigkeiten verkaufen. So auch jetzt.

M

Vechte River Goods, Gaststätte Timmer, Ohne (DE)
Tuinen Mien Ruys, Dedemsvaart (NL)
The Vechte or Vecht River flows between the Münsterland and IJsselmeer. One branch of the International Village Shop *with two shops is named after it:*

Gaststätte Timmer, Dorf 19, Ohne, County of Bentheim
Daily from 10:30 – 12:30 a.m. and starting from 3 p.m.
closed on Tuesdays
At the Gaststätte Timmer (Timmer Inn), there is a permanent shop for Vechte River Goods. *On offer:* Embroidered Workware, *linen notebooks, linseed, and* Confectie Boxes *from Dedemsvaart. A photo album with pictures of the flax field of Ohne lies on the counter next to the innkeepers. One can eat a Strammer Max sandwich upon request.*

Tuinen Mien Ruys, Moerheimstraat 84, Dedemsvaart, Overijssel
Open from April to October,
Tuesday – Saturday 10 a.m. – 5 p.m.,
Sundays 12 a.m. – 5 p.m.
In the warm months, in addition to gardening implements and books, the Tuinen Mien Ruys Confectie Boxes *– Shadow Box, Sunny Box, Acid Box, Chalky Box, and Bee Box – can also be purchased in the teahouse of the renowned garden.*

Vechtewaren, Gaststätte Timmer, Ohne (DE)
Tuinen Mien Ruys, Dedemsvaart (NL)
Zwischen dem Münsterland und dem IJsselmeer fließt die Vechte oder Vecht. Nach ihr heißt ein Zweig des International Village Shop *mit zwei Läden:*

Gaststätte Timmer, Dorf 19, Ohne, Grafschaft Bentheim
Täglich 10:30 – 12:30 und ab 15 Uhr
dienstags Ruhetag
In der Gaststätte Timmer gibt es einen permanenten Laden für die Vechtewaren, *im Angebot:* bestickte Arbeitsanzüge, *Notizbücher aus Leinen, Leinsaat und* Confectie Boxes *aus Dedemsvaart. An der Theke liegt bei den Wirten ein Fotoalbum mit Bildern vom Ohner Flachsfeld. Auf Anfrage kann man Strammen Max essen.*

Tuinen Mien Ruys, Moerheimstraat 84, Dedemsvaart, Overijssel
Geöffnet von April bis Oktober,
Dienstag – Samstag 10 – 17 Uhr,
sonntags 12 – 17 Uhr
Im Teehaus des berühmten Gartens werden in den warmen Monaten neben Gartengeräten und Büchern die Tuinen Mien Ruys Confectie Boxes *angeboten: Shadow Box, Sunny Box, Acid Box, Chalky Box und Bee Box.*

M

International Village Shop, Accra Open Air Stock Exchange, Accra (GH)
March 2015

A market takes place each month in the courtyard of the Goethe-Institut in Accra. Shea butter cream, fabric, black honey, and glass beads are sold; there is grilled food to eat and music to listen to. The youth dance group from Ekumfi provides the stage programme. At this market, Mustafa Nkrumah presented the first bamboo bowls from Ekumfi Ekrawfo. It was still not possible to buy the bowls, only to order them, since just a few were finished.

International Village Shop, Accra Open Air Stock Exchange, Accra (GH)
März 2015

Im Hof des Goethe-Instituts Accra findet monatlich ein Markt statt. Verkauft werden Sheabuttercreme, Stoffe, schwarzer Honig und Glasperlen; es wird gegrillt und Musik gehört. Auf diesem Markt präsentierte Mustafa Nkrumah die ersten Bambusschüsseln aus Ekumfi Ekrawfo. Die Tanzgruppe der Jugendlichen aus Ekrawfo bestritt das Bühnenprogramm. Die Schüsseln konnten noch nicht gekauft, aber bestellt werden, denn es waren nur wenige fertig.

Meschdunarodnij Celski Magasin, Archstoyanie Festival, Zvizzchi (RU), and Bogorodskoe Exhibition Hall, Moscow (RU)

Magasin, Zvizzchi, Oblast Kaluga
Open daily, when the shop is open

A pale green glass display case stands in the grocer's shop of Zvizzchi, built for products – "Made in Zvizzchi", for instance, baskets, ceramics, and t-shirts. Here, individuals who would like to purchase vegetables, fruit, marmalade, or mushrooms find the telephone numbers of villagers who offer them.

Meschdunarodnij Celski Magasin, Archstoyanie Festival, Zvizzchi (RU), und Bogorodskoe Galerija, Moskau (RU)

Magasin, Zvizzchi, Oblast Kaluga
Täglich geöffnet, wenn der Laden geöffnet ist

Im Lebensmittelgeschäft von Zvizzchi steht ein blassgrüner Vitrinenschrank, gebaut für Produkte »Made in Zvizzchi«, Körbe etwa, Quilts, Keramik und T-Shirts. Wer Gemüse, Obst, Marmelade oder Pilze kaufen möchte, findet hier die Telefonnummern derer, die es anbieten.

M

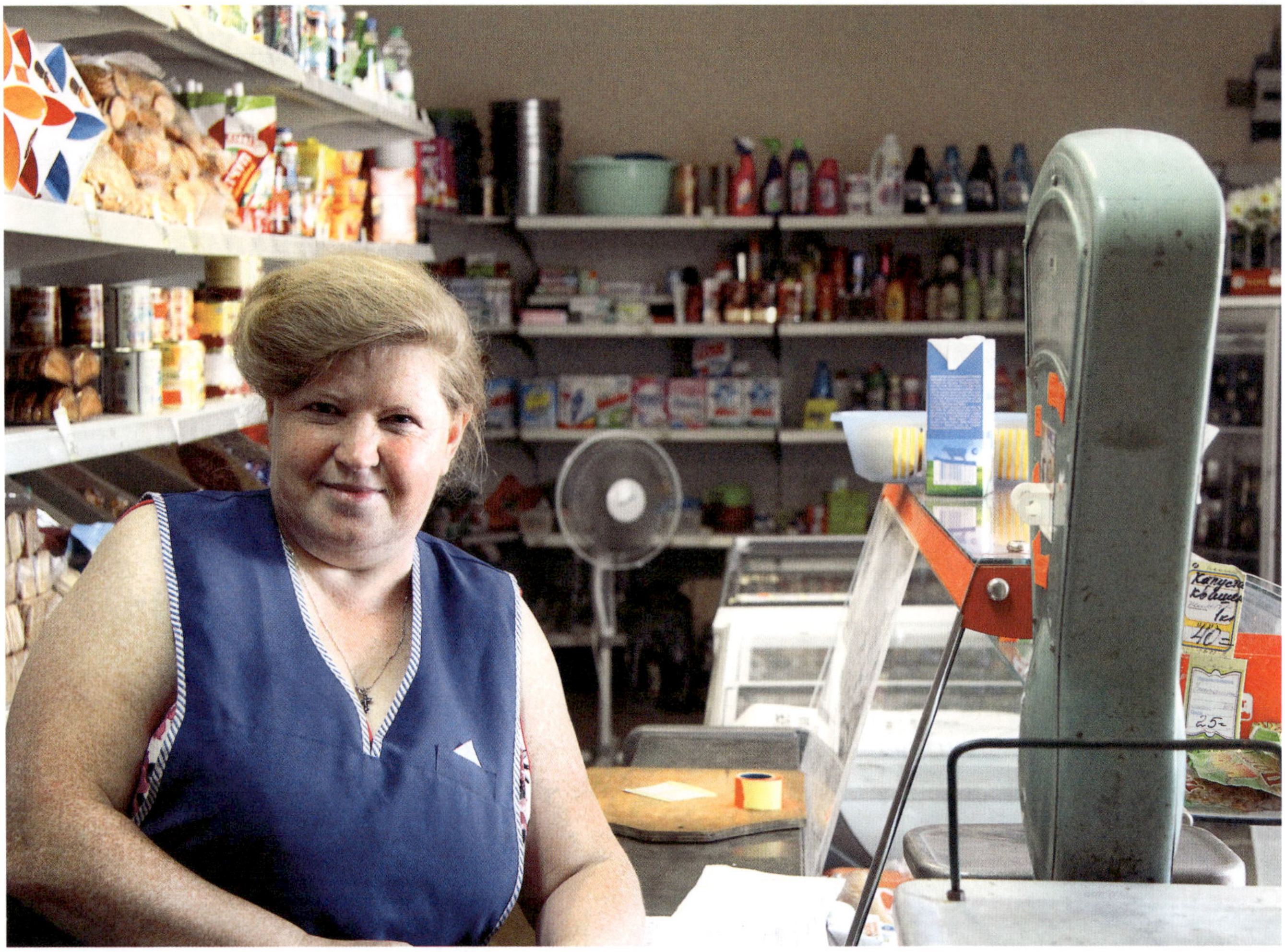

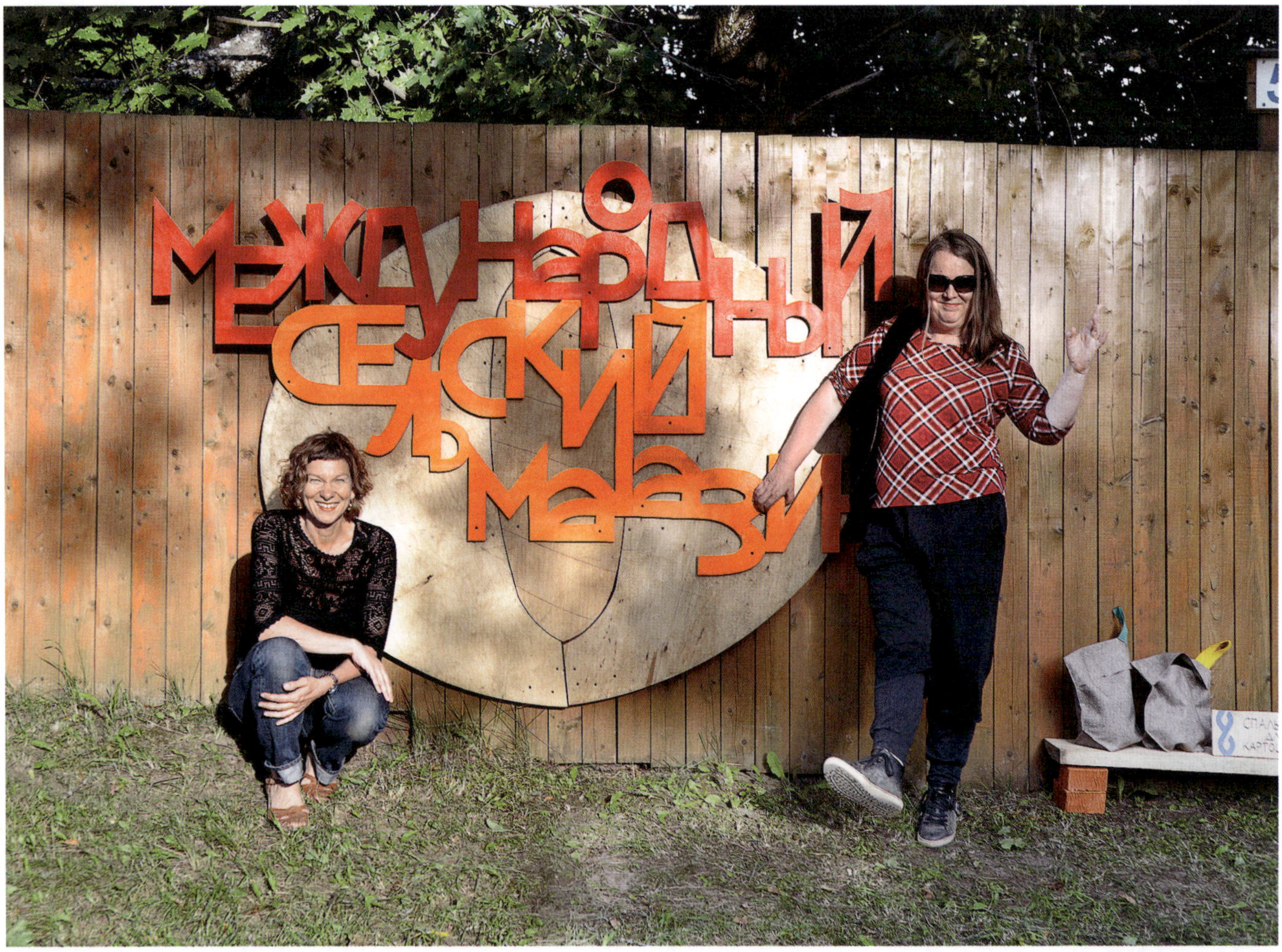
МЕЖДУНАРОДНЫЙ
СЕЛЬСКИЙ
МАГАЗИН

Meschdunarodnij Celski Magasin in the gateway to Oleg's courtyard, Zvizzchi Archstoyanie Festival, 31 July – 2 August 2015

Archstoyanie is an important festival for architecture, land art, and music in Russia. It takes place each year in the village next to Zvizzchi, in Nikola-Lenivetz. Our shop in the gate to the courtyard of Oleg's house was open for three days; sales went well, and were also made from the car and from our storage space in the Banja (bathhouse) in the early morning hours.

Meschdunarodnij Celski Magasin, Bogorodskoe Exhibition Hall, Moscow (RU) 18 September – 25 October 2015

As part of the Moscow Biennale, the shop moved from Oleg's courtyard in Zvizzchi to the rooms of the Bogorodskoe Galerija.

Meschdunarodnij Celski Magasin im Tor von Olegs Hof, Zvizzchi Archstoyanie Festival, 31. Juli – 2. August 2015

Archstoyanie ist ein wichtiges Festival für Architektur, Land Art und Musik in Russland. Es findet jährlich im Dorf neben Zvizzchi statt, in Nikola-Lenivetz. Drei Tage lang war unser Laden im Hoftor des Hauses von Oleg geöffnet; die Verkäufe liefen gut, auch aus dem Auto heraus wurde gekauft und in den frühen Morgenstunden aus unserem Lager in der Banja.

Meschdunarodnij Celski Magasin, Bogorodskoe Galerija, Moskau (RU) 18. September – 25. Oktober 2015

Als Teil der Moskau-Biennale zog der Laden von Olegs Hof in Zvizzchi um in die Räume der Bogorodskoe Galerija.

M

International Village Shop at the Parco Arte Vivente (PAV) in Turin 2015 – 2017

Most of our bestsellers filled the shop at the Grow It Yourself *exhibition at the PAV in Turin in the summer of 2015. Because the shop was so popular, a garden was laid out, from which unexpected beauty and health projects were supplied, underway throughout Turin with a newly constructed PAV pop-up shop.*

Two-Day Shop, Kunsthuis SYB, Beetsterwaag (NL), 2016

The Beestachtige Schat *was presented in the village for two days, along with yellow beans from De Wouden, rhubarb liqueur, cake, and good Opsterland cheese. We counted 750 guests; they liked the* Beestachtige Schat *so much that we now have a waiting list.*

International Village Shop im Parco Arte Vivente (PAV) in Turin 2015 – 2017

Die meisten unserer Bestseller füllten den Laden in der Ausstellung Grow It Yourself im PAV in Turin im Sommer 2015. Weil der Laden so beliebt war, wurde ein Garten angelegt, aus dem sich unerwartete Beauty- und Health-Produkte speisen, unterwegs mit einem neu gebauten PAV-Pop-up-Stand in ganz Turin.

Two-Day Shop, Kunsthuis SYB, Beetsterwaag (NL), 2016

Zwei Tage lang wird der Beestachtige Schat im Dorf vorgestellt, zusammen mit gelben Bohnen aus De Wouden, Rhabarberlikör, Kuchen und gutem Opsterlandkäse. Wir zählen 750 Gäste; sie mögen den Beestachtige Schat so sehr, dass wir jetzt eine Warteliste führen.

M

КЕВО
ТАРЕ ИЗ БАМБУКА
NEUENKIRCHEN
HINOJOSA D
РАБОЧАЯ ОДЕЖДА
ЖАКЕТ „ТРАВЫ"
ЖАКЕТ „КАРТОШКА"
КОМБИНЕЗОН „ЗЕРНО"
ДЕТСКИЙ КОМБИНЕЗОН „ЖУК"

M

ACID BOX
CHALKY BOX
BEE BOX
SHADOW BOX
SUNNY BOX
ACID BOX
CHALKY BOX
BEE BOX
SHADOW BOX
SUNNY BOX
EschF6
ANTHROPOGENE SCHWARZERDE
EschF6
ANTHROPOGENE SCHWARZERDE
EschF6
ANTHROPOGENE SCHWARZERDE
EschF6
ANTHROPOGENE SCHWARZERDE
SHADOW BOX
CHALKY BOX
BEE BOX
ACID BOX
SUNNY BOX
SHADOW BOX
CHALKY BOX
BEE BOX
ACID BOX
SUNNY BOX
EschF6
ANTHROPOGENE SCHWARZERDE
EschF6
ANTHROPOGENE SCHWARZERDE
EschF6
ANTHROPOGENE SCHWARZERDE
EschF6
ANTHROPOGENE SCHWARZERDE

EschF6
ANTHROPOGENE SCHWARZERDE

International Village Shop, Museum of Contemporary Art (GfZK), Leipzig (DE), 2015 – 16

IVS 1/8

Höfen and Ekumfi Ekrawfo
February – May 2015
The first of our shows in the Gartenhaus of the GfZK presented a selection of goods from the years 2006 to 2015 behind the counter in the shop. On offer in particular were two new products: lace by the metre from Höfen and bamboo bowls from Ekumfi Ekrawfo, of which there are only a few.

IVS 2/8

Region around Leipzig and Spanish villages
May – September 2015
The shop was cleared out: there were Farmers' Chinaware *and* Seville Orange Marmalade *from Spain, and stones from the region around Leipzig. Stones are good business.*

IVS 3/8

Brezoi and Friesland
September – November 2015
The shop offered baskets, textiles, and stools, produced near Brezoi.

IVS 5/8

Ballykinlar and Zvizzchi
March – June 2016
We take over the shops from Moscow and Zvizzchi with signs and a promotional film. The marmalade is sold out, but two products from Northern Ireland have been added: the Caravan Pot *with potted plants and our shiny* Twisted Bugles.

International Village Shop, Galerie für Zeitgenössische Kunst (GfZK) Leipzig (DE), 2015 – 16

IVS 1/8

Höfen und Ekumfi Ekrawfo
Februar – Mai 2015
Die erste unserer Shows im Gartenhaus der GfZK zeigt im Laden hinter der Theke eine Auswahl von Waren aus den Jahren 2006 bis 2015. Besonders vorgestellt werden zwei neue Produkte: Höfer Spitze vom Meter *und* Bambusschüsseln aus Ekumfi Ekrawfo, *von denen es nur wenige gibt.*

IVS 2/8

Leipziger Umland und spanische Dörfer
Mai – September 2015
Der Laden wird ausgeräumt: Es gibt ein bäuerliches Geschirr aus Spanien, Orangenmarmelade und Steine aus dem Leipziger Umland. Steine sind ein gutes Geschäft.

IVS 3/8

Brezoi und Fryslân
September – November 2015
Der Laden bietet Körbe, Textilien und Hocker an, gefertigt auf den Odai in den Bergen von Brezoi.

IVS 5/8

Ballykinlar und Zvizzchi
März – Juni 2016
Wir übernehmen den Laden aus Moskau und Zvizzchi mit Schildern und Werbefilm. Die Marmelade ist ausverkauft, aber zwei Produkte aus Nordirland kommen hinzu: der Caravan Pot *mit Topfpflanzen und unsere schimmernden* Twisted Bugles.

M

M

IVS 6/8

Vechte and Schelde
June – September 2016
Sacks of black earth, seeds, work clothes: we offer garden and agricultural products.

IVS 6/8

Vechte und Schelde
Juni – September 2016
Säcke mit Schwarzerde, Saatgut, Arbeitskleidung: Wir führen Garten- und Landwirtschaftsbedarf.

IVS 7/8

Kent and Franschhoek Valley
September – December 2016
Beverage trade

IVS 7/8

Kent und Franschhoek Valley
September – Dezember 2016
Getränkehandel

MYVILLAGES

SINCE / SEIT 2003

M

Being familiar with rural life but disconnected from the daily life in the villages, Antje Schiffers, Wapke Feenstra and Kathrin Böhm are both insiders and outsiders. This distance allows a different perspective on local skills and knowledge, communal work, and communities, and last but not least, on the relationship between art and the countryside. It also allows the group to establish connections beyond the actual site – connections that respond to and also mirror the dispersed spatial structure and social relationships that are a significant part of rural living today. Production in the respective villages is connected to production in other places. Everybody involved in the project becomes part of a smaller and larger community in equal measure, the one on site, in the village, and the one established by the joint space Myvillages.

Myvillages creates shared space, shaped by the activities of many individuals and groups. It draws attention to the various forms community can take. In this regard, it suggests a "utopian approach to community building". With this approach, they not only ask what kind of community we can imagine, but also where it might be located, what its relations to other communities and to the larger construct society might be, and finally, how communities can have the opportunity to shape themselves. Most importantly, it drafts a community that is itself heterogeneous and polyphonic, yet interrelated. Perhaps one way of reading Myvillages is to see their concrete actions, activities and projects, as a way of allowing a utopia to momentarily come into view, and of airing the possibility of community-oriented attitudes and behaviour in an increasingly diverse, and spatially and socially dispersed society.

Extracts from an essay written by **Barbara Steiner** for Myvillages' 10th Anniversary Newsletter, published in London and Rotterdam, December 2013

Antje Schiffers, Wapke Feenstra und Kathrin Böhm sind zwar mit dem Landleben vertraut, aber inzwischen selbst dem Alltag in den Dörfern entrückt. Sie sind gleichermaßen Eingeweihte und Außenseiterinnen. Diese Distanz eröffnet eine andere Sicht auf lokale Fertigkeiten und Kenntnisse, auf die gemeinsame Arbeit und das Leben in Gemeinschaft sowie nicht zuletzt auf die Beziehung zwischen Kunst und Land. Auf dieser Basis kann die Gruppe auch Verbindungen knüpfen, die über den eigentlichen Schauplatz hinausgehen und den weitläufigen Raumordnungen und Sozialbeziehungen entsprechen, die heute wesentlich zum Leben auf dem Land gehören. Jede Produktion im jeweiligen Dorf wird mit den Produktionen anderswo verknüpft. Alle Beteiligten des Projekts werden gleichermaßen Teil einer kleineren oder größeren Gemeinschaft – der einen an Ort und Stelle, im Dorf, der anderen in Form eines gemeinsam geschaffenen Raums.

Myvillages schafft diesen gemeinsamen Raum, der seine Gestaltung durch das Handeln zahlreicher Einzelpersonen und Gruppen erfährt. Die Gruppe weist uns darauf hin, welche verschiedenen Formen eine Gemeinschaft haben kann, und vertritt darin einen »utopischen Ansatz der Gemeinschaftsbildung«. Die drei Gründerinnen stellen nicht nur die Frage, welche Art von Gemeinschaft wir uns vorstellen können, sondern auch, wo diese beheimatet sein sollte, welche Beziehungen sie zu anderen Gemeinschaften und zum umfassenderen Konstrukt einer Gesellschaft unterhalten sollte, und schließlich, wo Gemeinschaften überhaupt eine Chance zum Werden und Wachsen haben. Vor allem pflegt Myvillages die Vorstellung einer Gemeinschaft, die in sich vielfältig, vielstimmig und doch eng geknüpft ist. Man kann Myvillages auch so verstehen, dass die konkreten Aktionen, Aktivitäten und Projekte für Momente eine Utopie in den Blick rücken sollen, dass sie in einer räumlich immer vielfältigeren und breiter gestreuten Gesellschaft die Möglichkeit gemeinschaftsorientierter Haltungen und Verhaltensweisen behaupten wollen.

Auszug aus einem Aufsatz von **Barbara Steiner** für den 10th Anniversary Newsletter von Myvillages, London und Rotterdam, Dezember 2013

M

НАШИ ПРОДУКТЫ

For the Meschdunarodnij Celski Magasin at the Bogorodskoe Exhibition Hall within the framework of the 6th Moscow Biennale, we needed Russian sellers for our products. For this purpose, we made a film in Zvizzchi in which goods from our shop are explained and advertised: Naschi Produkti.

Für das Meschdunarodnij Celski Magasin in der Bogorodskoe Exhibition Hall im Rahmen der 6. Moskau-Biennale brauchten wir russische Produktverkäufer. Darum haben wir in Zvizzchi einen Film gemacht, in dem Waren aus unserem Laden erklärt und angepriesen werden: Naschi Produkti.

Potato Sleeper (*with Natalia Serova*)
Our friends from the village of Neuenkirchen in Northern Germany offer such a sleeping bag for potatoes. It can also be used for other vegetables: for carrots, red beets, apples. Do you know why they invented it? Today, people in the city do not have anywhere to store vegetables appropriately. It's not possible to store potatoes in the fridge, since they turn sweet. Things are no better on the balcony, since light turns them green. That's why this beautiful sleeping bag was invented. And would you like to show off a little bit? It's also a fashionable and modern handbag.

Kartoffelbeutel(*mit Natalja Serowa*)
Unsere Freunde aus dem Dorf Neuenkirchen in Norddeutschland bieten einen solchen Schlafsack für Kartoffeln an. Man kann ihn auch für andere Gemüse verwenden: für Möhren, rote Rüben, Äpfel. Wissen Sie, warum sie das erfunden haben? Heute haben die Leute in der Stadt keinen Platz, um Gemüse angemessen aufzubewahren. Man kann Kartoffeln nicht im Kühlschrank aufbewahren, sie werden süß. Auf dem Balkon ist es nicht besser, vom Licht werden sie grün. Deshalb hat man diese schönen Schlafsäcke erfunden. Und wollen Sie sich ein bisschen aufspielen? Es ist auch eine modische und moderne Handtasche.

Farmers' Chinaware (*with Vadim Iakushin*)
I'm not a great expert on porcelain. This porcelain is interesting for me because it was made at a factory in Spain that is more than 150 years old. This *Farmers' Chinaware* was produced in this factory as an exclusive product. It's *Farmers' Chinaware* because there are drawings of ears of grain and harvesters on it. People who buy this porcelain will surely be very satisfied, with the quality and also with the drawings. It's an exclusive product, which has only been produced in limited quantities. Nearly all of the residents of our village have bought a piece of this *Farmers' Chinaware* from Spain. We also recommend that you purchase a piece, and are sure you won't regret it.

Farmers' Chinaware (*mit Vadim Jakuschin*)
Ich bin kein großer Porzellanexperte. Dieses Porzellan ist für mich deswegen interessant, weil es in Spanien in einer Fabrik gemacht wurde, die mehr als 150 Jahre alt ist. In dieser Fabrik hat man dieses Bauernporzellan als exklusives Produkt hergestellt. Es ist ein »Bauernporzellan«, weil darauf Zeichnungen von Ähren und Mähdreschern sind. Wer dieses Porzellan kauft, wird sicher sehr zufrieden sein, mit der Qualität und auch mit der Zeichnung. Es sind exklusive Waren, die nur in begrenzter Menge hergestellt worden sind. Fast alle unsere Dorfbewohner haben ein Stück von diesem Bauernporzellan aus Spanien gekauft. Wir raten auch Ihnen, eins zu kaufen, und sind sicher, dass Sie es nicht bedauern werden.

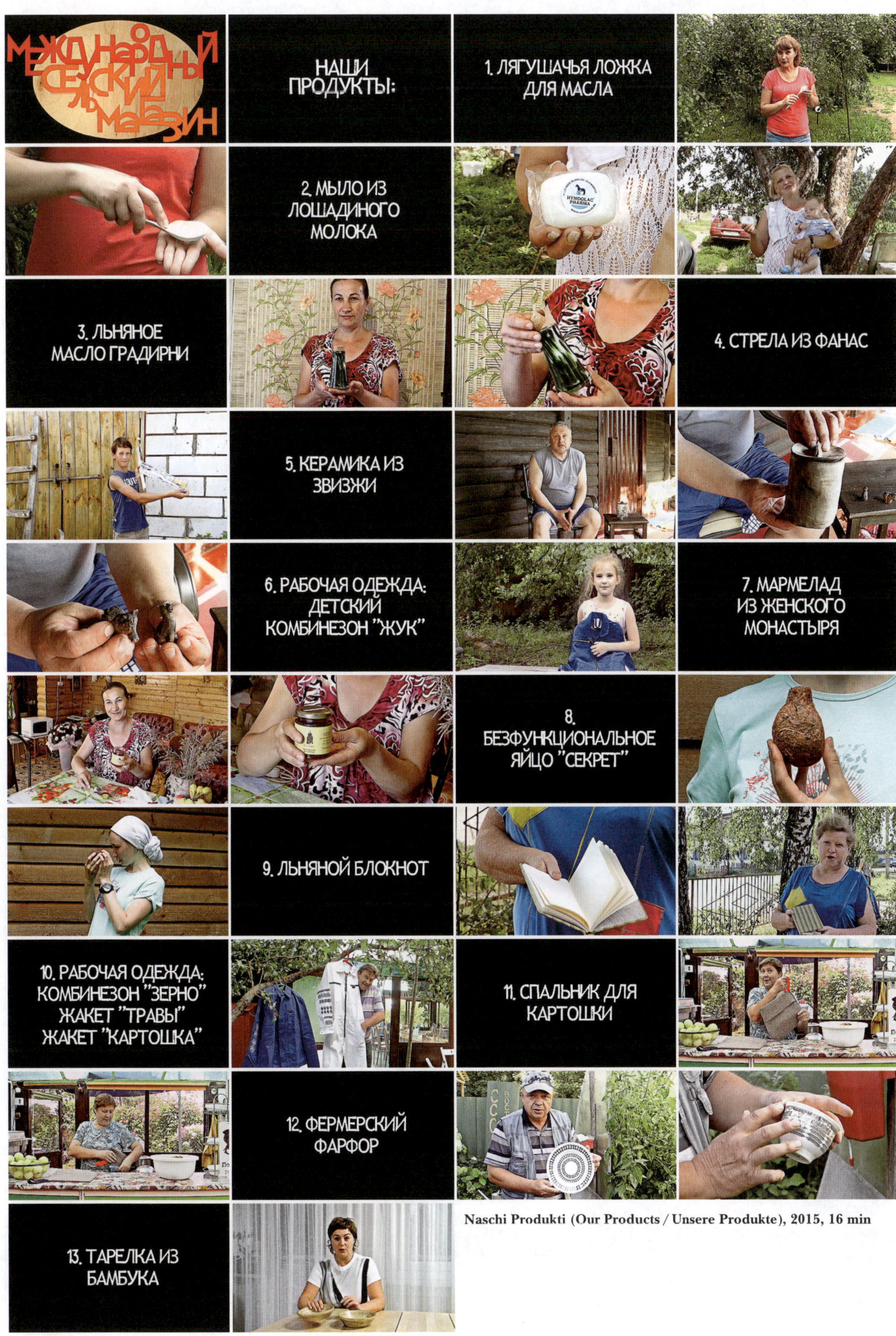

Naschi Produkti (Our Products / Unsere Produkte), 2015, 16 min

N

ФЕРМЕРСКИЙ ФАРФОР
ЛЬНЯНОЙ БЛОКНОТ
МЫЛО
ИЗ ЛОШАДИНОГО МОЛОКА

PERIPHERIE

Ninety-two per cent of the area of the European Union comprises agrarian areas. Fifty-six per cent of the population lives in them. The village and the land cannot be such outlandish topics.

Farming, forestry, water management, energy generation, and raw material extraction primarily take place here.

92 Prozent der Flächen der Europäischen Union sind ländliche Räume. 56 Prozent der Bevölkerung leben in ihnen. Das Dorf und das Land können keine so abwegigen Themen sein.

Landwirtschaft, Forstwirtschaft, Wasserwirtschaft, Energieerzeugung, Rohstoffabbau finden primär hier statt.

PLEIN

Cyclists and ramblers looking for a pavement cafe are a common sight in Vlassenbroek during the tourist season. But, suddenly, in 2014 and 2015, many people armed with sketchpads descended on the Schelde. Amateurs and professionals, young and old – you ran into them in groups, or alone, perched on a camping stool, deep in thought, contemplating a view, or grappling with central perspective. They ventured out in all weathers. But artistic interest was not exactly new to Vlassenbroek, for it was here that the Dendermonde School found inspiration at the end of the 19th century.

P

The recent plein air project was prompted by the events of 1 February 1953 – the day the dyke collapsed, leaving the whole of Vlassenbroek and Broekkant underwater.

Rosa Vermeir and her family were lodging with her parents. As the floodwater rose, they took refuge on the first floor. Luckily, her father managed to arrange a boat. He mounted a horse, which swam to Mechelsesteenweg, where he raised the alarm. They were rescued through a window.

Later, everything was covered in mud. That was a setback. But all the cows survived, except one.

The plans to control the river tides have had to be brought forward in the last decade to keep pace with climate change. Soon, some of the land along the Schelde will

Radfahrer und Wanderer auf der Suche nach einem Straßencafé sieht man während der Urlaubszeit in Vlassenbroek häufig. Doch 2014 und 2015 fielen plötzlich mit Zeichenblöcken bewaffnete Leute über die Ufer der Schelde her: Amateure und Berufskünstler jeden Alters, in Gruppen oder einzeln, kauerten tief in Gedanken auf Angelhockern, erwogen eine Ansicht, rangen mit der Zentralperspektive. Auch bei Wind und Wetter wagten sie sich hinaus. Allerdings ist künstlerische Neugier für die Leute von Vlassenbroek nichts Neues, denn hier suchte schon im späten 19. Jahrhundert die Dendermonde-Schule ihre Inspiration.

Das jüngste Plein-Air-Projekt nahm auf die Ereignisse vom 1. Februar 1953 Bezug, als der Deich brach und die ganze Gegend um Vlassenbroek und Broekkant überflutet wurde.

Rosa Vermeir kam mit Mann und Kindern im Haus ihrer Eltern unter. Als die Flut weiter stieg, flohen sie in den ersten Stock. Zum Glück gelang es ihrem Vater, ein Boot zu besorgen. Er setzte sich auf ein Pferd, das bis nach Mechelsesteenweg schwamm, und rief dort um Hilfe. Alle wurden durch ein Fenster aus dem Haus gerettet.

Danach war alles im Schlamm versunken. Das war ein Rückschlag. Doch sämtliche Kühe, bis auf eine, überlebten.

In den vergangenen zehn Jahren musste der Hochwasserschutz ausgebaut werden, um mit dem Klimawandel mitzuhalten. Bald werden manche Weiden und Felder an der Schelde wieder zu einem Überschwemmungsgebiet. Die

AIR

become a flood plain again. The surroundings are changing dramatically. This calls for a response that incorporates vision and imagination. Everyone is joining in; civil engineers, landscape architects, artists, and even anglers are taking notes. The *Drawing in Vlassenbroek* project challenged artists and dabblers to return to the dyke and take a fresh look at the polder. The specially organized drop-in drawing classes at the Baasrode Maritime Museum and the scouts' hut were popular.

Anglers are well-practiced in sitting motionless, so it was only to be expected that they would be asked to pose for a drawing. The Orcas' angling club was happy to sit for a sketch artist. This drawing will be a welcome memory, as their pond and clubhouse will be forced to relocate.

When the drawings are finished, everyone comes to the conservatory at the café, where I am waiting with an A3 scanner. We drink Belgian beer and eat toasted sandwiches while the scanner whirs. Scanning takes a long time. The resolution is 600 DPI to make sure that we have top-quality graphics for the book that is planned. The constantly changing landscape is an important theme. New observations appear at every scanning session. Dreams of the future are shared, interspersed with discussions on global issues. Not everyone can draw; so 16 drawings with a good story have been made at the request of local residents. These have been framed and have a museum index number glued to the back. Together, they form a collection entitled *Drawing in Vlassenbroek*, which

Umgebung verändert sich dramatisch. Damit umzugehen erfordert Weitsicht und Vorstellungsvermögen. Alle beteiligen sich: Bauingenieure, Landschaftsarchitekten, Künstler, sogar die Angler machen sich Notizen. Das Projekt *Zeichnen in Vlassenbroek* rief Künstler und Amateure auf, wieder zum Deich zu kommen und den Polder mit anderen Augen zu betrachten. Auch im Werftmuseum von Baasrode wurden eigens Zeichenkurse organisiert, und die Pfadfinderhütte entwickelte sich zum Treffpunkt.

Angler sind geübt darin, stillzusitzen, und so war es nur eine Frage der Zeit, bis jemand sie bat, für eine Zeichnung Modell zu sitzen. Der Anglerverein Orcas posierte bereitwillig für einen Künstler. Diese Zeichnung wird für den Verein eine schöne Erinnerung bleiben, zumal er sich mitsamt Fischteich und Vereinshaus einen anderen Standort suchen muss.

Wenn die Zeichnungen fertig sind, kommen alle zum Wintergarten des Cafés, wo ich mit einem A3-Scanner warte. Wir trinken belgisches Bier und essen getoastete Sandwiches, während der Scanner surrt. Das Abtasten dauert lange. Die Auflösung beträgt 600 dpi, denn für das Buch, das wir veröffentlichen wollen, brauchen wir bestmögliche Grafiken. Der anhaltende Wandel der Landschaft ist ein Hauptthema. Neue Beobachtungen treten bei jeder Scan-Runde zutage. Zukunftsträume äußern sich, durchzogen mit Debatten über allgemeine Themen. Nicht alle können zeichnen, also wurden 16 Zeichnungen auf Bitte einiger Anwohner, die eine gute Geschichte zu erzählen haben, von anderen angefertigt. Sie wurden gerahmt und bekamen auf der Rückseite

P

is the property of the city of Dendermonde. They now hang on people's walls as loaned exhibits.

The ring dyke stands on the plot of agricultural land that Lucia inherited from her grandfather. The happy childhood memories, including the family picnics, are a subject for a commissioned pen-and-ink drawing.

We scanned handwritten poetry about a view.

One artist made a drawing from the place where the compartment dyke and the river dyke meet, which offers an excellent view of the church in the village of Kastel, on the opposite bank. Beaver tracks were followed and replicas of old ships appeared to be patient models.

The drawing sessions ended in the spring of 2015 and I compiled a visual narrative from the hundreds of drawings scanned in the past year. The ground rules dictate that everyone who participated must be represented in the book with at least one drawing.

The story told by the drawings ends with a tropical beach on the Schelde. The owner of the Artists Studio, a local pub, says that a tropical climate is inevitable in this age of global warming. He is looking forward to welcoming sun-seekers. **WF**

eine Archivnummer des Museums aufgeklebt. Alle zusammen bilden eine Sammlung namens *Zeichnen in Vlassenbroek*, die der Stadt Dendermonde gehört. Die Zeichnungen hängen zurzeit als Leihexponate an den Wänden der Anwohner.

Der Deichring zieht sich über ein Feld, das Lucia von ihrem Großvater geerbt hat. Erinnerungen an eine glückliche Kindheit mit Picknicks im Familienkreis sind das Thema einer Auftragsarbeit in Tusche.

Wir scannen handgeschriebene Gedichte über eine Aussicht.

Ein Künstler zeichnet von der Stelle aus, wo der Flussdeich und der Rückhaltedeich aufeinandertreffen. Von hier aus hat man einen hervorragenden Blick auf die Kirche im Dorf Kastel am anderen Flussufer. Biberspuren werden verfolgt, und Nachbauten alter Schiffe erscheinen als geduldige Modelle.

Die Zeichensaison endet im Frühjahr 2015, und ich stelle aus den Hunderten im vorangegangenen Jahr eingescannten Zeichnungen eine Bildererzählung zusammen. Eine Grundregel lautete, dass jeder, der mitgemacht hat, mit mindestens einer Zeichnung im Buch vertreten sein muss.

Die von den Zeichnungen erzählte Geschichte endet mit einem Tropenstrand an der Schelde. Der Besitzer von »Atelier«, einer örtlichen Kneipe, hält ein tropisches Klima für unausweichlich in diesem Zeitalter globaler Erwärmung. Er freut sich schon auf sonnenhungrige Gäste. **WF**

VOLVO
95
VOLVO

PRO-
GRAMM
LEIPZIG

P

P

6.2.2015
For the opening of the first International Village Show *in the Gartenhaus, we had the women of Höfen as our guests. They travelled by train from Upper Franconia with suitcases packed with cold board goodies for the evening and "Geschnittene Hasen" (fried pastries, a regional specialty) and cakes for the coffee afternoon the next day. Nana Esi Nisin VIII, Queen Mother, represented Ekumfi Ekrawfo in official clothing over her winter jacket. Tinatin Eppmann gave a welcoming address on behalf of the Kulturstiftung des Bundes (German Federal Cultural Foundation). There was beer in kegs from Freudeneck and palm wine with Guinness. We made a fire in the snow.*

7.2.2015
After the coffee drinking: conversation with Elisabeth Meyer-Renschhausen, a sociologist, about future investments and dowry chests.

21.3.2015
We sell rocks in the vending machines at the Gartenhaus. Geological excursion to where they were found, along with Ronny Schmidt of the GeoWerkstatt Leipzig.

P

25.4.2015
The suitability for food, tightness, and heat resistance of the Fufu Bowls *had to be tested. Test meal with fufu, Thuringian dumplings, goulash, and stew.*

6.2.2015
Zur Eröffnung der ersten International Village Show *im Gartenhaus haben wir die Höfer Frauen zu Gast – angereist aus Oberfranken mit Brotzeitplatten für den Abend und Geschnittenen Hasen für das Kaffeetrinken am Nachmittag darauf. Für Ekumfi Ekrawfo repräsentiert Nana Esi Nisin VIII, Queen-mother, in offizieller Kleidung über der Winterjacke. Tinatin Eppmann spricht ein Grußwort der Kulturstiftung des Bundes. Es gibt Bier in Fässern aus Freudeneck und Palmwein mit Guinness. Wir machen Feuer im Schnee.*

7.2.2015
Im Anschluss an das Kaffeetrinken: Gespräch mit Elisabeth Meyer-Renschhausen, Soziologin, über Zukunftsinvestitionen und Mitgifttruhen.

21.3.2015
Im Automaten am Gartenhaus verkaufen wir Steine. Geologischer Ausflug zu ihren Fundorten mit Ronny Schmidt von der GeoWerkstatt Leipzig.

25.4.2015
Die Nahrungsmitteltauglichkeit, Dichtigkeit und Hitzebeständigkeit der Fufu-Schüsseln müssen erprobt werden. Testessen mit Fufu, Thüringer Klößen, Gulasch und Stew.

P

8.5.2015
We opened the second show on a warm evening, with red wine and local tapas.

9.5.2015
Conversation about vegetables with the people at Annalinde, a community garden and market garden in Leipzig.

20.6.2015
"Long Night of Farmer' Films" – with films from the archive of I like being a farmer and I would like to stay one.

10.7.2015
GfZK had a rather unpopular platform in the garden in front of our Gartenhaus – used by groups of joggers every evening for their stretches, by students for sunbathing, by parents with small children for a break, but nevertheless not ideal. Pupils from the school centre in Grossbardau became our experts for contemporary rural hanging out; in cooperation with them, the platform was modified and opened ceremoniously for the GfZK's summer party, with fast food and a lounge for chilling.

4.9.2015
In Friesland, it is common to scatter shells in courtyards and on paths. For a footpath that meanders from the main entrance of the GfZK through bushes and evergreens to the Gartenhaus, we ordered two cubic metres of shells in Harlingen on the Wadden Sea, shells that accrue through the dredging of channels to the islands. The young male and female Frisian farmers quickly poured a shell path with them. It was trodden down. It is called Frysk Skelpepaad.

Afterward, Frisian-Romanian scything under the guidance of Mircea Onică from Brezoi and Thomas Thiele from Leipzig, equipped with wooden scythe handles and forged blades, with whetstone holders and peening hammers: always glide close to the ground with a swift swing! We opened

8.5.2015
An einem warmen Abend eröffnen wir die zweite Show mit Rotwein und heimischen Tapas.

9.5.2015
Gemüsegespräch mit Annalinde, Gemeinschaftsgarten und Gärtnerei in Leipzig.

20.6.2015
»Lange Nacht des Bauernfilms« – mit Filmen aus dem Archiv von Ich bin gerne Bauer und möchte es auch gerne bleiben.

10.7.2015
Die GfZK hatte im Garten vor unserem Gartenhaus eine ungeliebte Plattform – genutzt jeden Abend von Jogginggruppen für ihre Dehnübungen, von Studenten zum Sonnenbaden, von Eltern mit Kleinkindern für eine Pause, aber dennoch nicht ideal. Schüler und Schülerinnen des Evangelischen Schulzentrums in Großbardau wurden unsere Experten für zeitgenössisches ländliches Rumhängen; gemeinsam mit ihnen wird die Plattform umgebaut und zum Sommerfest der GfZK festlich eröffnet, mit Fast Food und Lounge zum Chillen.

4.9.2015
In Friesland ist es üblich, Höfe und Wege mit Muscheln auszustreuen. Für einen Fußpfad, der sich vom Haupteingang der GfZK durch Sträucher und Immergrün zum Gartenhaus schlängelt, bestellen wir zwei Kubikmeter Muscheln in Harlingen am Wattenmeer, Muscheln, die beim Ausbaggern der Fahrrinnen zu den Inseln anfallen. Die jungen friesischen Bauern und Bäuerinnen schütten daraus schnell einen Muschelweg. Tritt sich fest. Er heißt Frysk Skelpepaad.

*Anschließend friesisch-rumänisches Sensen unter Anleitung von Mircea Onică aus Brezoi und Thomas Thiele aus Leipzig, ausgerüstet mit hölzernen Sensenbäumen und geschmiedeten Sensenblättern, mit Wetzsteinhalter und Dengelhammer: Immer dicht über dem Boden gleiten in zügigem Schwung!
Mit gemähten Wiesen und Muschelpfad*

P

the third show with a mowed meadow and a shell path, and presented the film Farmers & Ranchers *in a large projection. The Romanian guests grilled polenta. There were sausages from Franconia, Romania, and Leipzig, and from everywhere only the best. Pascal baked bread for us.*

5.9.2015
Harvest at Annalinde's, cooking zacuscă over the open fire with Theodor Teioșanu and Alexandra and Maria Onică. Tour through the large Osterland Agrar GmbH dairy farm in Frohburg near Leipzig with Dries van der Veen.

2.10.2015
For special occasions, we open our International Schnaps Bar, *a collection of mostly homemade schnapps – legal and illegal ones from all over the world. Wild berries were collected and prepared for fermenting a schnapps from Leipzig. Afterwards, Miriam Wiesel and Axel Schmidt from the "Kreuzberger Salon" were guests in the Gartenhaus. Naturally with* Schnaps Bar.

27.11.2015
We closed the Gartenhaus for the winter and invited people to a party in the remainder of the space behind the partition wall. No one noticed. Inside there was a landscape of kegs, outside a fire and chestnuts to warm our hands. In the old building of the GfZK, the Bibliobox, *a travelling archive in two crates, was ready for use, filled by Myvillages since 2005 with references to art projects in rural areas.*

11.3.2016
Some people baked blini, some quickly constructed a distillery. When the mash got stolen, the Irish distil Poitín from cheap wine.
In the evening, Lutz Nitsche gave a greeting on behalf of the Kulturstiftung des Bundes, a tradition at our cold spring openings. Phil Hession from Belfast sang. The

eröffnen wir die dritte Show und zeigen den Film Farmers & Ranchers *in großer Projektion. Die rumänischen Gäste grillen Polenta. Es gibt fränkische, rumänische und Leipziger Bratwürste, und von überall nur die besten. Pascal backt uns Brot.*

5.9.2015
Ernte bei Annalinde, Zacuscă einkochen über dem offenen Feuer mit Theodor Teioșanu und Alexandra und Maria Onică. Führung durch den großen Milchviehbetrieb der Osterland Agrar GmbH in Frohburg bei Leipzig durch Dries van der Veen.

2.10.2015
Zu besonderen Anlässen öffnen wir unsere International Schnaps Bar, *eine Sammlung zumeist hausgebrannter Schnäpse, legale und illegale Brände aus vieler Herren Länder. Für einen Leipziger Schnaps werden Wildbeeren gesammelt und zum Gären angesetzt. Anschließend sind Miriam Wiesel und Axel Schmidt mit dem »Kreuzberger Salon« zu Gast im Gartenhaus. Mit* Schnaps Bar *natürlich.*

27.11.2015
Wir schließen das Gartenhaus ab für den Winter und laden dafür zur Party im Restraum hinter der Trennwand. Fällt gar keinem auf. Drinnen gibt es eine Fasslandschaft, draußen Feuer und Maroni zum Händewärmen. Im Altbau der GfZK steht die Bibliobox *bereit zum Gebrauch, ein reisendes Archiv in zwei Kisten, von Myvillages mit Verweisen auf Kunstprojekte im ländlichen Raum gefüllt seit 2005.*

11.3.2016
Manche backen Blini, manche bauen schnell noch eine Destille. Als die Maische geklaut wird, brennen die Iren Poitín aus billigem Wein. Am Abend grüßt Lutz Nitsche für die Kulturstiftung des Bundes, eine Tradition zu unseren kalten Frühjahrseröffnungen. Phil Hession aus Belfast singt. Die Allunionslampe *strahlt. Im Wohnwagen wird Poitín getrunken, die Besucher wechseln, aber Paddy Bloomer erzählt, bis er umfällt. Im Grubenbrand brennen* Automateneulen *und* Automatenhasen *bis spät in die Nacht.*

P

P

TAILOR WEAR

P

All-Union Lamp *shone. Poitín was drunk in the caravan, the visitors alternated, but Paddy Bloomer told stories the bitter end. The ceramic owls and hares are being fired in the pit kiln until late in the night.*

12.3.2016
The "Coffee Morning Ballykinlar Style" had to take place indoors.

The owls and hares were still hot when we opened the pit. The Russian promotional video resulted in good sales in the shop. We constantly spent time looking for keys.

17.–20.3.2016
Olga Gartman from Moscow opened the Gartenhaus for three months and gave tours of the exhibition, thus also during the Leipzig Book Fair.

23.4.2016
"Night in the Village" with artists' films from Northern Ireland.

24.6.2016
Ten hours in the car on the way from Overijssel, with no air conditioning, but the flowers for the tulip vase were still beautiful. We celebrated a long, hot evening with guests from Belgium and the Netherlands. Children could eat as many chips as they wanted.

25.6.2016
Geological excursion to opencast pit mines and lakes with Ronny Schmidt.

Every Sunday afternoon from June to September: drawing lessons in the garden of the GfZK.

12.3.2016
Der »Coffee Morning Ballykinlar Style« muss drinnen stattfinden.

Die Eulen und Hasen sind noch heiß, als wir die Grube öffnen. Das russische Werbevideo führt zu guten Verkäufen im Laden. Ständig suchen wir Schlüssel.

17.–20.3.2016
Olga Gartman aus Moskau öffnet drei Monate lang das Gartenhaus und führt durch die Ausstellung, so auch zur Leipziger Buchmesse.

23.4.2016
»Nacht auf dem Dorf« mit nordirischen Künstlerfilmen.

24.6.2016
Zehn Stunden im Auto auf dem Weg von Overijssel, die Klimaanlage fällt aus, aber die Blumen für die Tulpenvase sind immer noch schön. Wir feiern einen langen heißen Abend mit Gästen aus Belgien und den Niederlanden. Kinder bekommen so viele Pommes, wie sie wollen.

25.6.2016
Geologische Exkursion zu Tagebauten und Seen mit Ronny Schmidt.

Von Juni bis September immer sonntags am Nachmittag: Zeichenunterricht im Garten der GfZK.

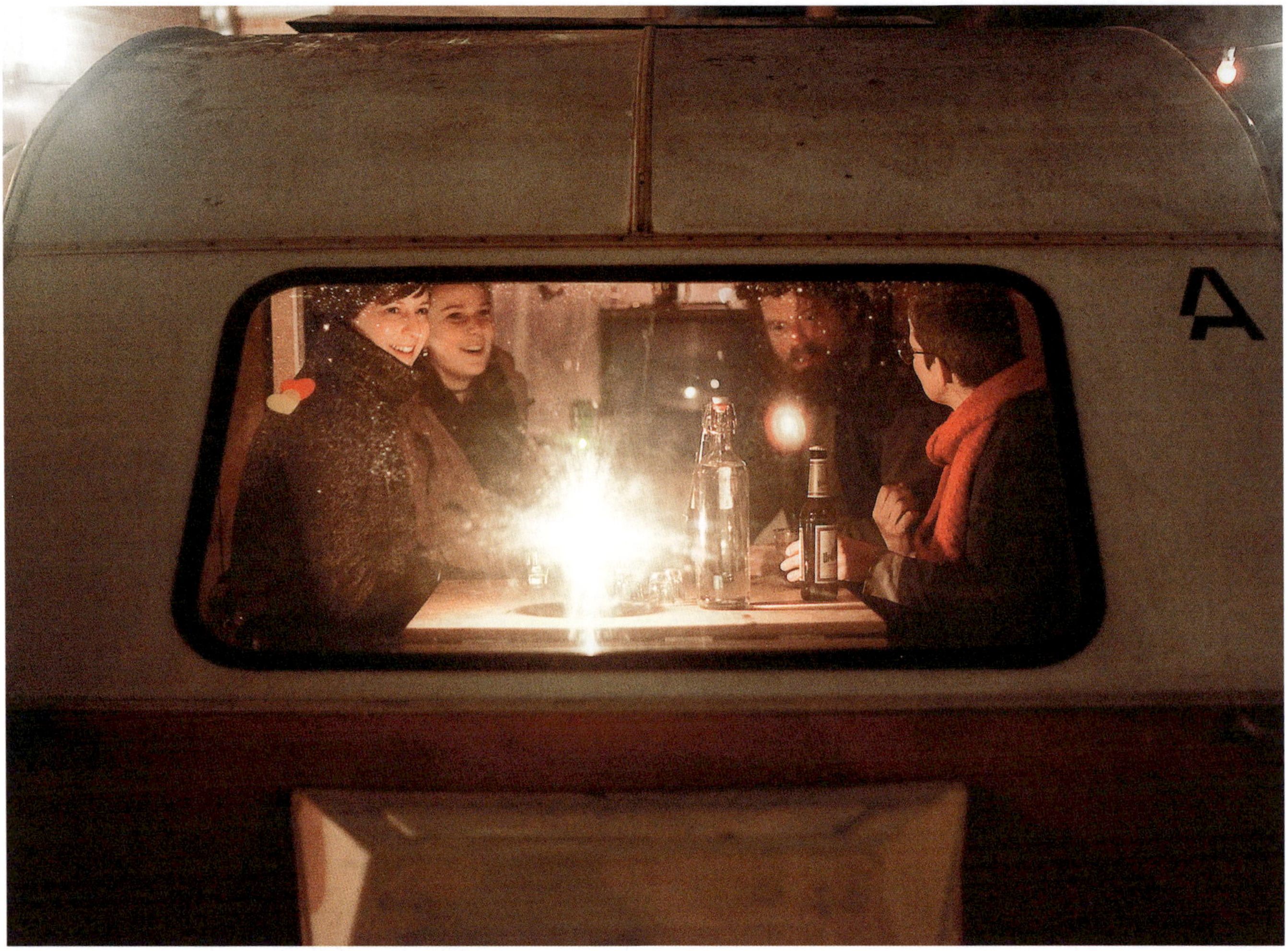

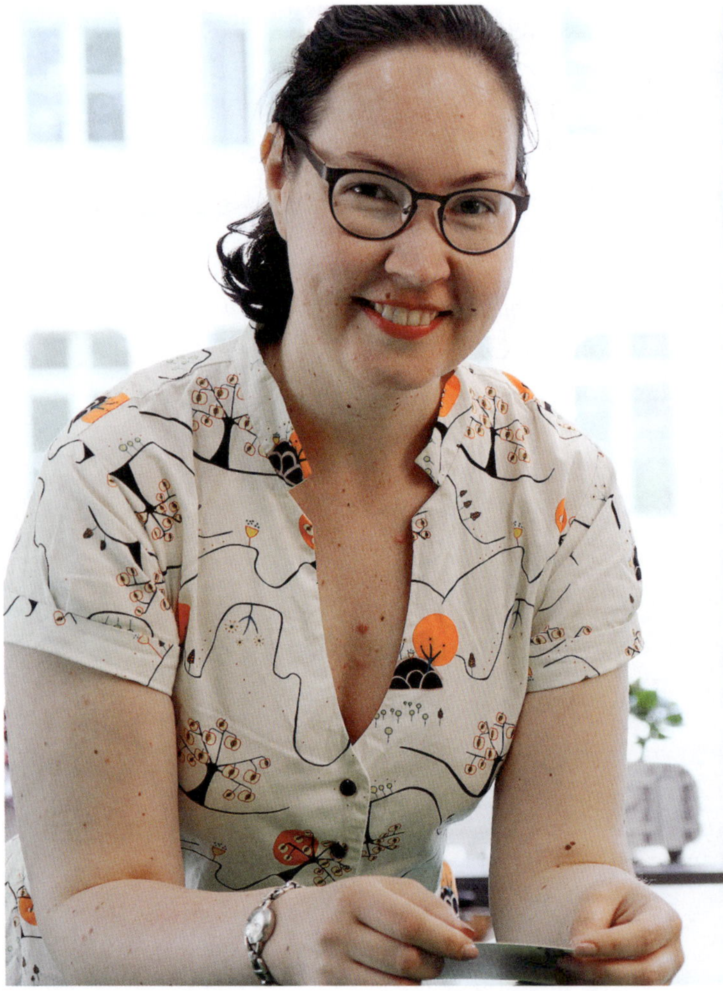

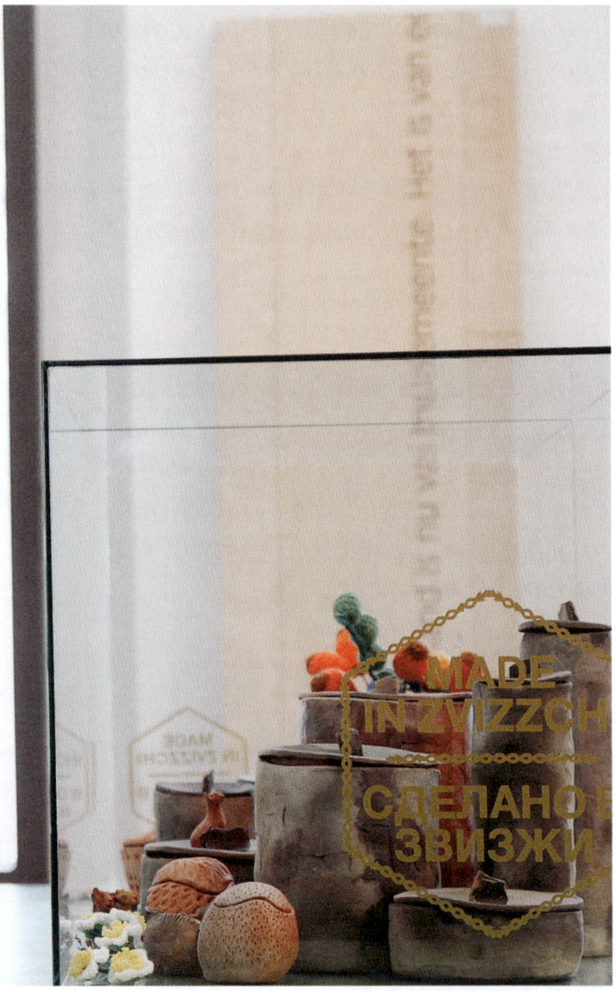

P

16.9.2016
Thinning Soda, Kent Cider, wine from Franschhoek – at the second to last opening, there was drinking, thematically motivated. Rain fell.

4.11.2016
Long Night of Farmers' Films – with films from the archive I like being a farmer and woult like to stay one.

2.12.2016
Festive Book Presentation.
Large International Village Shop *in the New Gallery with a new product from Beetsterzwaag.*

3.12.2016
Congress

AS

16.9.2016
Thinning Soda, Kent Cider, Wein aus Franschhoek – auf der vorletzten Eröffnung wird getrunken, thematisch motiviert. Der Regen fällt.

4.11.2016
»Lange Nacht des Bauernfilms« – mit Filmen aus dem Archiv von Ich bin gerne Bauer und möchte es auch gerne bleiben.

2.12.2016
Feierliche Buchpräsentation.
Großer International Village Shop *im Neubau mit einem neuen Produkt aus Beetsterzwaag.*

3.12.2016
Tagung

AS

P

PROTOKOLL

The village of Ohne has two inns, both located on the same square. For a long time, I always met with the committee from Ohne in one or the other by turns, for the sake of parity.

In Ekumfi Ekrawfo, eating together is not the most important aspect of festivities or community. When there is an achievement to celebrate, for instance, the success of a prototype for the coiled bamboo bowl or the production of the first bamboo bowls for sale, Everlove then invites the local dance group to drum and dance. Beverages for the dancers are stacked up into a tower. All the school children have to attend speeches and ceremonies. One waits until the representatives of all the important functions have come together. At the end there is palm wine in the palace; those who would like mix it with a Guinness from Kumasi, so it is very popular. Not everyone receives palm wine, certainly not: only exceedingly few. All of the others stand there, loiter, and look on.

The spectrum of difference in a village is probably smaller than in a city. On the other hand, one lives less in selected circles of friends and surroundings of people who are like oneself. The spectrum of difference may be smaller, but there is more contact with everyone within that spectrum.

Protocol determines, among other things, who belongs and to what degree. Nonchalance can be exclusive, and formality inclusive.

It seems to me as if delay and punctuality are aesthetic categories, hence, just like there is music that is deliberately drawn out or precise.

For an exhibition opening at the Centro Andaluz de Arte Contemporáneo in Seville, the museum and I invited the farmers with whom I had collaborated on the exhibition as guests of honour. They came from far away, from the Province of Málaga and from the Extremadura – all with children and grandchildren. For the exhibition, there was a joint buffet in the courtyard. The evening was warm and everyone brought their best food for the buffet. The farmers stayed in the exhibition for a long time, and I therefore did as well. They waited for hours for a speech; but no speech came, because speeches are never given in this museum, for the sake of freedom of interpretation; so the farmers and I missed the buffet. **AS**

Das Dorf Ohne hat zwei Gastwirtschaften, die am selben Platz liegen. Mit dem Komitee von Ohne treffe ich mich lange Zeit immer abwechselnd in der einen oder der anderen, wegen der Parität.

In Ekumfi Ekrawfo ist das gemeinsame Essen nicht das wichtigste Merkmal für Fest oder Gemeinschaft. Soll ein Erfolg gefeiert werden, etwa das Gelingen des Prototyps der gewickelten Bambusschüssel oder die Herstellung erster Bambusschüsseln für den Verkauf, dann lädt Everlove die lokale Tanzgruppe ein, zu trommeln und zu tanzen. Getränke in Dosen werden für die Tänzer zu einem Turm aufgebaut. Alle Schulkinder müssen den Reden und Zeremonien beiwohnen. Man wartet lange, bis Vertreter aller wichtigen Funktionen beisammen sind. Am Ende gibt es im Palast Palmwein; wer möchte, trinkt ihn mit Guinness aus Kumasi, so ist er sehr beliebt. Nicht alle bekommen Palmwein, beileibe nicht: die wenigsten nur. Alle anderen stehen dabei, lungern herum und gucken zu.

Das Spektrum der Verschiedenheit im sozialen Gefüge ist im Dorf wahrscheinlich kleiner als in der Stadt. Andererseits lebt man weniger in gewählten Freundeskreisen und Umgebungen von Menschen, die einem ähnlich sind. Das Spektrum der Differenz mag kleiner sein, aber die Berührung mit allen im Spektrum ist größer.

Das Protokoll entscheidet unter anderem darüber, wer dazugehört und in welchem Grad. Lässigkeit kann exklusiv sein, Förmlichkeit inklusiv.

Es kommt mir vor, als seien Verzögerung oder Pünktlichkeit ästhetische Kategorien, so wie es verschleppte und akkurat gewollte Musik gibt.

Zu einer Ausstellungseröffnung im Centro Andaluz de Arte Contemporáneo in Sevilla hatten das Museum und ich als Ehrengäste die Landwirte eingeladen, mit denen ich für die Ausstellung zusammengearbeitet hatte. Sie kamen von weiter her, aus der Provinz Málaga und aus der Extremadura, vollständig mit Kindern und Enkeln. Zur Ausstellung gab es ein gemeinsames Buffet im Hof. Der Abend war warm und zum Buffet hatten alle das Beste mitgebracht. Die Landwirte blieben lange in der Ausstellung, und so auch ich. Sie warteten auf die Rede, stundenlang; die Rede kam nicht, weil in diesem Museum nie Reden gehalten werden, der Freiheit der Interpretation wegen; so haben die Bauern und ich das Buffet verpasst. **AS**

P

RURAL AR

A conversation between Francien van Westrenen (**F**) and Kathrin Böhm (**K**)

F: Myvillages is many villages; there's more than one story to be told. Together they provide a way to understand Myvillages as an artist, spatial, productional, emancipatory, exhibited, open village. Myvillages takes on different formats and turns with each project. There's no physical structure, no centre or master plan, it functions through the three of you working in different places.

K: Sometimes I describe Myvillages by appropriating a rural art space model with a trajectory in art history, the artist village. When I use this term, I'm not describing a reclusive and exclusive geographical unit. I instead want to make people think of our practice as a new way of organizing and working as artists in rural environments.

F: The term artist village doesn't work for me. I like to think of Myvillages as an inclusive, open practice. You're not only working with the rural landscape, but also from within it.

K: We've talked about how the work of Myvillages can be read and discussed in terms of spatial production and architecture, referring to the discussion around architecture beyond actual buildings. In that sense, the spatial network we have established so far could be described as architectural production.

F: Yes, that makes sense to me as a way to describe what you're doing. It is a form of architecture, looked at as culture, as a spatial practice, as a place for cultural production. I would rather call it an applied attitude or spatial agency, a way of doing architecture, through building a social network, infrastructure, and product line.

K: So, if we've been making our own particular art space, why would we want to bring our work to a gallery or a museum? We think that we address some crucial assumptions, for example, that there is no art in the rural, and therefore counteract "urban cultural arrogance", which should be amplified by cultural organizations that see their role in publishing, explaining, and facilitating contemporary art practice.

T SPACE

Ein Gespräch zwischen Francien van Westrenen (**F**) und Kathrin Böhm (**K**)

F: Myvillages ist viele Dörfer. Es gibt mehr als nur eine einzige Geschichte zu erzählen. Insgesamt entsteht aus allen diesen Geschichten das Bild von Myvillages als einem künstlerischen, räumlichen, produktiven, emanzipatorischen, ausgestellten, offenen Dorf. Myvillages bedient sich unterschiedlicher Formate und wandelt sich mit jedem Projekt. Es hat keinen materiellen Unterbau, kein Zentrum und keinen Rahmenplan. Es funktioniert, indem ihr drei an unterschiedlichen Orten arbeitet.

K: Gelegentlich habe ich Myvillages als eigenen ländlichen Kunstraum beschrieben und dafür auch die kunstgeschichtliche Tradition des Künstlerdorfs vereinnahmt. Ich meine mit dieser Bezeichnung keinen geografisch gefassten, exklusiven Ort auf der Landkarte, sondern ich will damit vermitteln, dass es in unserer Praxis um eine neue Art und Weise geht, wie Künstlerinnen im ländlichen Raum arbeiten und sich gleichzeitig räumlich organisieren.

F: Der Begriff »Künstlerdorf« passt für mich nicht. Ich sehe Myvillages eher als eine inklusive, offene künstlerische Praxis. Ihr arbeitet nicht nur mit den ländlichen Schauplätzen, sondern mitten in ihnen.

K: Wir sprachen darüber, wie sich die Arbeit von Myvillages in Begriffe der Raumproduktion und Architektur fassen ließe, im Sinne einer »Architektur«, die nicht als gebauter Raum zu verstehen ist. In diesem Zusammenhang lässt sich das räumliche Netzwerk, das wir bislang geschaffen haben, als architektonische Produktion beschreiben.

R

F: Ja, das scheint mir eine zutreffende Beschreibung eurer Arbeit. Sie ist eine Form von Architektur im Sinne eines Schaffens in und mit dem Raum, als ein Ort für kulturelle Produktion. Am ehesten würde ich das, was ihr tut, eine angewandte Haltung oder ein Handeln im Raum nennen: Architektur als Konstruktion eines sozialen Netzwerks, einer Infrastruktur und einer Produktionsweise.

K: Wenn wir nun unseren eigenen Kunstraum geschaffen haben: Warum sollten wir dann unsere Arbeit überhaupt in einer Galerie oder einem Museum zeigen wollen? Wir finden, dass wir mit unserer Arbeit zentrale Voreingenommenheiten und Probleme des Kunstbetriebs ansprechen – etwa die überhebliche Annahme vieler Städter, es gebe auf dem Land

F: I'm interested in thinking about other kinds of public spaces where a similar discussion can be held. On the other hand, I can see that the rather established context of a cultural institution can take concentration, reflection, and discussion to another level.

K: You explained that the work of Stroom starts with artist practice (working from the arts) and finding the best space for it to become public.

F: True, that's how we work. We're an art and public space organization and need to think outside of the walls of our exhibition space. In trying to do this, we pay tribute to Otto Neurath[1], who believed in cultural space outside of a cultural place. As he wrote in 1931, we "have reached a point where in the great metropolis the decentralization of the museum is afoot ... These museums should not be treated as central, monumental locations, but as moving structures that one can transform depending on the purpose of the exhibition."[1]

K: To a degree, it is an institutional critique for us to ask a gallery or museum to collaborate with us on an exhibition or publishing format that shows the work of Myvillages appropriately. If our work doesn't fit into conventional structures – such as the six-week exhibition slot – then this doesn't mean the work shouldn't be shown, but rather that the structure needs to be adapted.

F: Myvillages is already a structure to show, to produce, to make public, to connect, to think – all of which can be said of exhibitions.

K: We – Myvillages – also see ourselves as coming from the arts . Therefore, the *International Village Show* offers a space where "our art world" is open and can be entered and visited by those whose rural spaces we normally visit and use. A reciprocal relationship between village and museum. The *International Village Show* claims the exhibition space/the museum as a format that should be owned by many.

R

F: These are very important notions, I think. The museum is an important space for knowledge production, a kind of neutral space where an unknown or unthinkable connection between people and practices can occur.

Francien van Westrenen works at the Stroom Den Haag centre for visual arts and architecture, as a curator of architecture exhibitions, projects, publications, and lectures based on an interdisciplinary and cultural approach to the urban environment.

1 **Otto Neurath** (1882–1945) was a sociologist and economist, and founder of the Museum of Society and Economy in Vienna. Quote: Nader Vossoughian, *Otto Neurath, The Language of the Global Polis* (Rotterdam: NAi Uitgevers, 2008), p. 79.

keine Kunst. Wie jede künstlerische Praxis sollte auch unsere von Kulturorganisationen, die ihre Aufgabe im Vertrieb, Erklären und Ermöglichen zeitgenössischer künstlerischer Arbeit sehen, öffentlich gemacht werden.

F: Mich interessieren andersgeartete öffentliche Räume, in denen eine solche Auseinandersetzung stattfinden kann. Ich sehe aber auch ein, dass der Kontext einer etablierten Kultureinrichtung das Niveau der Konzentration, Reflexion und Debatte heben kann.

K: Du hast mir erklärt, dass beispielsweise die Arbeit des Kunst- und Architekturzentrums Stroom Den Haag, wo du arbeitest, immer von einer künstlerischen Praxis ausgeht und dann nach dem bestmöglichen Raum ihrer öffentlichen Präsentation sucht.

F: Das stimmt, so arbeiten wir. Wir sind eine Organisation für Kunst und öffentlichen Raum und müssen außerhalb der vier Wände unseres Ausstellungsraums denken. Darin sind wir dem Wiener Soziologen, Nationalökonom und Museumsgründer Otto Neurath[1] verpflichtet, der an einen Raum für die Kultur außerhalb von Kultureinrichtungen glaubte: Er schrieb 1931, dass in den Großstädten eine Dezentralisierung der Museen überfällig sei, dass man sie nicht als Gedenkstätten, sondern als bewegliche, dem jeweiligen Zweck der Ausstellung anzupassende Orte betrachten sollte.

K: Wir sehen es bis zu einem bestimmten Grad als institutionelle Kritik, wenn wir eine Galerie oder ein Museum bitten, mit uns ein Veröffentlichungsformat zu erarbeiten, das der Arbeit von Myvillages gerecht wird. Dass unsere Arbeit sich nicht in konventionelle Strukturen wie den sechswöchigen Ausstellungszyklus fügt, heißt ja nicht, dass sie nicht gezeigt werden sollte, sondern dass die Struktur einer Anpassung bedarf.

F: Man könnte Myvillages als eigene Struktur beschreiben, in der ausgestellt, produziert, veröffentlich, verknüpft und gedacht wird – genau das, wofür Ausstellungsräume verantwortlich sind.

K: Myvillages kommt aus der Kunst, und die *International Village Show* eröffnet bewusst einen Raum in »unsere Kunstwelt«, der offen steht und von denjenigen betreten und besucht werden kann, deren ländliche Räume wir normalerweise besuchen und benutzen. Die Beziehung zwischen dem Dorf und dem Museum beruht hier auf Gegenseitigkeit. Die Show erhebt Anspruch auf den Ausstellungsraum beziehungsweise das Museum als öffentlichem Raum, der von vielen in Anspruch genommen werden kann.

F: Das scheinen mir sehr wichtige Überlegungen. Das Museum bleibt ein wichtiger Raum für Wissensproduktion. Es ist zugleich auch ein neutraler Raum, in dem unvorhergesehene und anderswo undenkbare Verbindungen entstehen können.

Francien van Westrenen erarbeitet als Architekturkuratorin am Kunstzentrum Stroom Den Haag (NL) Ausstellungen, Projekte, Publikationen und Vorträge, die auf einem interdisziplinären, kulturwissenschaftlichen Umgang mit dem städtischen Raum basieren. www.stroom.nl

1 **Otto Neurath** (1882–1945) war Soziologe und Nationalökonom. Er gründete das Gesellschafts- und Wirtschaftsmuseum Wien, das sich der Bildung der Arbeiterschaft widmete. Zitiert nach: Nader Vossoughian, *Otto Neurath: The Language of the Global Polis*, NAi Uitgevers Rotterdam, 2008, S. 79.

SCHNAPSBAR

Wapke brings clove cheese from Frisia, Antje liver pate from Heiligendorf, and Kathrin schnapps from Höfen. That's how things have been ever since the first public appearance of Myvillages at the 850-year anniversary of Heiligendorf. We've made a lot of friends.

Kathrin's father, Walter Böhm, has his schnapps distilled at the communal distillery in Unterzettlitz: quince, apple, plum. When you cultivate the fruit yourself, you can distil as much as you would like. The distiller charges 25 euro per 100 litres of mash. As far as the alcohol tax is concerned: plum is given a more favourable tax rate than cherry.

When people who keep reserves of food for feeding guests then bring food with them on a journey – with no known cold chain – they really appreciate schnapps. Schnapps never goes off. Today, we have a collection of spirits from many countries and hands, distilled legally and illegally.

Sergej produces his Samagon solely to serve it in the summer at his café, Kartoschkino. You cannot order it; it comes with the food. Vladimir has a secret production site in the cellar, and uses numerous herbs and roots. His Samagon is popular with neighbours and summer visitors; they come to visit discreetly. Samagon is an economic mainstay. Vladimir likes to fill it into fancy vodka, whisky, or brandy bottles, which he collects for this purpose.

From Goritsa, Bulgaria, where her mother married, Nathalie brings us Rakia in small plastic bottles.

Mircea distils Țuică at the Odaja, and we regularly receive a portion.

The oldest schnapps in our collection is an Orujo, a grape marc spirit, corked in the 1980s by Francisco Olveira in Xuño, Porto do Son, Galicia.

Wapke bringt Nelkenkäse aus Friesland, Antje Leberwurst aus Heiligendorf, Kathrin Schnaps aus Höfen. So war es seit unserem ersten öffentlichen Auftritt von Myvillages beim 850-jährigen Jubiläum von Heiligendorf. Hat uns viele Freunde gebracht.

Kathrins Vater, Walter Böhm, lässt seinen Schnaps in der Kommunalbrennerei in Unterzettlitz brennen, Quitte, Apfel, Pflaume. Wenn das Obst aus eigenem Anbau stammt, kann man so viel brennen, wie man will. Der Brenner verlangt 25 Euro pro 100 Liter Maische. Was die Branntweinsteuer betrifft: Pflaume ist steuerlich günstiger als Kirsche.

Wer Vorratshaltung betreibt, um Gäste daraus zu bewirten, mit diesen Vorräten auf Reisen geht – Kühlkette unbekannt –, der weiß Schnaps zu schätzen. Schnaps verkommt nie. Wir haben heute eine Sammlung von Bränden aus vielen Ländern und Händen, legal und illegal gebrannt.

Sergej produziert seinen Samagon nur, um ihn im Sommer in seinem Café Kartoschkino auszuschenken. Man kann ihn nicht bestellen, er kommt mit dem Essen. Vladimir hat eine geheimnisvolle Produktion im Keller, unter Nutzung zahlreicher Kräuter und Wurzeln. Sein Samagon ist bei Nachbarn und Sommerfrischlern bekannt, sie kommen unauffällig zu Besuch. Der Samagon ist ein wirtschaftliches Standbein. Vladimir füllt ihn gern in schicke Wodka-, Whisky- oder Weinbrandflaschen, die er zu diesem Zweck sammelt.

Aus Goritsa in Bulgarien, wo ihre Mutter verheiratet war, bringt uns Nathalie Rakia in kleinen Plastikflaschen.

Mircea brennt auf der Odaja Țuică, und wir bekommen stets ein Kontingent.

Der älteste Schnaps in unserer Sammlung ist ein Orujo, ein Tresterbrand, verkorkt in den Achtzigerjahren von Francisco Olveira in Xuño, Porto do Son, Galizien.

We also have Genever from Dordrecht and mint liqueur from the Preussische Spirituosenmanufaktur in Berlin-Wedding, a very strong one, which was supposedly quite popular with the sophisticated ladies of the 1920s. In Berlin, there was no surplus of fruit, which is why people specialized not in fine brandies, but rather in liqueurs.

We set up an *International Village Shop* at the Tate Britain one time and sold goods from our tables for an entire evening. Among other things, we had schnapps by Walter Böhm on offer, in a plastic bottle, lewdly labelled, actually a gift for his son-in-law, but made available for our product range in the morning. We also had fruit brandy by Christoph Keller, a very good fruit brandy, at the time with labels by Liam Gillick. The later was supposed to cost 80 pounds per bottle, and so we gave the schnapps by Kathrin's father the same price. A collector came to us to shop; he bought a lot, and he also wanted a bottle. He took a long time making his decision: the artist edition schnapps or the plastic bottle. To me, it was immediately clear: he could only take the plastic bottle; it was a question of style. **AS**

Wir führen auch Genever aus Dordrecht und Minzlikör von der Preussischen Spirituosenmanufaktur in Berlin-Wedding, sehr stark, der bei den mondänen Damen der Zwanzigerjahre beliebt gewesen sein soll. An Obst habe es in Berlin keinen Überschuss gegeben, weshalb man sich nicht auf Edelbrände, sondern vielmehr auf Liköre spezialisiert hat.

Einmal haben wir einen *International Village Shop* in der Tate Britain aufgebaut und einen Abend lang von unseren Tischen verkauft. Unter anderem hatten wir einen Schnaps von Walter Böhm im Angebot, in einer Plastikflasche, liederlich beschriftet, eigentlich ein Geschenk an seinen Schwiegersohn, aber am Morgen schnell fürs Sortiment zur Verfügung gestellt. Wir hatten auch Obstbrand von Christoph Keller, sehr guten Obstbrand, damals mit Etiketten von Liam Gillick. Letzterer sollte 80 Pfund die Flasche kosten, und so haben wir dem Schnaps von Kathrins Vater den gleichen Preis gegeben. Ein Sammler kam bei uns einkaufen; er kaufte viel, und er wollte auch eine Flasche haben. Er hat lange überlegt: der Künstlereditionsschnaps oder die Plastikflasche. Mir war gleich klar: Er konnte nur die Plastikflasche nehmen, das war eine Frage des Stils. **AS**

Show 1/8

February – May / Februar – Mai 2015

Höfen, Upper Franconia / Oberfranken (DE)
Ekumfi Ekrawfo, Central Region (GH)

Ekumfi Ekrawfo, 2015
Wood, painted, LED lamps /
Holz bemalt, LED-Lampen
42 × 38 × 4 cm

Fufu Bowls, 2015
Video, 14 min

Höfen, 2015
Steel rings, welded and powder-coated /
Stahlringe geschweißt und pulverbeschichtet
110 × 70 × 2 cm

Höfer Lace / Höfer Spitze, 2015
Video, 4:56 min

One-Street Village / Straßendorf, 2015
Digital print / Digitaldruck
dimensions variable / Maße variabel

One-Street Village / Straßendorf, 2015
Screen print on linen / Siebdruck auf Leinen
160 × 300 cm

Untitled (Ekumfi Paintings) /
o.T. (Ekumfi-Bilder), 2015
Acrylic on wood, 10 panels /
Acryl auf Holz, 10 Tafeln
1: 26 × 43 cm
9: each / je 21,4 × 36,5 cm

Pots with Noses (Thinking about
Höfen while Working Clay) /
Vasen mit Nasen (beim Lehmkneten
über Höfen nachdenken), 2015
Homage to / Hommage an Michael Back,
clay, partially glazed / Lehm, teilglasiert
3,5 – 19 × ø 4,2 – 8 cm

S

S

Hasselförde
Heiligendorf
Heino
Helchteren
Hinojosa del Valle
Höfen
Höflein
Hofstede
Holthone
Huins
Kimswert
Marrum
Mechow
Meseberg
Memmelsdorf
Mol
Montalvo
Mürsbach
Neuenkirchen
Nikola Lenivetz
Ohne
Oppenberg
Ornding
Seehausen
Sellendorf
Sexbierum
Sibculo
Simla
Slagharen
Sodupe
Sopuerta
Steg
Steinhöfel
Stolzenhagen
Stratford
Warnsveld
Warth
Wem
Wijk aan Zee
Wjelsryp
Wolimierz
Wommels
Workum
Worpswede
Zalla
Zvizzchi

S

S

Show 2/8

May–August / Mai–August 2015

Region around Leipzig / Leipziger Umland (DE) Spanish villages / spanische Dörfer (ES)

Transporte de Cabras, 2014
Oil on wood / Öl auf Holz
77 × 101 cm

Andaluces de Jaén, 2015
Wood veneer, mini-loudspeakers, paper /
Holzfurnier, Minilautsprecher, Papier
28 × 34 cm

Finca Yñiguez-Ovando / Laureano Rosario,
Hinojosa del Valle, 2015
(from the archive *I like being a farmer and I would like to stay one* /
aus dem Archiv *Ich bin gerne Bauer und möchte es auch gerne bleiben*, 2000–)
Video, 26 min

Geological Animation /
Geologische Animation Leipzig, 2015
Video, 4:36 min

Geological Collection /
Geologische Sammlung, 2015
with / mit Ronny Schmidt of the /
von der GeoWerkstatt Leipzig
Stone and lignite / Gestein und Braunkohle

Geological Drawings /
Geologische Zeichnungen Leipzig, 2015
Pigment print on paper, framed with Dibond /
Pigmentdruck auf Papier, Dibond gerahmt
22 × 33 cm

Juan García, Cuevas del Becerro, 2015
(from the archive *I like being a farmer and I would like to stay one* /
aus dem Archiv *Ich bin gerne Bauer und möchte es auch gerne bleiben*, 2000–)
Video, 24 min

MTL Meeting Point / MTL-Treffpunkt, 2015
Multifunctional furniture, wood /
multifunktionales Möbel, Holz
1200 × 1200 × 40 cm

Paisajes de Producción, 2015
3 drawings, felt pen, paper /
3 Zeichnungen, Faserstift, Papier
each / je 29,7 × 21 cm

The Grain Store is Full /
Das Getreidelager ist voll, 2015
Installation, *Farmers' Chinaware* with stones from the Geological Collection /
Installation, Geschirr mit Gestein aus der Geologischen Sammlung
dimensions variable / Maße variabel

Village Sign / Dorfschild MTL-Team, 2015
Metal, powder coated /
Metall pulverbeschichtet
15 × 45 cm

S

Das Getreidelager i

voll.
Wir b

Show 3/8

September–November 2015

Brezoi (RU), Deer Trail, Colorado (US) Fryslân (NL)

Photographs of / Fotografien von Colorado, 2012–2015
Digital print / Digitaldruck
various formats / verschiedene Formate

Deer Trail, 2014
Photo print on industrial curtain / Fotodruck auf Industrievorhang
268 × 310 cm

Farmers & Ranchers: Growing Up in Changing Landscapes, 2014
Video, 26 min

Fryslân, 2014
Photo print on industrial curtain / Fotodruck auf Industrievorhang
268 × 310 cm

Odaja, 2014
Video, 6:56 min

Raspberry Syrup / Himbeersirup, 2014
Video, 2:50 min

Zacuskă, 2014
Video, 3:40 min

Eco Nomadic School, 2015
Postcards / Postkarten DIN A6 and shelve / und Regal
110 × 60 × 12 cm

Stool / Sitzhocker, 2015
by / von Cimpoeru Dumitru,
Wood / Holz
40 × ø 42 cm

Village Sign for / Dorfschild Brezoi, 2015
Wood, untreated / Holz, unbehandelt
25 × 100 × 8 cm

Textiles / Textilien
Private collection of / Privatsammlung von Georgeta Onică and / und Mihaela Efrim

Wall Hanging from the Odaja / Wandteppich aus der Odaja
Loan / Leihgabe Mircea Onică

S

S

S

S

Show 4/8

November 2015 – March 2016 / November 2015 – März 2016

Winterdisplay and / und **Bibliobox**

Bibliobox, 2005
Travelling library / reisende Bibliothek
2 boxes / 2 Kisten
each / je 65 x 40 x 50 cm

Barrel Landscape / Fasslandschaft, 2015
Lidded plastic barrels and glasses /
Kunststoffdeckelfässer und Gläser
280 × 555 × 175 cm

Winter Lines / Winterzeilen, 2015
Digital text display / Laufschrift
26 × 317 cm

While ascending to the Odaja, it began to snow and the tranquil mountains became even quieter. — We drove behind a water cannon truck from the British army for 45 minutes. No one was able to overtake. It was still 12 miles to Ballykinlar. — There was nothing more to be found outside. The mice were looking for their way back into the Gartenhaus. — Windows are washed for Christmas. Never by the men, and never on Sunday. — Vladimir picks up his wife from the train from Moscow every Friday, drives one and a half hours to reach the train station. She does not come to Zvizzchi in winter. Vladimir stays home. — In Colorado, the fields need snow. Dust storms threaten the winter wheat. — The moor gave us a sunset hazy with fog. — He went into the apple yard with a small ladder to cut the longer branches. — It was now finally possible to repair the tractor seat, with new, black imitation leather. — Four horses no longer want to be milked; they are pregnant. — "This is my office," said Herr Leicht of the local distillery in Unterzettlitz and pointed to a fruit crate with a small roof. — Everybody looks forward to the Matanza. Three pigs are then slaughtered on a frosty day, and the work goes on until late in the night.

S

Beim Aufstieg zur Odaja fing es an zu schneien, und die ruhigen Berge wurden noch stiller. — Seit 45 Minuten fahren wir einem Wasserwerfer der britischen Armee hinterher. Keiner kann überholen. Nach Ballykinlar sind es noch zwölf Meilen. — Draußen ist nichts mehr zu holen. Die Mäuse suchen ihren Weg zurück ins Gartenhaus. — Zu Weihnachten werden die Fenster geputzt. Nie von den Männern und nie an einem Sonntag. – Jeden Freitag hat Vladimir seine Frau vom Zug aus Moskau abgeholt, eineinhalb Stunden ist er bis zum Bahnhof gefahren. Im Winter kommt sie nicht nach Zvizzchi. Vladimir bleibt zu Hause. — In Colorado brauchen die Felder Schnee. Staubstürme bedrohen den Winterweizen. — Das Moor schenkt uns einen im Nebel verschwommenen Sonnenuntergang. — Er geht mit einer kleinen Leiter in den Apfelhof, um die längeren Äste zu beschneiden. — Jetzt kann man endlich mal den Traktorsessel reparieren, mit neuem, schwarzem Kunstleder. — Vier Pferde werden nicht mehr gemolken, sie sind trächtig. — »Das hier ist mein Büro«, sagte Herr Leicht von der Kommunalbrennerei in Unterzettlitz und zeigte auf eine Obstkiste mit kleinem Dach. — Wir freuen uns auf die Matanza. An einem frostigen Tag werden drei Schweine geschlachtet, und alle arbeiten bis tief in die Nacht.

Vladimir
759

eibt zu hause

Show 5/8

March–June / März–Juni 2016

ЗВИЗЖИ (RU)
Ballykinlar, Northern Ireland / Nordirland (GB)

Photos of / Fotos Zvizzchi, 2012/13
Digital prints / Digitaldruck
various dimensions / verschiedene Maße

Caravan Pot, 2013
Ceramic, glazed / Keramik, lasiert
18 × 16 × 32 cm

Greetings from / Grüße aus Zvizzchi, 2013
Postcards, various motifs / Postkarten, verschiedene Motive
DIN A6

Made in Zvizzchi, 2012–2015
Display case, textiles, crocheted flowers, "golden shoes", and jewellery / Vitrine, Textilien, Häkelblumen, »Goldene Schuhe« und Schmuck (2012/13), miniature animals and ceramics / Miniaturtiere und Keramik (2015)
dimensions variable / Maße variabel

Geological Animation / Geologische Animation Zvizzchi, 2015
Video, 3:53 min

МЕЖДУНАРОДНЫЙ СЕЛЬСКИЙ МАГАЗИН, 2015
Wood, painted / Holz, bemalt
151 × 209 cm

Naschi Produkti, 2015
Video, 16 min

Water Tower and Wood / Wasserturm und Holz, 2015
Photo wallpaper / Fototapete
200 × 300 cm

All-Union Lamp / Allunionslampe, 2016
Electrical installation, various materials / Elektroinstallation, verschiedene Materialien
222 × 30 × 30 cm

Twisted Bugle, 2016
Bugles, bent by / Blashörner, gebogen von Paddy Bloomer, Glass / Glas, Stearin
40 × 12 × 27 cm

Twisted Bugle, 2016
Video, 5:42 min

S

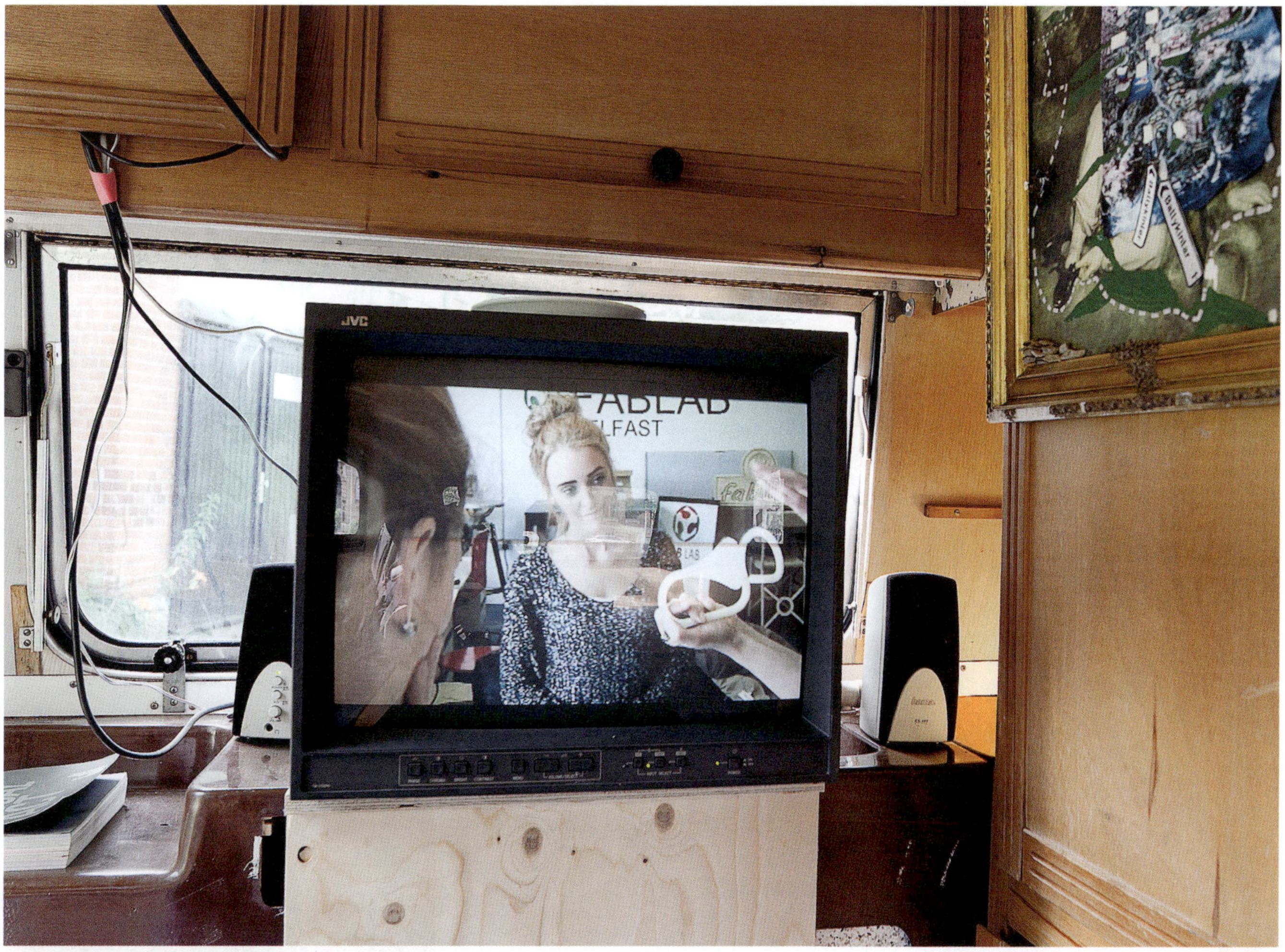
JVC
FABLAB
LFAST

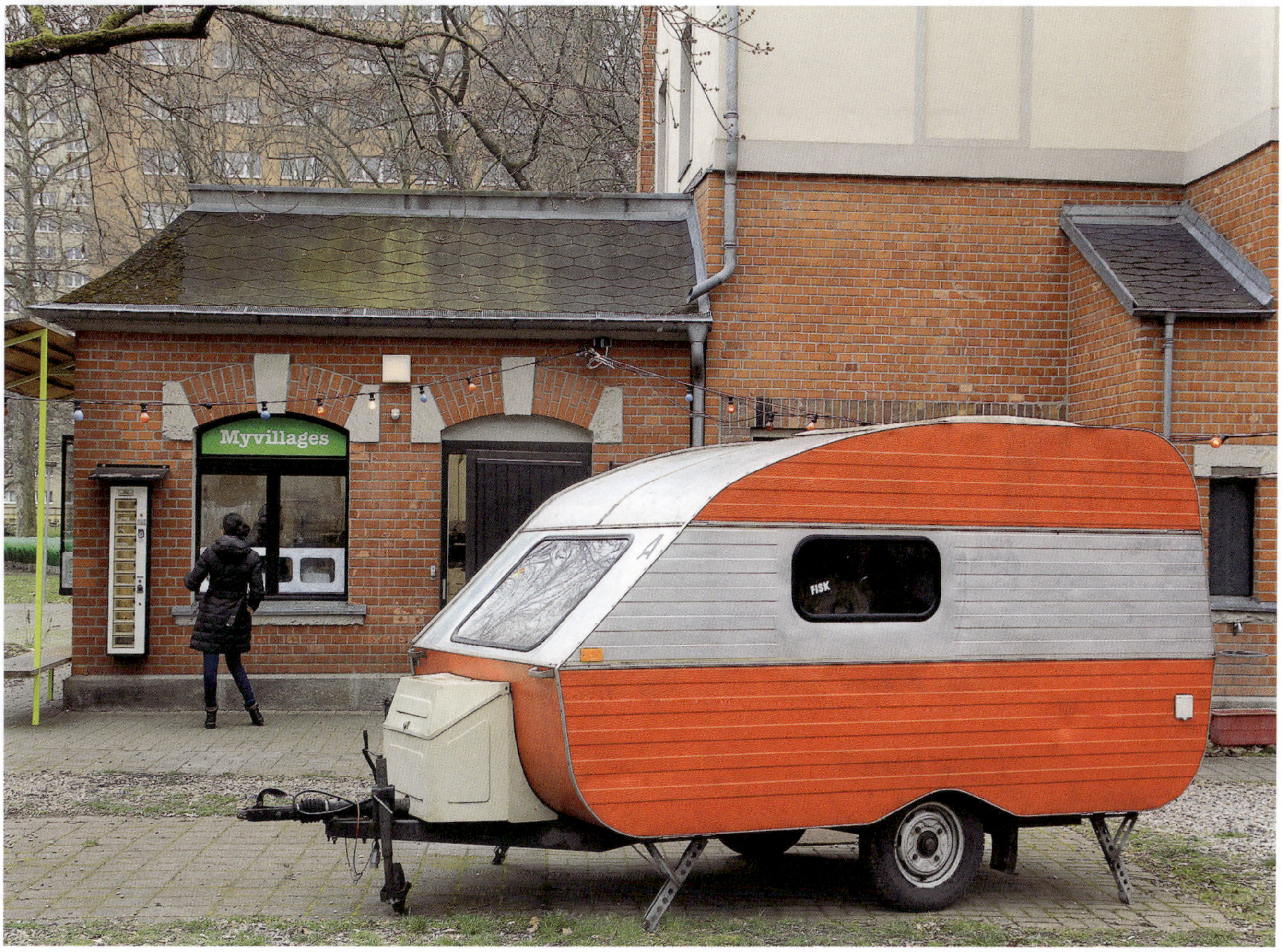
Myvillages
FISK

S

S

Show 6/8

June–September / Juni–September 2016

Vechte (DE / NL)
Schelde (BE)

Vinex Tulpenvaas, 2008
Tulip vase / Tulpenvase
Open Source Design by / von Roderick Vos
118 × 37 × 35 cm

Plein Air Drawing Set / Plein-Air-Zeichenset, 2014
10 sets consisting of each 1 A3 board and fishing stool / 10 Sets bestehend aus je 1 A3-Brett und Angelhocker

A Schelde Riverscape, 2016
4 books, each / 4 Bücher, je 21 × 27 cm, beer table / Biertisch

Baasrode, 2016
Wall painting based on the eponymous drawing by / Wandgemälde nach der gleichnamigen Zeichnung von Pieter Brueghel the Elder / dem Älteren (1556), acrylic on plaster / auf Putz
200 × 350 cm

Confectie Boxes, 2016
Video, 7:47 min

Esch F6, 2016
Video, 7:43 min

Mien Ruys Confectie Border, 2016
Flower bed, railway sleepers / Blumenbeet, Bahnschwellen
15 × 169 × 144 cm

Underbrush / Gestrüpp, 2016
various dimensions/verschiedene Maße

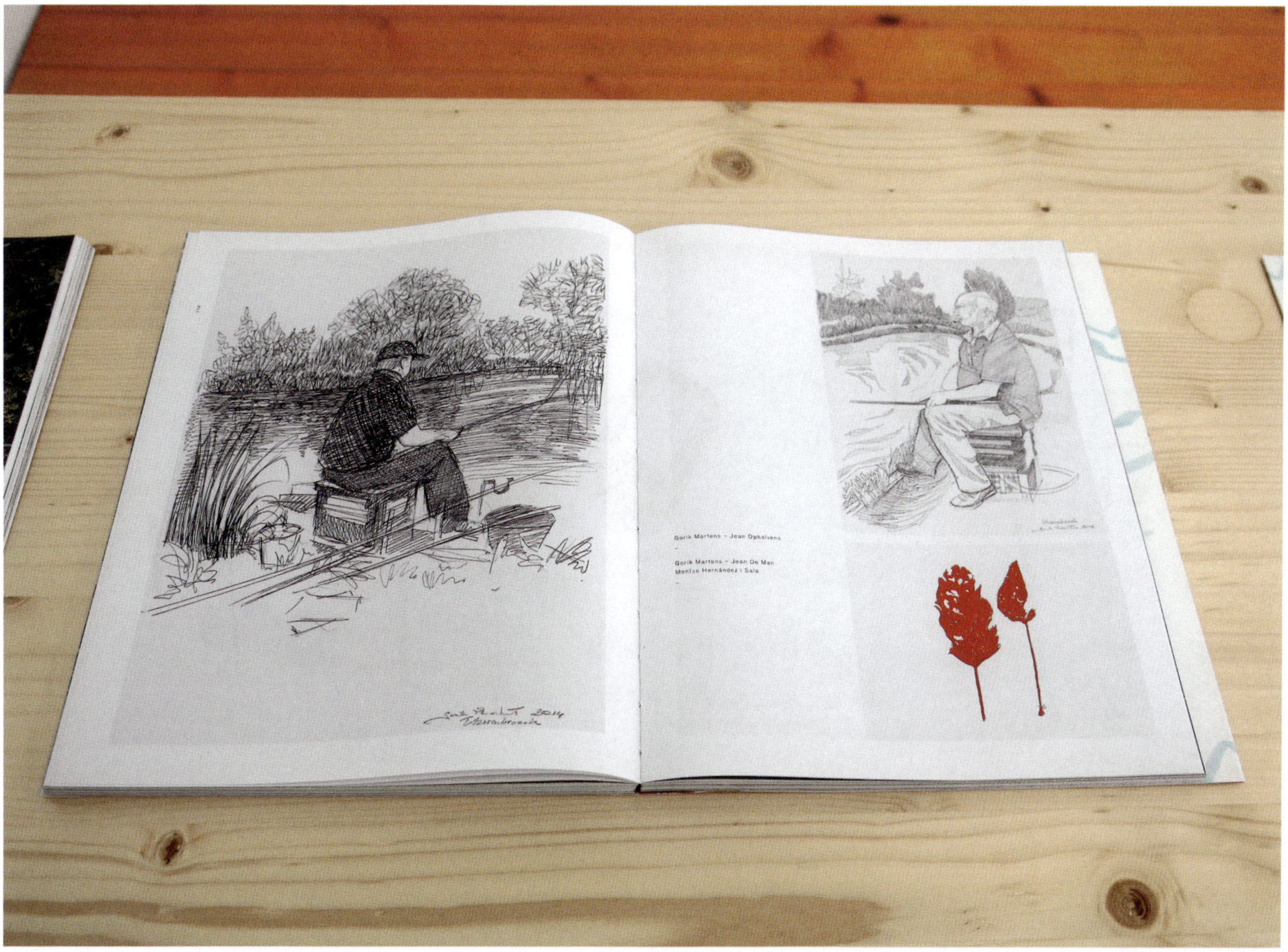

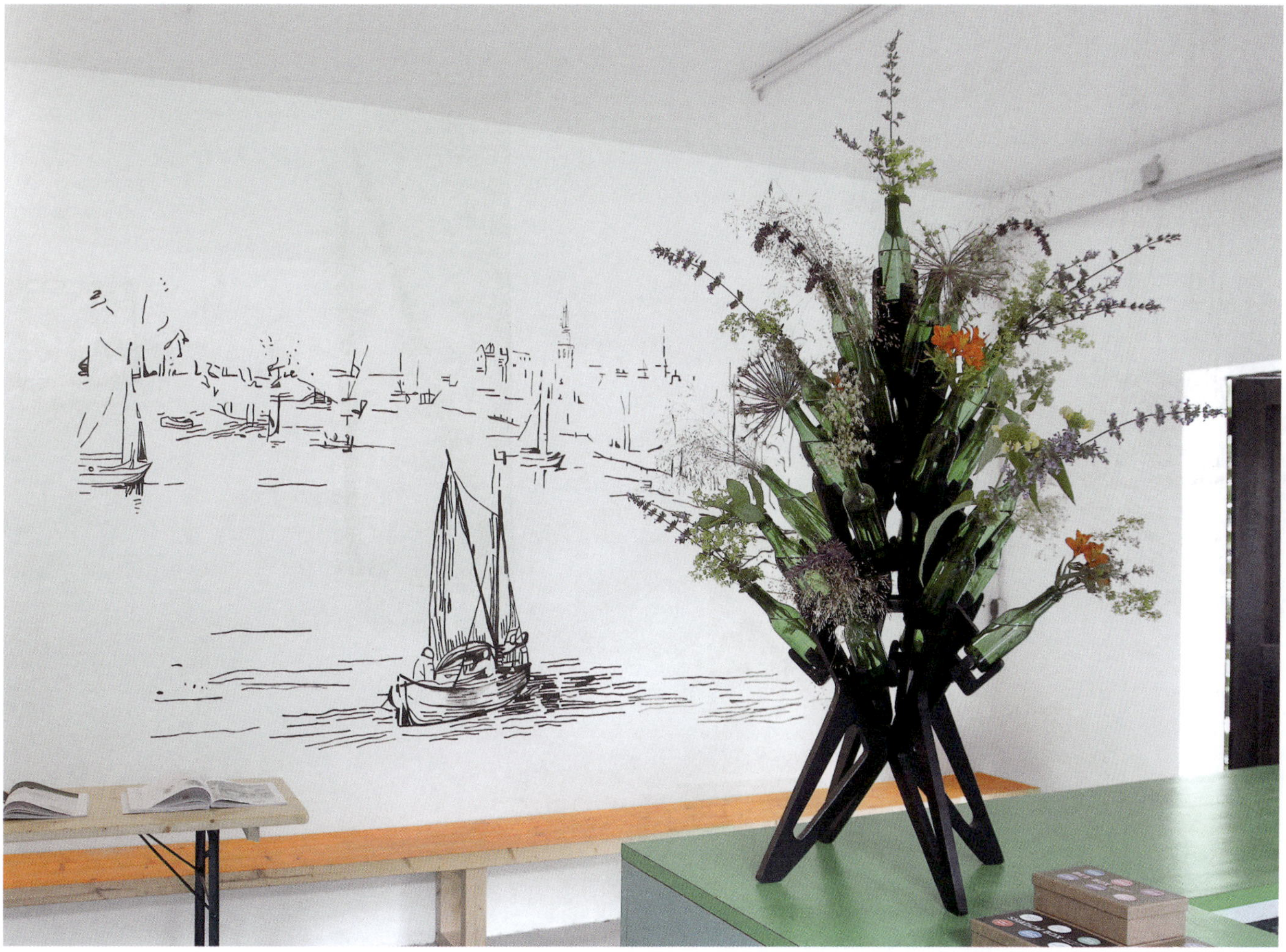

S

S

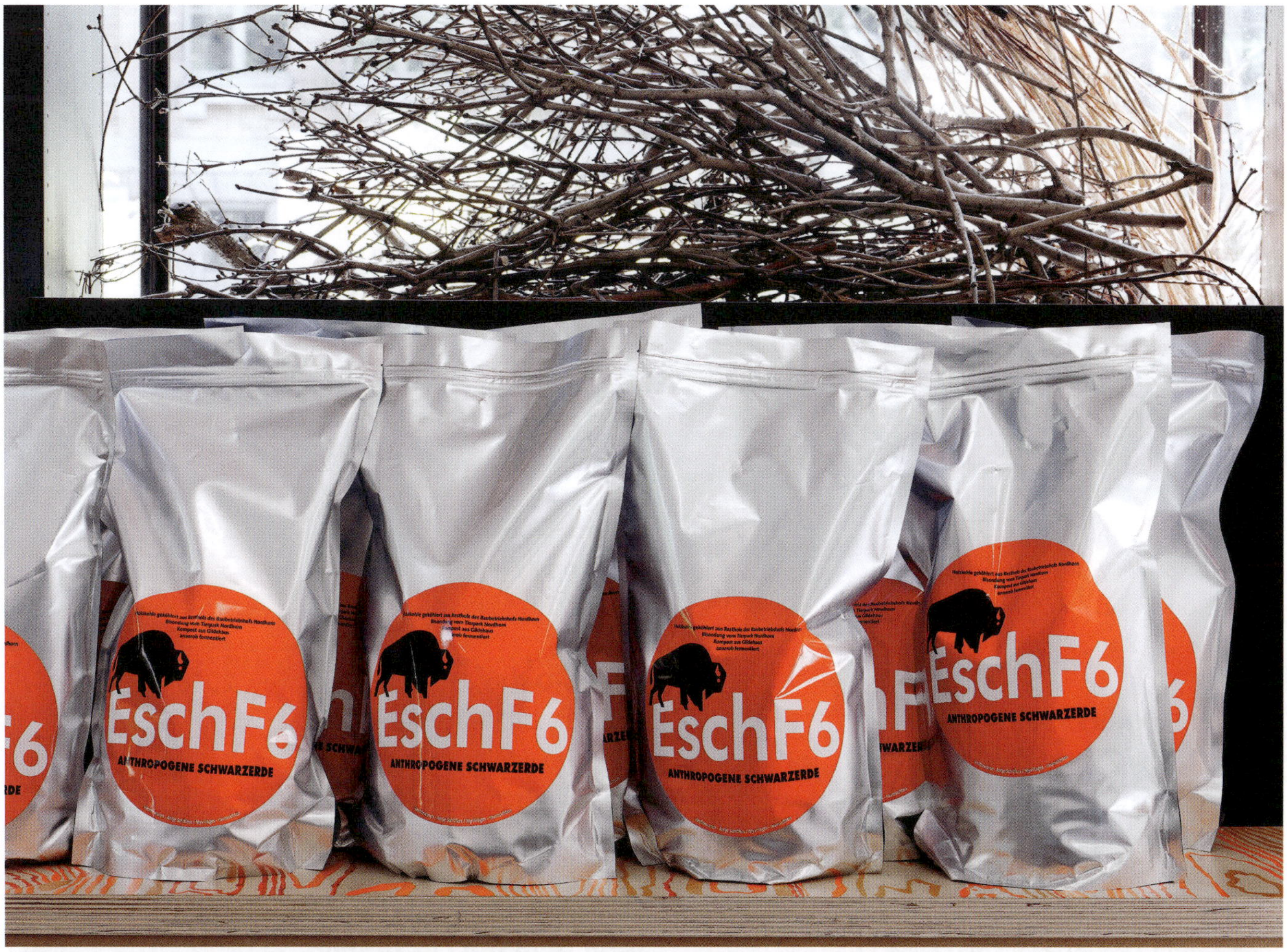

S

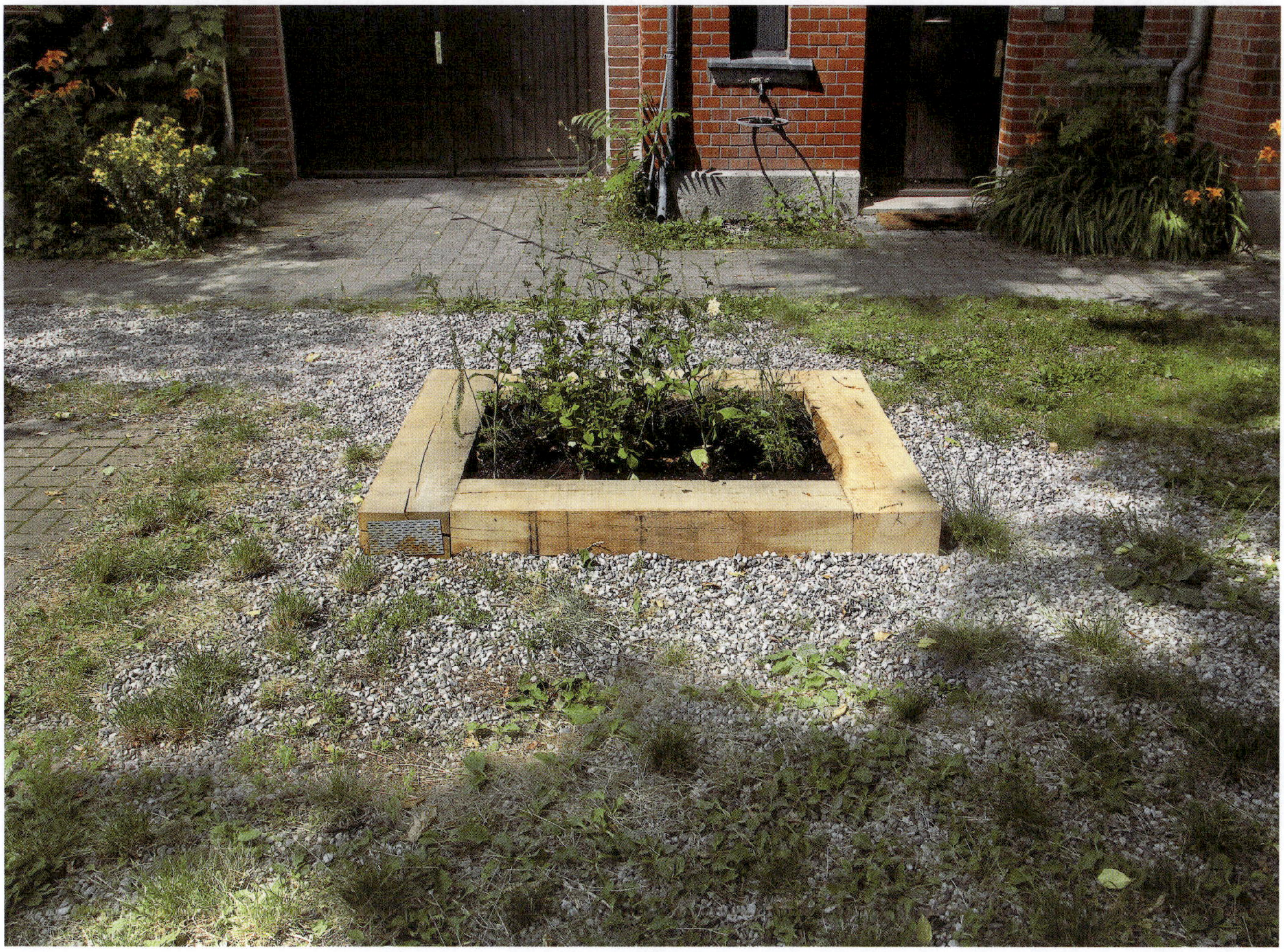

Show 7/8

September–November 2016

Franschhoek Valley (ZA)
Kent (GB)

Pfalz I und / and **II,** 2015
(from the series / aus der Serie *BASF*)
Acrylic on wood / Acryl auf Holz
each / je 21,3 × 37 cm

Foreign Pickers, 2016
Video, 23 min

Foreign Pickers, 2016
Installation: shelves, wood / Regale, Holz:
7: 12 × 120 × 10 cm
shelf, wood / Regal, Holz and / und Print:
1: 53 × 83 × 32 cm

Heiligendorf Juli I and / und
Heiligendorf Juli II, 2000–2016
Acrylic on wood / Acryl auf Holz
each / je 56 × 56 cm

Moldawien, 2016
Acrylic on wood / Acryl auf Holz
42,8 × 61,5 cm

Solms-Delta, 2016
Inkjet print / Inkjetdruck
16,5 × 27,7 cm

Solms-Delta, Franschhoek Valley, 2016
(from the archive *I like being a farmer and I would like to stay one* /
aus dem Archiv *Ich bin gerne Bauer und möchte es auch gerne bleiben*, 2000–)
Video, 23 min

Wall painting / Wandbild, 2016
Spray paint on wall / Sprühlack auf Wand

Company Drinks Kent Cider
330 ml bottle / Flasche

Company Drinks Thinning Soda
275 ml bottle / Flasche

Company Drinks Merchandise
Hops, beer coaster, advertising material /
Hopfen, Bierdeckel, Werbematerial

S

Show 8/8

December / Dezember 2016

SOCIAL FRO

So-called social practices – including Myvillages – often get reduced to social utility, whilst a convivial sociality is foregrounded as the main image and aesthetical expression of the work. To break down this double "social front" means detaching the work from purely social obligations and overcoming the group photo so as to foreground other ambitions and realities.

In his essay *Towards a Lexicon of Usership*, Stephen Wright, a theorist of contemporary art, discusses what happens when users deactivate the conceptual edifices of modernist art and submerge it in social relationships specific to usership. Artworks are then no longer stable entities entrenched in aesthetic conventions of spectatorship or rituals of collecting. Artists and users begin to activate a double ontology of certain objects or practices – something that is both art and not art at the same time. Similarly, the work of Myvillages often adopts familiar everyday or common structures such as a shop or a soft drink to activate their artistic coefficients. The social situations that emerge during these processes (gatherings, workshops, trips, discussions) are the more visible aspects of the whole piece. But the energy released during these interpersonal fusions might overshadow other qualities that remain inherent to the process. It is not Myvillages' intention to subordinate the conceptual, spatial, poetic, economic, or aesthetic to the socially utilitarian.

The "group" or a "collective" in the work is also what most closely resembles an authorial figure, on which aesthetic perception relies in order to make its judgments. Without an author, the elaborate edifice of contemporary art collapses. It fervently needs to define a social group as an authorial foreground, and a primary object of an experiment through authorship, relegating all other aspects of a work as unimportant background.

But isn't every form of authorship rooted in various forms of collectivity? We spend time exposed to ideas and art made by other people. We communicate. We exchange. And then we add our own voices to this massive stream of human creativity. Making a big fuss about authorship is a bit adolescent. People who support the limited notion of individual authorship do so in order to maintain archaic and overrated modes of artistic production. They insist that an individual author is a sole guarantor of rigor, boldness, style. But, in fact, the majority of what is spun out by the gallery-exhibition nexus is conformist pulp. It is in the realm of extended practice where we spot interesting and courageous work, and the authorship of this work is collective, uncertain, or even

NT

Sogenannte soziale Praxen – Myvillages inbegriffen – werden häufig auf ihren gesellschaftlichen Nutzen reduziert, während ein geselliges Miteinander als dominantes Bild und ästhetischer Ausdruck der Arbeit in den Vordergrund rückt. Um diese doppelte »soziale Front« aufzubrechen, muss das Werk von rein gesellschaftlichen Verpflichtungen befreit und der Gruppenbild-Charakter überwunden werden, um andere Ziele und Realitäten der Arbeit sichtbar werden zu lassen.

Stephen Wright, Kunsttheoretiker und Verfasser von *Towards a Lexicon of Usership*, beschäftigt sich mit der Frage, was passiert, wenn Benutzer die konzeptuellen Überbauten moderner Kunst links liegen lassen und sie stattdessen in einen benutzerspezifischen, gesellschaftlichen Kontext stellen. Kunstwerke sind dann keine fest umrissenen Entitäten mehr, die mit bestimmten ästhetischen Konventionen der Kunstbetrachtung oder Ritualen des Sammelns einhergehen. Künstler und Benutzer fangen an, ein doppeltes Repräsentationssystem für bestimmte Gegenstände oder Praxen zu entwickeln – etwas, was gleichzeitig Kunst und Nichtkunst ist. Ähnlich bedient sich auch Myvillages alltäglicher oder »gewöhnlicher« Strukturen, zum Beispiel eines Ladens oder einer Limonade, um deren künstlerische Koeffizienten zu aktivieren. Die sozialen Situationen, die aus diesem Prozess resultieren (Treffen, Workshops, Ausflüge, Diskussionen), sind der augenfälligere Aspekt des Ganzen. Aber die bei diesen zwischenmenschlichen Kontakten freigesetzte Energie lässt möglicherweise andere Eigenschaften übersehen, die mit dem Prozess einhergehen. Myvillages hat nicht die Absicht, Konzeptuelles, Räumliches, Poetisches, Ökonomisches oder Ästhetisches auf einen sozialutilitaristischen Nenner zu bringen.

In dem Werk kommt die »Gruppe« oder ein »Kollektiv« der autoritären Instanz des Einzelkünstlers am nächsten, auf die sich die ästhetische Wahrnehmung beruft, wenn sie ihre Urteile fällt. Ohne einen Urheber bricht das ganze kunstvolle Gebäude der zeitgenössischen Kunst zusammen. Es ist also ungeheuer wichtig, eine soziale Gruppe als auktorialen Vordergrund zu definieren und den primären Gegenstand eines Experiments mit einer Urheberschaft zu versehen, während man alle übrigen Aspekte des Werks als unwichtig in den Hintergrund verbannt.

Aber geht nicht jede Form von Urheberschaft auf unterschiedliche Formen von Kollektivität zurück? Wir werden pausenlos mit den Ideen und der Kunst von Anderen konfrontiert. Wir kommunizieren. Wir tauschen uns aus. Und wir lassen auch unsere eigenen Stimmen in diesen gewaltigen Strom menschlicher Kreativität einfließen. Das Gerangel um die Urheberschaft ist eher pubertär. Wer den engen Begriff einer individuellen Urheberschaft verteidigt, tut das, um eine archaische und überschätzte künstlerische Produktionsform aufrechtzuerhalten.

S

totally diffused. But insisting that the value of such practices should be measured by their convivial collectivity misses the point, too. It would be like evaluating the beauty of rippling waves by measuring their water content. The function of expanded authorship is different. It opens up our understanding of the world and possible ways of interacting with it.

It still seems impossible for many art professionals to avoid thinking and judging in binary codes. There is such a strong desire and habit of wanting to think of things as either art or not-art. Something is either art or a utilitarian service, an artistic practice or a community enterprise; it is autonomous or exploited, individually authored or collectively negotiated. This fundamental desire to draw lines, to think in binary terms and make fronts emerge from power struggles fundamental to the gallery-exhibition nexus, is the dominant mode of producing and distributing contemporary art. The restrictive definitions of art legitimize the production of market-friendly works, and anchor their value in such concepts as authorship, aesthetic purposelessness, or contemplative spectatorship. Moreover, many art professionals still like to think of their own field as a realm of experimentation and imagination. But, in fact, the concepts and rituals mentioned above limit the horizon of what is imaginable, desirable, and doable in the art world. In this way, the wider spectrum of hybrid practices, which can be both art and something else, is forcefully devalued. In fact, people working in the extended field of artistic practice have totally different ideas about what art actually is.

Myvillages, for instance, consider the value of art in relation to its interruptive and imaginary potential, beyond the ideological framings of contemplation, ownership, or collectability. The prime interest of Myvillages is to work with emergent, potentially consensual but always contestable, collective situations and processes. Such practices are both art and something else. They evade the art police, who like art to be segmented and marketed. They are expedient. They permeate various domains of life. They can be instruments of critique, playful props, cartographic devices, or enjoyable consumables. The real stake in these discussions is to extend our understanding of art beyond narrow definitions and binary codes. We need to look beneath the “social front”, a convenient yet misleading cognitive scheme, and foreground more principal questions and suggestions of what art is and wants to be.

KB with **Kuba Szreder** (curator, sociologist, and writer. His recent exhibitions include *Making Use: Life in Postartistic Times* (Museum of Modern Art in Warsaw, 2016), curated along with Sebastian Cichocki and Stephen Wright (as shadow curator).

Ihre Verteidiger lassen nur einen einzelnen Urheber als Garanten für Strenge, Kühnheit und Stil gelten. Dabei sind die meisten Inhalte, die von dem Galerie-Ausstellung-Nexus in Umlauf gebracht werden, einfach nur konformistischer Unsinn, während die interessanten und mutigen Arbeiten im Bereich einer entgrenzten künstlerischen Praxis zu finden sind, deren Urheberschaft kollektiv, ungewiss oder überhaupt nicht nachweisbar ist. Aber es wäre auch falsch, das gesellige Miteinander als den Maßstab aller Dinge zu betrachten. Das käme dem Versuch gleich, die Schönheit von Wellenbewegungen durch das Wasservolumen erklären zu wollen. Eine erweiterte Urheberschaft funktioniert anders. Sie beschert uns ein neues Weltverständnis und Möglichkeiten, mit ihr zu interagieren.

Viele Kunstexperten scheinen immer noch nur in binären Codes denken und urteilen zu können. Das Bedürfnis und der zur Gewohnheit gewordene Wunsch, die Dinge in Kunst oder Nichtkunst einteilen zu wollen, sind einfach übermächtig. Etwas ist entweder Kunst oder Dienstleistung, eine individuelle, künstlerische Praxis oder ein Gemeinschaftsunternehmen, ein autonomer Gegenstand oder Mittel zum Zweck, individuell autorisiert oder kollektiv verhandelt. Dieses Urbedürfnis zu trennen, in binären Codes zu denken und Fronten zu bilden, entspringt den Machtkämpfen, bedingt durch den Nexus Galerie und Ausstellungsort als dem beherrschenden Produktions- und Distributionsmodus zeitgenössischer Kunst. Die restriktiven Definitionen von Kunst legitimieren eine marktgerechte Kunst und setzen auf Konzepte wie Urheberschaft, ästhetische Zweckfreiheit oder kontemplatives Zuschauerverhalten. Hinzukommt, dass viele Kunstexperten ihren Bereich immer noch gerne als Terrain für Experimente und Kreativität sehen möchten. Leider ist es aber so, dass der Horizont dessen, was in der Welt der Kunst vorstellbar, wünschenswert und machbar ist, durch die genannten Konzepte und Rituale eher eingeschränkt wird. Gleichzeitig wird damit auch das ganze Spektrum hybrider Praxen, die sowohl Kunst als auch etwas anderes sein können, nachdrücklich diskreditiert. Tatsächlich haben aber diejenigen, die in dem erweiterten Feld künstlerischer Praxis arbeiten, völlig andere Vorstellungen von dem, was Kunst bedeutet.

Myvillages sieht zum Beispiel die Bedeutung der Kunst jenseits von ideologischem Beiwerk wie Kontemplation, Besitz oder Sammeltauglichkeit. Was zählt, sind ihr Störpotenzial und ihre Visionen. Myvillages kommt es vor allem darauf an, sich mit sich entwickelnden kollektiven Situationen und Prozessen auseinanderzusetzen, die akzeptiert, immer aber auch infrage gestellt werden können. Solche Praxen sind zugleich Kunst und etwas anderes. Sie meiden jede künstlerische Kontrolle, die Kunst segmentiert und vermarktet sehen möchte. Und sie sind auch sehr findig. Sie durchdringen alle möglichen Lebensbereiche und können sowohl Instrumente der Kritik, verspielte Requisiten, kartografische Verfahren oder amüsante Konsumartikel sein. Uns kommt es bei diesen Diskussionen vor allem darauf an, die Kunst auch außerhalb enger Begriffe und binärer Codes zu sehen. Wir müssen hinter die »soziale Front« blicken, die zwar ein praktisches, aber auch irreführendes Denkschema ist, und uns stattdessen mit wichtigeren Fragen und Vorschlägen die Kunst betreffend auseinandersetzen – mit dem, was Kunst ist und was sie sein möchte.

KB mit **Kuba Szreder** (Kurator, Soziologe, Autor. In jüngster Zeit kuratierte er zusammen mit Sebastian Cichocki und Stephen Wright – als Schattenkurator – die Ausstellung *Making Use. Life in Postartistic Times*, Museum of Modern Art, Warschau 2016.)

S

Coca-Cola

SYMBOLISC ÜBERDETERI

Three of us, Marc Weiland, Prof. Werner Nell, and I, were sitting in a café in Halle on a hot afternoon. We had sought out a dark corner and, being so engrossed in conversation, did not consume very much.

Let us proceed from the assumption that the village has less cultural capital than the city. With "cultural capital" we are following Bourdieu's model of differing authority of disposal over the four types of capital: economic, symbolic, social, and cultural, and we therefore mean cultural according to a bourgeois concept of culture, high-culture, culture as an asset that one is able to leverage. The village has less of such capital, though it does have its own everyday culture, internally generated spaces for fellowship and encounters, forms for celebrating festivals, bidding farewell to the deceased, or caring for shared resources: hence culture according to ethnologists' concept of culture. The high-culture dimension is based on specialization on the part of the actors; participating in it and being familiar with its complexity is a sought-after, distinguishing characteristic.

It can be seen that peripheral regions have less power in the cultural discourse, and thus less power to represent the concept of culture that is practiced in them in discussions.

As a topos, however, the village and the land are very present. To what one perceives as a cultural tabula rasa, one can attribute what one would like – from the idyll to the anti-idyll; a concentration on symbolic contents. We can ascribe a discomfort with modernity or a state of being overstrained by modern life. The village and the manageable number of actors in it invite relating stories and making something comprehensible.

In his classic *The Country and the City*, Raymond Williams traces the idea of the land as simple, natural, and unspoilt, as an antithesis to the idea of the capitalistic, exploitative, alienating city, back over the centuries. This myth and its polar explanatory model obstruct any view of a more complex relationship, of mutual dependencies, class conflicts, and enmities.

IE

INIERUNG

An einem heißen Nachmittag sitzen wir zu dritt in einem Café in Halle, Marc Weiland, Prof. Werner Nell und ich. Wir haben uns eine dunkle Ecke gesucht und konsumieren wenig, so vertieft sind wir ins Gespräch.

Gehen wir einmal davon aus, das Dorf habe ein geringeres kulturelles Kapital als die Stadt. Mit »kulturellem Kapital« folgen wir Bourdieus Modell der unterschiedlichen Verfügungsmacht über die vier Kapitalsorten: ökonomisches, symbolisches, soziales und eben kulturelles Kapital, und wir meinen dabei kulturell nach einem bürgerlichen Kulturbegriff, hochkulturell, kulturell als Pfund, mit dem man wuchern kann. Das Dorf hat weniger von diesem Kapital, wenn es auch Alltagskultur haben mag, selbst geschaffene Räume von Gemeinschaft und Begegnung, Formen, Feste zu feiern, Beerdigungen zu begehen oder Gemeinbesitz zu pflegen, also Kultur nach dem Kulturbegriff der Ethnologen. Die hochkulturelle Dimension beruht auf Spezialisierung vonseiten der Akteure; an ihr teilzuhaben und ihrer Komplexität gewachsen zu sein ist ein gesuchtes Distinktionsmerkmal.

Man kann feststellen, dass periphere Regionen wenig Macht haben im kulturellen Diskurs, und von daher wenig Macht, den Kulturbegriff, der in ihnen praktiziert wird, in der Diskussion zu vertreten.

Als Topos dagegen sind das Dorf und das Land präsent. Was man als kulturelle Tabula rasa wahrnimmt, dem kann man zuschreiben, was man möchte, von der Idylle bis zur Anti-Idylle; eine Verengung auf symbolische Inhalte. Wir können ein Unbehagen an der Moderne konstatieren und eine Überforderung durch die Moderne. Das Dorf und die Überschaubarkeit seiner Akteure laden dazu ein, Dinge zu erzählen und etwas fassbar zu machen.

In seinem Klassiker *The Country and the City* verfolgt Raymond Williams die Idee vom Land als einfach, natürlich und unverdorben, als Gegenpol zur Idee von der kapitalistischen, ausbeutenden und entfremdenden Stadt, über die Jahrhunderte zurück. Dieser Mythos und sein polares Erklärungsmodell verstelle den Blick auf ein komplexeres Verhältnis, auf gegenseitige Abhängigkeit, Klassenkonflikte und Feindseligkeit.

In *Chamissos Schatten* by Ulrike Ottinger, a woman is filmed digging up potatoes in a village on the Kamchatka Peninsula. We see volcanoes, thickets, rivers, and isolation. The woman asks the filmmaker whether she has also been to where she had her summer camp and fished and gathered berries, 80 kilometres away, or a ride of two days: it is peaceful and beautiful there, the air fresh, and all stress is left behind.

We take pleasure in telling stories about how we drank beer at the bar in the evening with the tractor drivers. In the 1970s, an invitation to a Greek country wedding was a popular narrative and contemporary continuation of the idyll. Only just a few elements suffice for symbolic over-determination.

The situation of being stylized to comprise certain characteristics does not remain hidden from the thing or person stylized and also has an effect on their self-perception and self-presentation. With this reverse stylization the narrowing of both sides is reinforced.

The images that we receive when we search for the authentic are artificial. Since artificial, the arts can actually only work analytically in such cases.

The "Farmer Wants a Wife" television format is popular around the world. The farmers are gladly presented as good-natured, awkward, bumbling, and those who best correspond to this can become popular gimmick farmers. This differs only in Australia. On Australian television the farmers are well built and manage their operations optimistically and energetically. One can see things as one would like. **AS**

This text is based on a conversation with **Marc Weiland** and **Prof. Werner Nell** of the Department of Comparative Literature and Cultural Studies at Martin-Luther-University, Halle-Wittenberg.

Pierre Bourdieu, *La distinction. Critique sociale du jugement* (Paris, 1979)
Ulrike Ottinger, *Chamissos Schatten*, 720 min., Germany, 2016
Raymond Williams, *The Country and the City* (New York, 1973)

In *Chamissos Schatten* von Ulrike Ottinger wird eine Frau in einem Dorf in Kamtschatka gefilmt, die Kartoffeln ausgräbt. Wir sehen Vulkane, Dickichte, Flüsse und Einsamkeit. Die Frau fragt die Filmemacherin, ob sie auch dort gewesen sei, wo sie ihr Sommerlager hätten und fischten und Beeren sammelten, 80 Kilometer oder einen Ritt von zwei Tagen entfernt: Dort sei es friedlich und schön, die Luft frisch, und aller Stress bleibe hinter einem.

Wir erzählen gern Geschichten davon, wie wir am Abend mit dem Traktoristen an der Theke Bier getrunken haben. In den Siebzigerjahren war die Einladung zur griechischen Bauernhochzeit eine beliebte Narration und zeitgenössische Fortsetzung der Idylle. Für die symbolische Überdeterminierung reichen wenige Elemente.

Die Stilisierung auf bestimmte Merkmale bleibt den Stilisierten nicht verborgen und wirkt sich aus auf ihre Selbstwahrnehmung und Selbstdarstellung. Mit dieser Rückstilisierung verstärkt sich die Verengung von beiden Seiten.

Die Bilder, die wir bekommen, wo wir Authentisches suchen, sind künstliche. Die Künste, als künstliche, können da eigentlich nur analytisch arbeiten.

Das Fernsehformat »Bauer sucht Frau« ist international beliebt. Die Bauern werden gern als gutmütig, ungeschickt und plump dargestellt, und diejenigen, die dem am besten entsprechen, können zu populären Gimmick-Bauern werden. Nur in Australien ist das anders. Im australischen Fernsehen sind die Bauern gut gebaut und managen optimistisch und tatkräftig ihren Betrieb. Man kann die Sache sehen, wie man will. **AS**

Dieser Text beruht auf einem Gespräch mit **Marc Weiland** und **Prof. Werner Nell** von der Abteilung Komparatistik an der Martin-Luther-Universität, Halle-Wittenberg.

Pierre Bourdieu, *La distinction. Critique sociale du jugement*, Paris 1979
Ulrike Ottinger, *Chamissos Schatten*, 720 min, Deutschland 2016
Raymond Williams, *The Country and the City*, New York 1973

S

THESEN A

The *International Village Show* is a hybrid form of exhibition, event location, and shop. In the freely accessible Gartenhaus of the Galerie für Zeitgenössische Kunst (Museum of Contemporary Art) Leipzig, it presents pictures, filmic reports, and products from rural areas, created in collaboration with village communities and farmers around the world. The "product range" is handpicked and is revamped again and again in thematic presentations. The changing selection is interesting in connection with the storage space and archives of the three Myvillages artists, where numerous additional stories, objects, and materials can be found. What does one present and what does one leave out? How can processes of getting to know one another, coming to an understanding, and cooperation be represented? Who is involved and who speaks about it? Through juxtaposing various voices and forms of expression next to one another on an equal basis, the *International Village Show* addresses the fascinating and at times contentious relationship between process and result, participation and authorship, action and representation.

The development and multidimensionality of creative processes are presented: The *International Village Show,* which advertises itself with a show window facing the street, comprises a series of transcultural encounters and activities, which change with the season of the year. The linking and presentation of – generally two – different locations therefore not only reflect the stages in the development of this project, but also make it possible to recognize the various actors and the diverse participation of the three artists, their individual interests and ways of working. It is therefore not about defining locations or an always similar form of cooperation with communities. The *International Village Show* instead provides an opportunity to examine the interplay of artistic approaches and everyday realities in various contexts.

From subjectivity, interaction, and changeability, arises a place for shared reflection, where one's surroundings and one's own actions are called in question in exchange with others, and where mutual assumptions,

TRESEN

Die *International Village Show* ist eine Mischform aus Ausstellung, Veranstaltungsort und Ladenlokal. Im frei zugänglichen Gartenhaus der Galerie für Zeitgenössische Kunst Leipzig zeigt sie Bilder, filmische Berichte und Produkte aus dem ländlichen Raum, die in Zusammenarbeit mit Dorfgemeinschaften und Bauern weltweit entstanden sind. Das »Sortiment« ist handverlesen und wird in thematischen Präsentationen immer wieder neu gefasst. Interessant ist die wechselnde Auswahl in Hinblick auf den Lagerraum und auf die Archive der drei Myvillages-Künstlerinnen, wo sich zahlreiche weitere Geschichten, Gegenstände und Materialien befinden. Was zeigt man und was lässt man weg? Wie bildet man Prozesse des Kennenlernens, der Verständigung und der Zusammenarbeit ab? Wer ist beteiligt und wer spricht darüber? Indem sie verschiedene Stimmen und Ausdrucksformen gleichberechtigt nebeneinander stellt, adressiert die *International Village Show* das spannungsreiche Verhältnis von Prozess und Ergebnis, von Partizipation und Autorschaft, von Handlung und Repräsentation.

Gestalterische Prozesse werden in ihrem Verlauf und in ihrer Vielschichtigkeit vorgestellt: Die *International Village Show*, die mit einem zur Straße gerichteten Schaufenster für sich wirbt, umfasst eine Reihe von transkulturellen Begegnungen und Aktivitäten und verändert sich zu jeder Jahreszeit. Die Verknüpfung und Präsentation von – meist zwei – verschiedenen Orten spiegelt dabei nicht nur die Entwicklungsstadien des Projekts wider, sondern lässt auch die unterschiedlichen Akteure und die unterschiedliche Beteiligung der drei Künstlerinnen, ihre individuellen Interessen und Arbeitsweisen, erkennen. Es geht also nicht um die eindeutige Bestimmung von Orten oder um die immer gleichförmige Zusammenarbeit mit Gemeinschaften. Vielmehr bietet die *International Village Show* eine Gelegenheit, die Wechselwirkung von künstlerischen Ansätzen und Lebenswirklichkeiten in unterschiedlichen Zusammenhängen zu untersuchen.

Aus Subjektivität, Interaktion und Wandelbarkeit entsteht ein Ort der gemeinsamen Reflexion, an dem das eigene Umfeld und das eigene Tun im Austausch mit anderen hinterfragt wird und wo gegenseitige Annahmen, Erwartungen und Betrachtungsweisen durcheinander geraten können. Die Rolle und Position der Beteiligten verändert sich dabei fortwährend: Künstlerinnen und Dorfbewohner*innen tauschen ihre Kenntnisse untereinander aus, im Gespräch mit

T

expectations, and approaches can become jumbled. The role and position of the individuals involved therefore undergoes constant change: artists and village residents exchange their knowledge with one another; in conversation with visitors and GfZK staff members, they are non-professionals and experts at the same time. In the end, different skills are necessary for cooking, animal husbandry, geological surveys, and presentation.

While the work of Myvillages questions the visibility, perception, and appreciation of cultural production in rural areas, these approaches can also be transferred without difficulty to the art scene. What topics are popular, what (conceptual) images are passed on, what importance is given to artistic work, and how is it gauged? What role does the object character of artworks play, and how can their implicit availability be subverted? What significance do open, process-based artistic approaches have in institutions, and what impulses do they provide?

The *International Village Show* challenges classic forms of art production, exhibiting, receiving, and mediating art. It combines well-known spatial situations – the exhibition, the shop, the garden, and the clubroom – to offer other operational models beyond looking and buying. Designing, producing, showing, negotiating, encounter and exchange are defined as elements of equal value in artistic work, and the boundaries between art and non-art, to which mechanisms of attributing value and desire are affixed, become more permeable through the reception of the products exhibited. Since, in them, experiences, spontaneous ideas, and experiments are consolidated, just as are traditional production techniques and forms of processing. They tell of landscapes and climate, of raw materials, local knowledge, and social relationships.

Depending on when and with whom you visit the *International Village Show*, a new narrative emerges and one learns about different aspects of the work process. As a result of the wide-ranging social, economic, and non-material barter transactions that the *International Village Show* initiates, the process remains open and can also be continued beyond the presentation in Leipzig.

Julia Schäfer, curator and art-educator at the Museum of Contemporary Art Leipzig. 2000 Assistant at the New Museum of Contemporary Art, New York, 1999–2001 freelance at the Kunstmuseum Wolfsburg, 2001–2003 assistant curator Museum of Contemporary Art Leipzig. Julia Schäfer studied fine arts, art education and German literature at the University of Osnabrück and Academy for Fine Art Dresden. Schäfer focuses on the possibilities of art mediation in curatorial strategies. Since 2014 she has been a member of the Board the Cultural Foundation of Saxony. She has published several books.

Franciska Zólyom has been the Director of the Museum of Contemporary Art, Leipzig since 2012. Following her studies in Cologne and Paris, she was first a curator at the Museum Ludwig Budapest and later Director of the Institute of Contemporary Art – Dunaújváros in Hungary. Since 2003, she has been a member of the Hungarian Section of the International Association of Art Critics (AICA; board member from 2006 to 2008); since 2005, member of the board of tranzit.hu, an initiative of the Erste Stiftung, since 2012, Member in the University Council of the Bauhaus-Universität Weimar, and, since 2013, Senator in the Kultursenat (Cultural Senate) of Saxony.

den Besucher*innen und GfZK-Mitarbeiter*innen sind sie Laien und Expert*innen zugleich. Schließlich sind beim Kochen, bei der Tierzucht, bei geologischen Untersuchungen und beim Präsentieren unterschiedliche Fertigkeiten erforderlich.

Fragt die Arbeit von Myvillages nach der Sichtbarkeit, Wahrnehmung und Wertschätzung der kulturellen Produktion im ländlichen Raum, so lassen sich diese Ansätze unschwer auch auf den Kunstbetrieb übertragen. Welche Themen sind angesagt, welche (Denk-)Bilder werden tradiert, welche Bedeutung wird künstlerischen Arbeiten zugeschrieben und woran wird sie gemessen? Welche Rolle spielt die Objekthaftigkeit von Kunstwerken und wie lässt sich die damit einhergehende Verfügbarkeit anders denken? Welchen Stellenwert haben offene, prozessbasierte künstlerische Ansätze in Institutionen und welche Impulse geben sie?

Die *International Village Show* fordert klassische Formen der Kunstproduktion, des Ausstellens, der Kunstrezeption und der Kunstvermittlung heraus. Sie kombiniert wohl bekannte räumliche Situationen – die Ausstellung, den Laden, den Garten und das Vereinszimmer –, um jenseits von Schauen und Kaufen weitere Handlungsmodelle anzubieten. Das Entwerfen, Produzieren, Zeigen, Verhandeln, die Begegnung und der Austausch werden als gleichwertige Teile der künstlerischen Arbeit definiert, und auch die Grenze zwischen Kunst und Nichtkunst, an der sich Mechanismen der Wertzuschreibung und des Begehrens festmachen lassen, wird durch die ausgestellten Produkte durchlässiger. Denn in den Produkten verdichten sich Erfahrungen, spontane Ideen und Experimente genauso wie tradierte Herstellungstechniken und Verarbeitungsformen. Sie erzählen von Landschaften und vom Klima, von Rohstoffen, lokalem Wissen und sozialen Verhältnissen.

Je nachdem, wann und mit wem man die *International Village Show* besucht, entsteht eine neue Erzählung und man lernt unterschiedliche Aspekte des Arbeitsprozesses kennen. Durch die vielseitigen sozialen, ökonomischen und ideellen Tauschgeschäfte, welche die *International Village Show* initiiert, bleibt der Prozess offen und auch über die Leipziger Präsentation hinaus fortführbar.

Julia Schäfer, Kuratorin und Kunstvermittlerin an der Galerie für Zeitgenössische Kunst Leipzig, war nach einer Assistenzzeit am New Museum of Contemporary Art, New York, freie Mitarbeiterin am Kunstmuseum Wolfsburg, bevor sie 2001 zunächst als Volontärin an die GfZK kam. Nach einem Studium der Freien Kunst, Kunstpädagogik und Germanistik an der Universität Osnabrück und der Hochschule der Bildenden Künste Dresden untersucht sie Vermittlungsstrategien im kuratorischen Feld der zeitgenössischen Kunst. Seit 2014 ist sie Beiratsmitglied der Kulturstiftung des Freistaates Sachsen. Sie hat mehrere Publikationen herausgegeben

Franciska Zólyom ist seit 2012 Direktorin der Galerie für Zeitgenössische Kunst Leipzig. Nach ihrem Studium in Köln und Paris war sie zunächst Kuratorin am Museum Ludwig Budapest und später Direktorin des Institute of Contemporary Art – Dunaújváros in Ungarn. Seit 2003 ist sie Mitglied der ungarischen Sektion des Internationalen Kunstkritikerverbandes AICA (von 2006 bis 2008 Vorstandsmitglied); seit 2005 Vorstandsmitglied von tranzit.hu, einer Initiative der Erste Stiftung, seit 2012 Mitglied im Universitätsrat der Bauhaus-Universität Weimar und seit 2013 Senatorin im Sächsischen Kultursenat.

TYRANNY O

The competition for localness can be fierce.

"We've lived here 26 years."
"You're not from this village."
"That's how we do it here."

The lure of the local gets nasty when it becomes competitive. Exclusive.

Greg Sharzer[1] even accuses the concept of the local of nihilism – a practiced lack of faith in the possibility that changes can take place on a larger scale.

However, the local remains the place for possible one-to-one action and therefore the place for the imaginary to become reality. Referring to J.K. Graham-Gibson[2], it allows us to make changes and create politics with a new kind of dispersed collective action that does not depend upon established radical politics.

I work locally and sometimes I am local.
I'm local in Höfen.
I'm local in Hackney.

KB

T

1 **Greg Sharzer**, *No Local: Why Small-Scale Alternatives Won't Change the World* (Aylesford: Zero Books, 2012).
2 **J.K. Gibson-Graham** is a pen name shared by the feminist economic geographers Julie Graham and Katherine Gibson.

THE LOCAL

Geht es um das Lokale, darum, zu behaupten, man selbst, ein Gebrauch, eine Norm oder ein Ding seien lokal, wird mit harten Bandagen gekämpft.

»Wir leben schon seit 26 Jahren hier.«
»Sie sind nicht aus diesem Dorf.«
»Das machen wir hier so.«

Schlimm wird die Sache, wenn der Wettbewerb um das Lokale zu Ignoranz und Exklusion führt.

Greg Sharzer[1] wirft der Idee des Lokalen sogar vor, eine Weltsicht zu sein, die sich auf das Kleine beschränkt, weil Veränderungen in größerem Umfang angeblich nicht möglich seien.

Dennoch ist das Lokale der überschaubare Raum, in dem direkte Interaktion möglich ist, und deshalb auch der Raum, wo Imaginäres Realität werden kann. Laut J.K. Gibson-Graham[2] ermöglicht er uns, mit dezentralem gemeinschaftlichen Handeln, unabhängig von etablierter linker Politik, Veränderungen herbeizuführen und politische Strategien zu entwickeln.

Ich arbeite lokal und bin manchmal lokal.
Ich bin es in Höfen.
Ich bin es in Hackney.

KB

1 **Greg Sharzer,** *No Local: Why Small-Scale Alternatives Won't Change The World*, Zero Books, Alresford 2012.
2 **J.K. Gibson-Graham** ist das gemeinsame Pseudonym der beiden feministischen Wirtschaftsgeografinnen Julie Graham und Katherine Gibson.

T

Vlassenbroek

Dendermonde, Flanders, BE

Population: 160

Einwohner: 160

Climate change is causing the River Schelde to flood more frequently. Heavy rainfall is pushing up the water levels to unprecedented heights. Flood plains are being laid out to monitor the flooding and make space for the water, while retaining some control over the river at the same time. In the past few years the landscape between the village of Vlassenbroek and the district of Broekkant in Baasrode, where the river polder is situated, has undergone some radical changes, designed and developed by engineers. A dyke is being built along the edge of the village. Although only the older residents can still recall the devastation wreaked by the flood disaster in 1953, everyone appreciates the need to make changes to the polder in this naturally wet area. These changes will keep the residents and their homes dry. And experts predict more biodiversity. But will this attract more tourists? Vlassenbroek has been well-known as an artists' village since the end of the 19th century. In the slipstreams of Barbizon and inspired by the spirit of the river landscape, people used to flock to the old dyke to draw and paint en plein air.

I met the engineer at the church in Vlassenbroek and we got into a four-wheel drive to take a look at the work on the ring dyke. I am deeply impressed by stories about new technology and soil tests on dredged sludge. People can get quite passionate about dyke technology. We walked close to the work and everyone warned us to watch out for the big yellow dumper trucks. The drivers' senses are dulled by the monotonous task of loading and unloading, and driving containers of sludge back and forth, so we had to be extra careful. **WF**

Infolge des Klimawandels tritt der Fluss Schelde häufiger über die Ufer. Starker Regen lässt den Wasserstand auf nie gekannte Pegel steigen. Zurzeit werden Überschwemmungsgebiete angelegt, um das Hochwasser steuern und ableiten und gleichzeitig den Fluss einigermaßen beherrschen zu können. Die Landschaft zwischen dem Dorf Vlassenbroek und dem Bezirk Broekkant in Baasrode, wo der Hochwasserpolder liegt, hat sich in den letzten Jahren teilweise radikal verändert. Geplant und gebaut wird das alles von Ingenieuren. Rund um das Dorf errichten sie einen Deich. Obwohl sich nur die älteren Bewohner noch an die Verwüstung durch die Flutkatastrophe von 1953 erinnern, ist allen klar, dass der Polder in dieser von Wasser durchzogenen Naturlandschaft verändert werden muss. Diese Arbeiten werden dafür sorgen, dass Bewohner und Häuser trockene Füße behalten. Fachleute erwarten sogar eine größere Artenvielfalt. Aber werden dann auch mehr Touristen kommen? Vlassenbroek ist seit Ende des 19. Jahrhunderts als Künstlerdorf bekannt. Im Windschatten der Schule von Barbizon strömten die Menschen zum alten Deich und zeichneten und malten dort en plein air.

Vor der Kirche von Vlassenbroek lernte ich den Ingenieur kennen, und wir stiegen in einen Geländewagen, um uns die Arbeiten am Deichring anzusehen. Ich bin schwer beeindruckt von den Erzählungen über neue Technologien und Bodenproben des ausgebaggerten Scheldeschlicks. Deichbautechnik ist für manche Menschen eine große Leidenschaft. Wir nähern uns der Baustelle, und alle ermahnen uns, auf die großen gelben Kipplaster zu achten. Die Sinne der Fahrer seien von der eintönigen Arbeit des Auf- und Abladens und Hin- und Herfahrens mit Mulden voller Schlick abgestumpft, also müssten wir besonders achtgeben. **WF**

→ PLEIN AIR

V

VORSTELLU

Translators are familiar with both sides. They are not able to translate into a void.

Each language keeps silent differently. (*José Ortega y Gasset*)

When I talk about Zvizzchi, I often mention that many men do not drink. Perhaps the men once drank too much, and therefore now no longer drink. Russia and boundless drinking is a familiar topos. It is harder for a story without drinking to meet with acceptance than for a story with drinking. At the same time, this is still a simple case: Although there is no drinking, the topic is familiar. Better a cliché than no idea at all.

When translating, we do something I call "sliding". When nothing can be found for a word or a sentence in the translation, we say: a dark sound, a clattering rhythm, or a connotation of stench, and we then slide this into another sentence or into other words nearby.

One may doubt whether it is possible to recognize something that is truly alien, something for which there is still no pattern in one's own thinking, hence epistemologically impossible. But let's assume that it is possible on occasion. If I would like to show and translate something that is alien, alien in another way than expected, is it not necessary to have something in the head of the other person onto which I can dock?

That is perhaps more of a problem for narrators than for translators.

V

Do I have to explain things more precisely to those who are far away than to those who are familiar with the context?

I am not sure whether I have to evoke something more closely because I am farther away. I have to have every little flower in it, indeed, but I do not have to explain the little flower more precisely than it is explained in the original. The poet finds the right balance, and the translator retains it.

Der Übersetzer kennt beide Seiten. Er kann nicht ins Leere übersetzen.

Alle Sprachen schweigen verschieden. (*José Ortega y Gasset*)

Wenn ich von Zvizzchi erzähle, erwähne ich oft, dass viele Männer nicht trinken. Die Männer haben vielleicht einmal zu viel getrunken, und darum trinken sie jetzt nicht mehr. Russland und das grenzenlose Trinken, das ist ein bewährter Topos. Es ist schwieriger, für eine Erzählung ohne Trinken Billigung zu finden, als für als eine Erzählung mit Trinken. Dabei ist das sogar noch ein einfacher Fall: Es wird zwar nicht getrunken, aber das Thema ist bekannt. Besser ein Klischee als gar keine Vorstellung.

Beim Übersetzen machen wir etwas, das ich »schieben« nenne. Wenn für ein Wort oder einen Satz in der Übersetzung etwas nicht zu erreichen ist, sagen wir mal: ein dunkler Klang, ein trappelnder Rhythmus oder eine Konnotation von Gestank, dann schieben wir das in einen anderen Satz oder in andere Wörter im Umfeld.

Man kann bezweifeln, dass es möglich ist, etwas wirklich Fremdes zu erkennen, etwas, für das noch keine Muster im eigenen Denken bestehen, also erkenntnistheoretisch unmöglich. Nehmen wir an, manchmal kann man es. Wenn ich das zeigen und übersetzen möchte, was fremd ist, anders fremd als erwartbar – braucht es da nicht etwas im Kopf des anderen, wo ich ansetzen kann?

Das ist wohl mehr ein Problem des Erzählers als des Übersetzers.

Muss ich demjenigen, der weit weg ist, die Dinge genauer beschreiben als dem, der den Kontext kennt?

V

Ich bin mir nicht sicher, ob ich näher evozieren muss, weil ich ferner bin. Ich muss jedes Blümchen darin haben, ja, aber ich muss das Blümchen nicht genauer erklären, als es im Original erklärt ist. Das richtige Maß findet der Dichter, und der Übersetzer hält sich daran.

In exile, many storytellers become essayists; they explain the things about which they tell stories, they explain the places. They can no longer assume that people know what associations they have when they make one of their characters, for instance, walk over a particular square in Prague.

I give students texts about which they cannot know whether they are original texts or translations. Ninety per cent of students then think that Goethe's original is a translation. The most original texts are also alien, or more precisely: produce the alien.

When you say that it is glorious to swim in a Russian river – that says nothing to me. People bathe in French rivers; people bathe in Swiss rivers. You must tell me something about the Russian river so that I can begin to envision what you see in your mind's eye.

When I think of Russian rivers, I see on the map the great streams that flow into the Norwegian Sea, the Irtysh, the Yenisei, the Lena. The river is clear; it is not a green river, not an amber-coloured river, it is transparent down to its sandy bed. The banks go uphill, with wild, high steppe meadows full of wormwood, meadowsweet, and bellflowers, and there are red-trunked pines. We swim in the wildness like a herd of elk, a fast herd, since the current is strong. We swim downstream to the bathing area with the shade of birch trees in the neighbouring village and swat the horseflies away from our foreheads from time to time.

You translate a project for yourself from the idea into your language – you begin in your language. You arrive in another country with one language and have already crossed a border. When you have transported your language with you yourself, you then look: Where has it then actually arrived? How do you speak in the foreign language and culture so that what YOU have in your head in your language lands there, is understood there, and can be transposed into concrete action, so that it inspires the other? The other then also translates it into his or her deed. He or she does it. He or she has translated it into his or her language. It then has to come back to you again: to be translated in your understanding and your inner world, to travel back to a certain extent, you formulate your thoughts and experiences here, and they once again encounter eye and ear, and behind them an imaginary world.

Either the translator does leave the writer in peace as much as possible, and moves readers against him; or the translator leaves readers in peace as much as possible and moves the writer against them.

V

One can bring a story to an audience, or an audience to a story. (*Friedrich Schleiermacher*) Or both, said Marie. **AS**

Written based on a conversation with **Marie Luise Knott**.
She provided the paraphrases of the **Ortega y Gasset** and **Schleiermacher** quotes.
Marie is a translator and author. Her book *Verlernen. Denkwege mit Hannah Arendt* (Unlearning with Hannah Arendt) was nominated for the Leipzig Book Fair Prize in 2011.

Im Exil werden viele Erzähler zu Essayisten; sie erklären die Dinge, über die sie erzählen, sie erklären die Orte. Sie können nicht mehr davon ausgehen, dass die Menschen wissen, was sie damit verbinden, wenn sie eine ihrer Figuren zum Beispiel über einen bestimmten Platz in Prag gehen lassen.

Ich gebe den Studenten Texte, von denen sie nicht wissen können, ob sie Originaltexte oder Übersetzungen sind. 90 Prozent der Studenten halten Goethes Original dann für Übersetzung. Auch die originellsten Texte sind fremd, oder besser: produzieren Fremde.

Wenn du sagst, es sei herrlich, im russischen Fluss zu baden – das sagt mir nichts. In französischen Flüssen wird gebadet, in Schweizer Flüssen wird gebadet. Du musst mir etwas zum russischen Fluss sagen, damit ich anfangen kann, mir vorzustellen, was du dir vorstellst.

Wenn ich an russische Flüsse denke, sehe ich auf der Landkarte die großen Ströme, die ins Nordmeer gehen, Irtysch, Jenissej, Lena. Der Fluss ist klar; er ist kein grüner Fluss, kein bernsteinfarbener Fluss, er ist durchsichtig bis auf sein Bett aus Sand. Die Ufer gehen hügelan mit wilden hohen Steppenwiesen voller Wermut, Mädesüß und Glockenblumen und mit rotstämmigen Kiefern. Wir schwimmen wie eine Herde Elche in der Wildnis, eine schnelle Herde, denn die Strömung ist stark. Wir schwimmen flussabwärts bis zur Badestelle mit dem Birkenschatten im Nachbardorf und schlagen uns ab und an die Bremsen von der Stirn.

Du übersetzt dir ein Projekt aus der Vorstellung in deine Sprache – du beginnst es in deiner Sprache. Du kommst im anderen Land an mit einer Sprache und hast schon eine Grenze passiert. Wenn du deine Sprache mit dir selbst dahin transportiert hast, dann guckst du: Auf welchen Boden gelangt sie da eigentlich? Wie sprichst du in der fremden Sprache und Kultur so, dass das, was DU in deiner Sprache im Kopf hast, dort anlandet, dass es dort verstanden wird und sich umsetzen lässt in konkretes Handeln, so, dass es den anderen inspiriert? Der andere übersetzt es sich ja dann noch in sein Tun. Er tut es. Er hat es sich in seine Sprache übersetzt. Dann muss es wieder zurück zu dir: sich übersetzen in dein Verständnis und deine innere Welt, zurückreisen gewissermaßen, du formulierst deine Gedanken und Erfahrungen ja hier, wieder treffen sie auf Auge und Ohr und dahinter auf eine Vorstellungswelt.

Entweder der Übersetzer lässt den Schriftsteller möglichst in Ruhe und bewegt den Leser ihm entgegen; oder er lässt den Leser möglichst in Ruhe und bewegt den Schriftsteller ihm entgegen.

Man kann die Geschichte zum Publikum bringen, oder das Publikum zur Geschichte. (*Friedrich Schleiermacher*) Oder beides, sagt Marie. **AS**

Geschrieben nach einem Gespräch mit **Marie Luise Knott**.
Die Zitate von **Ortega y Gasset** und **Schleiermacher** übernehme ich von ihr.
Marie ist Übersetzerin und Autorin. Ihr Buch *Verlernen. Denkwege bei Hannah Arendt* wurde 2011 für den Leipziger Buchpreis nominiert.

ЗВИЗЖИ

Oblast Kaluga (RU)

Population: 150

Einwohner: 150

It's 10 April and we're standing at the edge of the Russian village of Zvizzchi, the taxi can't go any further because the roads are bad and the snow is piled up in drifts. But, despite everything, nature is gently awakening from hibernation. We can see meltwater and, in front of us, an adult fox crosses the road in the dusky twilight. I let out a yell, but Olga Gartman – from the Russian Association of Cultural Managers – looks up from her smart phone too late. Olga is the manager.

As we tuck into the meal that was waiting for us in the village pub we joke about the biceps you get from clearing snow. Everybody agrees: "Far too much snow has been cleared this winter!" Then it's time to get out the art plans. In the parcel of books that I sent to Zvizzchi last November, there was also a DVD of short films about how items are produced for the International Village Shop. *They want to hear more about it. Together, we look at a large screen, at the farm where I grew up, which is now a horse milkery. We watch ladies in Southern Germany sitting at the kitchen table making Höfer goods.*

We have been working in Zvizzchi, a village on the Ugra River, a four-hour drive to the southwest of Moscow, when the Moscow traffic jams are manageable, for four years. First Wapke, then Antje, sometimes both of them together.

The kolkhoz of Zvizzchi was closed at the beginning of the 1990s. It specialized in milk and meat production. The veterinarians, agronomists, and civil engineers have kept themselves afloat through self-sufficiency. Natalja says that they then got round and plump when they had a private cow and did not want to let any of their milk, their cream and butter go to waste.

Es ist der 10. April, und wir stecken am Rand des russischen Dorfs Zvizzchi fest. Das Taxi kann nicht weiterfahren, weil die Straße zu schlecht und voller Schneeverwehungen ist. Wir sehen Schmelzwasser, und vor uns quert ein ausgewachsener Fuchs in der späten Dämmerung die Straße. Ich stoße einen Warnschrei aus, aber bis Olga Gartman von der Association of Cultural Managers (ACM) von ihrem Smartphone aufschaut, ist es zu spät. Olga ist die Managerin.

Während das Essen im Dorfwirtshaus auf uns wartet, machen wir Witze über den Bizeps, den man vom Schneeschaufeln bekommt. Alle sind sich einig: »In diesem Winter gab es zu viel Schnee zum Schaufeln.« Dann ist es Zeit, unsere Kunstpläne hervorzuholen. Im Paket mit den Büchern, die ich im vergangenen November nach Zvizzchi geschickt habe, war auch eine DVD mit Kurzfilmen über die Herstellung von Artikeln für den International Village Shop. *Die Leute wollen mehr darüber wissen. Gemeinsam sehen wir auf einem großen Bildschirm den Bauernhof, auf dem ich aufgewachsen bin und der inzwischen ein Pferdemilchbetrieb ist. Dann sehen wir ein paar Frauen in Süddeutschland, die an einem Küchentisch Höfer Waren erzeugen.*

Vier Jahre lang haben wir in Zvizzchi gearbeitet, einem Dorf an der Ugra, vier Stunden Autofahrt südwestlich von Moskau, wenn die Moskauer Staus sich im Rahmen halten. Zuerst Wapke, dann Antje, und manchmal beide zusammen.

Anfang der Neunzigerjahre wurde der Kolchos von Zvizzchi geschlossen. Er war auf Milch- und Fleischproduktion spezialisiert. Die Tierärztinnen, Agronomen und Bauingenieurinnen hielten sich mit Selbstversorgung über Wasser. Natalja sagt, rund und prall seien sie damals geworden, als sie eine private Kuh hatten

The village nearest to Zvizzchi is Nikola-Lenivets, which is known in Russia for its large Land art festival in summer. Over time, the residents of Zvizzchi have gone from people who worked in production, to service providers: for the festival, the maintenance of the houses and gardens of the summer visitors, with guided walks, and car journeys.

What do the villagers know about the Netherlands and what do you pack in your suitcase? Their answer is simple: flowers and vegetable seeds. I fill my suitcase and look for a sponsor. Suddenly I am offered a field for crop trials, loads of seeds, and an agronomist to advise us. No trouble finding a location, because learning to grow your own veg conjures up visions of the lost school allotments of the Soviet era. Kohlrabi is new and extra lettuce is planted for tourists and festival-goers. Lettuce is apparently trendy in Moscow.

In Zvizzchi's school, seven teachers work with 15 children. Sturdy shoes are taken off in the vestibule, and stylish shoes are put on. The walls have colours and trim, there is an exhibition on the Second World War, whose frontline passed closeby, and a photo wall made with a coping saw: "Nasch Schisn", our life. During breaks, the teachers pass sweets around in the teachers' room and eat soup from the school kitchen. They are convinced that they will never be able to hold a candle to big schools, capital city schools. Cabbage, potatoes, and turnips are kept in the storeroom. The children search out particularly difficult words and teach them to us: водонапорная башня, water tower, приложение, attachment, or библиотекарь, librarian, the last word is naturally easy for us Germans.

Who makes what? In which seasons are feasts celebrated? Photos that schoolchildren and local residents make for us show the seasonal rhythm in the village. We carefully sift through the harvest of photos while tucking into a plate of blinis, and select the subjects for the seven postcards. Labels are made for the jam, pickles, and hand-woven baskets. The open source brand "Made in Zvizzchi" is a fact. "Made in Zvizzchi" spotlights the village culture and produce – both having been ignored up to now by the culture crowd in Nikola-Lenivets. Our central point of sale will be in the village shop next to the post office. I paint signs that will be strategically

und nichts von ihrer Milch, ihrer Sahne und Butter umkommen lassen wollten.

Das Nachbardorf von Zvizzchi ist Nikola-Leniwetz, bekannt in Russland für sein großes sommerliches Land-Art-Festival. Im Laufe der Zeit wurden die Bewohner von Zvizzchi von Menschen, die in der Produktion arbeiten, zu Dienstleistern: für das Festival, die Pflege der Häuser und Gärten der Sommerfrischler, mit geführten Spaziergängen und Autofahrten.

Was wäre ein gutes Gastgeschenk aus den Niederlanden? Die Antwort ist einfach: Blumen- und Gemüsesamen. Ich fülle meinen Koffer und sehe mich nach einem Sponsor um. Überraschend werden mir ein Feld für Anbauversuche, Saatgut in Massen und ein Agrarwissenschaftler als Berater angeboten. Ohne Mühe finden wir einen Ort für unsere Versuche, denn eigenes Gemüse anbauen lernen erinnert viele an die Schulgärten aus der Sowjetzeit. Der Kohlrabi ist neu, und für Touristen und Festivalbesucher wird zusätzlich grüner Salat angebaut. Offenbar ist grüner Salat in Moskau gerade angesagt.

In der Schule von Zvizzchi arbeiten sieben Lehrerinnen für 15 Kinder. Derbe Schuhe werden im Vorraum ausgezogen, schicke Schuhe angezogen. Die Wände haben Farben und Borten, es gibt eine Ausstellung zum Zweiten Weltkrieg, dessen Frontlinie in der Nähe verlief, und eine mit der Laubsäge gefertigte Fotowand: »Nasch Schisn«, unser Leben. In den Pausen geben die Lehrerinnen im Lehrerzimmer Konfekt herum und essen Suppe aus der Schulküche. Sie sind überzeugt, großen Schulen, Hauptstadtschulen, niemals das Wasser reichen zu können. Kohl, Kartoffeln und Rüben lagern in der Vorratskammer. Die Kinder suchen besonders schwere Wörter aus und bringen sie uns bei: водонапорная башня, Wasserturm, приложение, Anhang, oder библиотекарь, Bibliothekar, mit Letzterem haben wir es natürlich leicht.

Wer macht was? Zu welcher Jahreszeit wird welches Fest gefeiert? Schülerinnen und Schüler und Dorfbewohner machen für uns Fotos, die den Jahreszeitenwechsel im Dorf veranschaulichen. Sorgfältig sieben wir die Bilderernte, während wir einen Teller mit Blini aufessen und Motive für die Ansichtskarten auswählen. Für die Marmeladen, das eingelegte Gemüse und die handgeflochtenen Körbe entstehen Etiketten. Die Open-Source-Marke »Made in Zvizzchi« ist geboren. »Made

Заказ продукции:
Тел.: (495) 549-69-00
www.mosagro.ru
ВЫРАЩЕНО
В ПОДМОСКОВЬЕ

placed on the main street. The large photo exhibition in the club is only the second exhibition ever hosted by Zvizzchi. We celebrate the opening with grapes and champagne.

The club is located nearby the school and already at the edge of the steep slope going down to the river, at the beginning of the avenue. Natalja sits in the library every day and keeps it open. There is a hall with an old table tennis table and a dancehall with parquet flooring for the disco on Saturdays.

In our fourth year in Zvizzchi, ceramics are made; they are supposed to be the centrepiece of the presentation of the International Village Shop at the Archstoyanie Festival and the wood-burning kiln established as a new means of production in the village. We travel there with friends and children and take care of the rough work: digging up clay, drying clay, dissolving and filtering clay in water, and letting clay dry into mouldable masses on plasterboard. Heavy storms make the work exciting. Martin chops wood into thin sticks. Vadim builds a kiln with Thomas. They have been reading books about this, but this is the first actual attempt.

We put the ceramics into the hands of the professionals: Sascha, from Moscow, and Chajim, who travelled from Berlin along with his wife. Chajim will be giving pottery classes every day in the week before the festival, mostly attended by women and children. Many women from the dachas treat us like a team of welcome child-minders on rainy days.

We're building the stand for the presentation at the Archstoyanie Festival. This year Zvizzchi will host the entire festival – and Zvizzchi is also the theme. As a result of the festival, the Club has received a new, sophisticated entrance, a seashell made of wood. There is no skimping on wood for the follies and architectures for the festival, and that also applies in the case of this seashell.

More and more new construction is appearing in the village. Discussions are afoot about village development and about selling village produce on tables in the main street during the festival. The village shop has stocked

in Zvizzchi« rückt eine Dorfkultur und ihre Produkte ins Rampenlicht, die bisher von der Kulturszene in Nikola-Leniwetz ignoriert wurden. Unser wichtigster Verkaufsposten wird der Dorfladen neben dem Postamt sein. Ich male Schilder, die an strategisch günstigen Stellen entlang der Hauptstraße angebracht werden. Die große Fotoausstellung im Klub ist erst die zweite Ausstellung, die jemals in Zvizzchi stattgefunden hat. Wir feiern die Eröffnung mit Weintrauben und Champagner.

Der Klub steht nah bei der Schule und schon an der Kante des Steilhanges, der zum Fluss abfällt, am Anfang der Allee. Jeden Nachmittag sitzt Natalja in der Bibliothek und hält sie geöffnet. Es gibt einen Saal mit einer alten Tischtennisplatte und einen Tanzsaal mit Parkett für die samstägliche Disco.

In unserem vierten Jahr in Zvizzchi wird Keramik gemacht; sie soll das Herzstück der Präsentation des Internationalen Dorfladens beim Archstoyanie-Festival sein und den Holzbrandofen als neues Produktionsmittel im Dorf etablieren. Wir reisen an mit Freunden und Kindern und kümmern uns um die grobe Arbeit: Ton ausgraben, Ton trocknen, Ton in Wasser lösen und sieben, Ton auf Gipsplatten zu formbarer Masse trocknen lassen. Gewaltige Gewitter machen die Arbeit spannend. Martin hackt Holz zu schmalen Stiften. Vadim baut mit Thomas einen Ofen. Sie haben Bücher darüber gelesen, aber dieses ist der erste Versuch.

Die Keramik geben wir in die Hände von Professionellen: Sascha aus Moskau und Chajim, der mit seiner Frau aus Berlin anreist. Chaijm wird in der Woche vor dem Festival täglich Töpferkurse anbieten. Etliche Mütter aus den Datschen nutzen uns an Regentagen als eine willkommene Kinderbetreuung.

Wir bauen den Stand für die Präsentation auf dem Archstoyanie-Festival auf. In diesem Jahr wird Zvizzchi das gesamte Festival veranstalten – und selbst dessen Thema sein. Der Klub hat durch das Festival einen neuen, mondänen Eingang bekommen, eine hölzerne Muschel. An Holz wird nie gespart bei den Follies und Architekturen des Festivals.

Immer mehr Bauten entstehen im Dorf. Es entzünden sich lebhafte Debatten über dessen Entwicklung. Es werden mehrere Tausend Besucher erwartet. Die Bewohner spüren die Anspannung, denn alle wollen auf dem Festival irgendetwas anbieten. Da jeder mit jedem

up on extra supplies of soft drinks. The local residents are feeling the strain, because everyone has something to sell at the festival – they're expecting a few thousand visitors. People start bickering because they are all vying with one another. The festival offers excellent opportunities for earning money through selling catered dishes from the garden, chanterelle mushrooms gathered in the woods, and homemade vodka from clandestine sheds, and by doing all sorts of odd jobs for the organizers. There has been a love-hate relationship with the culture crowd ever since the festival started and locals got involved in catering and caring for the sculpture park. Even now, with Zvizzchi as the festival's main subject and location, the locals are assigned a pretty clear role and there are territorial interactions on all fronts. We are making Russian nameplates for our International Village Shop, and the festival organizers are putting pressure on us to sell the goods from their standardized tables. We maintain a distance and find a lovely location in the gateway to Oleg's courtyard.

In Zvizzchi, people meet on the street. The paths have space: There are gravelled paths, like the one that leads from the water tower past the shop to the buildings and stall ruins of the old kolkhoz, and there are wide summer paths, four-lane, with ruts from muddy periods. The flock of geese is aggressive. Mascha, the school director, lets her horses graze during the day. The evenings are dark. It is best to take along a torch.

The kiln is a popular hangout during the festival. The outside kiln burns around the clock, and everything comes out of it in one piece – much to everyone's delight. The freshly fired "Made in Zvizzchi" pottery is on show as an example: everyone can produce pottery here in the future. In our shop we praise the local clay. On the second day a woman pulls up in a black Range Rover, rolls down the window, and chooses her favourite items from the wares her husband has preselected. Yes, looks like we have clocked up our first-ever drive-in sale.

Our catering during the Moscow Biennale comes from Zvizzchi. People squeeze into a medium-size bus along with food and catering supplies. On the way back, they pass the time singing. **WF** *and* **AS**

wetteifert, wird ab und zu auch gezankt. Das Festival ist eine hervorragende Gelegenheit, mit Gerichten aus dem Garten Geld zu verdienen, außerdem mit Pfifferlingen aus dem Wald, mit schwarz in diversen Schuppen gebranntem Wodka und mit Gelegenheitsarbeiten für die Organisation. Seit es das Festival gibt und die Einwohner Zvizzchis sich an der Gastronomie und Pflege des Skulpturenparks in Nikola-Leniwetz beteiligen, gibt es eine Hassliebe zur Kulturszene. Selbst jetzt noch, da Zvizzchi Hauptthema und Veranstaltungsort des Festivals ist, wird den Ansässigen eine erstaunlich klar beschränkte Rolle zugeschrieben. Wir malen russische Namensschilder für unseren Internationalen Dorfladen, und die Organisatoren des Festivals drängen uns immer heftiger, unser Sortiment von ihren Standardtischen zu verkaufen. Wir halten Distanz und finden einen schönen Ort im Hoftor von Olegs Haus.

In Zvizzchi trifft man sich auf der Straße. Die Wege haben Raum: Es gibt geschotterte wie den, der vom Wasserturm am Laden vorbei und zu den Gebäuden und Stallruinen des alten Kolchos führt, und es gibt ausgefahrene Sommerwege, vielspurig in Schwüngen aus matschigen Zeiten. Die Gänseherde ist aggressiv. Mascha, die Schuldirektorin, lässt am Tage ihre Pferde grasen.

Die Abende sind dunkel. Besser, man nimmt eine Taschenlampe mit.

Der Brennofen ist ein beliebter Treffpunkt während des Festivals. Er steht im Freien, wird rund um die Uhr befeuert, und zur allgemeinen Erleichterung kommt am Ende alles heil wieder heraus. Die frisch gebrannte Töpferware »Made in Zvizzchi« ist ein Mustersortiment: Künftig kann hier jeder seine Keramik herstellen. In unserem Laden loben wir den Ton aus der Gegend. Am zweiten Tag fährt eine Frau in einem schwarzen Range Rover vor, lässt das Fenster herunter und wählt ihre Favoriten aus der engeren Auswahl, die ihr Mann zuvor getroffen hat. Sieht ganz so aus, als hätten wir unseren allerersten Drive-in-Verkauf im Kasten.

Unser Catering für die Moskau-Biennale kommt aus Zvizzchi. Die Leute aus dem Dorf quetschen sich mitsamt dem Essen und den Catering-Utensilien in einen mittelgroßen Bus. Auf dem Heimweg singen sie. **WF** *und* **AS**

INTERNATIONAL VILLAGE SHOW
Funded by / gefördert durch The German Federal Cultural Foundation / die Kulturstiftung des Bundes

EXHIBITIONS / AUSSTELLUNGEN
1/8 – 8/8
Stiftung Galerie für Zeitgenössische Kunst Leipzig
Karl-Tauchnitz-Straße 9 – 11
04107 Leipzig
06.02.2015 – 23.12.2016

gfzk

Concept / Konzept: Myvillages
Curators / Kuratorinnen: Julia Schäfer & Franciska Zólyom
Assistance / Assistenz: Katrin Kappenberger, Daniel Niggemann
Technical support and installation / Technik und Aufbau: Lars Bergmann, Bernd Fattich, Michael Hahn, Martin Reich

Supported by / Gefördert durch: The Culture Foundation of the Free State of Saxony / Kulturstiftung des Freistaates Sachsen

WEBPAGE / WEBSEITE
Design: An Endless Supply
www.internationalvillageshow.myvillages.org

GARTENHAUS
Remodelling / Umbau: Weis & Volkmann Architekten, Leipzig
Site management / Bauleitung: Ilona Brauer

With the financial support of the Ikea Foundation / **Mit finanzieller Unterstützung der** Ikea Stiftung.

Interior construction and furnishings / Innenausbau und Möbel: Lars Bergmann, Michael Hahn

PROGRAMM LEIPZIG
With the regular support of the / Mit regelmäßiger Unterstützung von Anna Linde Gärtnerei und Gemeinschaftsgarten, GeoWerkstatt Leipzig and / und Leipziger Gartenprogramm.

A warm thank you to all the guests for the food and beverages they brought with them / **Dank an** die angereisten Gäste für mitgebrachte Speisen und Getränke.
For the QEK thanks to / Für den QEK Dank an Martin Liebscher.

PROJECTS / PROJEKTE

COMPANY DRINKS & FOREIGN PICKERS
Company Drinks is a drinks company set up by / ist eine Getränkefirma von Kathrin Böhm/Myvillages.
The apples for the Company Drinks Kent Soda and Cider come from / Die Äpfel für das Kent Soda und Cider kommen von Moat Farm in Five Oak Green & Gleaning Network Kent.
The soda is produced at / Das Soda wurde hergestellt bei Square Root Soda in East London / Ostlondon.
Realized within the framework of / Realisiert im Rahmen von Company: Movements, Deals and Drinks.
www.companydrinks.info

FILM FOREIGN PICKERS
The film / Der Film Foreign Pickers was commissioned by the / wurde in Auftrag gegeben von der Delfina Foundation London **within the framework of the / im Rahmen der** »Politics of Food« series / Serie**, with additional support from the / mit zusätzlicher finanzieller Unterstützung durch die** University of East London and / und Art in Romney Marshes.
Direction / Regie: Kathrin Böhm, Sue Giovanni
Camera / Kamera: Richard Gillespie
Editing / Schnitt: Sue Giovanni
Research / Recherche: Tom James
Archive material / Archivmaterial: British Pathé

DELFINA FOUNDATION  

ECO NOMADIC SCHOOL
Odaja Films / Filme
Camera and editing / Kamera und Schnitt: Ciprian Cimpoi, Dragos Hanciu, Alexandru Popescu
With the support of / Mit Unterstützung von: Erasmus +

FARMERS & RANCHERS
Farmers & Ranchers is a coproduction by / ist eine Koproduktion von Wapke Feenstra/Myvillages with the / mit dem M12 Collective, Byers, Colorado.
Curator / Kuratorin: Kirsten Stoltz
Farmers & Ranchers was financed by the / wurde finanziert von National Endowment for the Arts, Gates Family Foundation, Colorado Creative Industries, Stichting Doen (BankGiro Loterij Fonds), Tijl Fonds (BPC), Omrop Fryslân and the / und dem Fries Museum.

FILM FARMERS & RANCHERS
Direction / Regie: Wapke Feenstra
Camera / Kamera: Gerco Jonker, Kim Shively
Editing / Schnitt: Ismael Lotz, Kim Shively

WEBPAGE / WEBSEITE FARMERS & RANCHERS
Design: Ariënne Boelens
Equipment / Technik: Grobbel & Dreis
www.farmersandranchers.nl

With additional support from the / Mit zusätzlicher Unterstützung der University of Colorado, Boulder, Nordwin College, Veehouderij, Leeuwarden, Future Farmers of America, Deer Trail, and the parents of the participants / und den Eltern der Teilnehmerinnen.

GEOLOGY / GEOLOGIE LEIPZIG
Geologische Animation Leipzig, the / die Geologische Sammlung and the geological excursions are a production of / und die geologischen Ausflüge sind eine Produktion von Wapke Feenstra / Myvillages and the / und der GeoWerkstatt Leipzig, **with the financial support of** The Embassy of the Kingdom of the Netherlands / **mit finanzieller Unterstützung durch die** Niederländische Botschaft.
Thanks to / Dank an Ronny Schmidt of the / von der GeoWerkstatt Leipzig.

GeoWerkstatt Leipzig — Koninkrijk der Nederlanden

I LIKE BEING A FARMER AND I WOULD LIKE TO STAY ONE / ICH BIN GERNE BAUER UND MÖCHTE ES AUCH GERNE BLEIBEN in Andalusia and / Andalusien und Extremadura, Spain / Spanien, 2014
Supported by the / Unterstützt vom Centro Andaluz de Arte Contemporáneo (CAAC), Sevilla
Thanks to / Dank an Manuel Olveira, Raquel Lopez and the / und die Cartuja de Sevilla.

I LIKE BEING A FARMER AND I WOULD LIKE TO STAY ONE / ICH BIN GERNE BAUER UND MÖCHTE ES AUCH GERNE BLEIBEN in Western Cape, South Africa / Südafrika, 2016
Thanks to / Dank an Justin Brett.

I LIKE BEING A FARMER AND I WOULD LIKE TO STAY ONE / ICH BIN GERNE BAUER UND MÖCHTE ES AUCH GERNE BLEIBEN is a project by / ist ein Projekt von Antje Schiffers / Myvillages and / und Thomas Sprenger.
www.ichbingernebauer.eu

INTERNATIONAL VILLAGE SHOP
www.internationalvillageshop.net

BEESTACHTIGE SCHAT
A collaboration between / Eine Zusammenarbeit von Wapke Feenstra/Myvillages, Kunsthuis SYB in Beetsterzwaag in Fryslân and the work group / und der Arbeitsgruppe Beestachtige Schat.
The Kunsthuis SYB is supported by the / Das Kunsthuis SYB wird unterstützt vom Mondriaan Fonds.
The product development for the / Die Produktentwicklung für den International Village Shop was supported by the / wurde unterstützt vom BankGiro Loterij Fonds. **The workshops were financed by / Die Workshops wurden finanziert von** Erasmus+

BankGiro Loterij FONDS 

FILM BEESTACHTIGE SCHAT
Camera and editing / Regie und Schnitt: Murk-Jaep van der Schaaf
Camera / Kamera: Jorrit Meinsma

FUFU BOWLS
A project by / Ein Projekt von Antje Schiffers/Myvillages, **on the invitation and with the financial support of the / auf Einladung und mit finanzieller Unterstützung des** Goethe-Instituts in Accra, **curated by / kuratiert von** Susanne Altmann.

FILM FUFU BOWLS
Camera / Kamera: Francis Brown, Antje Schiffers, Thomas Sprenger
Editing / Schnitt: Thomas Sprenger
Thanks to / Dank an Nana Obaahemaa Esi Nisin VIII., Ekumfi-Ekrawfo, and / und Robert Sobotta / Goethe-Institut Accra.

HÖFER WAREN
Höfer Goods / Höfer Waren are a project by / sind ein Projekt von Kathrin Böhm / Myvillages in cooperation with the women of Höfen / in Zusammenarbeit mit den Höfer Frauen.
The Höfer Lace was created in cooperation with / Die Höfer Spitze entstand in Zusammenarbeit mit der Spitzenstickerei Hofer in Rattelsdorf and / und Nina Hofer.

FILM HÖFER SPITZE
Camera / Kamera: Nina Hofer, Martin König
Editing / Schnitt: Martin König
With the support of / Mit Unterstützung des Bauernmuseums Bamberger Land and the / und der Eco Nomadic School (EU Grundtvig Lernpartnerschaft).

TWISTED BUGLE
Twisted Bugle is a collaboration between / ist eine Zusammenarbeit von Kathrin Böhm/Myvillages, Peter Mutschler of / von PS2 in Belfast, and the / und den "Army Wives", Abercorn Barracks, in Ballykinler / Ballykinlar.
Production / Produktion Twisted Bugle: Paddy Bloomer, J. Lie, Daniel Rous

FILM TWISTED BUGLE
Camera / Kamera: Kathrin Böhm, Phil Hession, Christopher Wideside
Editing / Schnitt: Phil Hession
Thanks to / Dank an Anne-Marie Dillon.

VECHTEWAREN
Vechte River Goods / Vechte Waren is a collaboration between / ist eine Zusammenarbeit von Antje Schiffers / Myvillages and / und Thomas Sprenger within the framework of / im Rahmen von kunstwegen / raumsichten.

OHNER LEINEN and / und **ESCH F6 are financed by / sind finanziert durch die** kunstwegen EWIV.

CONFECTIE BOXES from / aus **DEDEMSVAART were created with the additional support of the / entstanden mit zusätzlicher Förderung des** BankGiro Loterij Fonds, NL.

FILM CONFECTIE BOXES
Camera / Kamera: Antje Schiffers
Editing / Schnitt: Thomas Sprenger

BankGiro Loterij | FONDS

FILM ESCH F6
Camera and editing / Kamera und Schnitt: Thomas Sprenger

MTL PLATTFORM
MTL Plattform is a collaboration between / ist eine Zusammenarbeit von Kathrin Böhm / Myvillages, the art teacher / der Kunsterzieherin Dorit Löffler and students in year 9 and 10 of the / sowie Schülern und Schülerinnen der Jahrgangstufe 9 und 10 des school centre / Evangelischen Schulzentrums Großbardau, as well as / sowie Till Richter, architect and furniture maker / Architekt und Möbelbauer.

The remodelling of the platform was financed by / Der Umbau der Plattform wurde finanziert von Michael Berninger and / und Arthur Bruls.

TEKENEN IN VLASSENBROEK
(Drawing in / Zeichnen in Vlassenbroek) is a project by / ist ein Projekt von Wapke Feenstra / Myvillages with the / mit dem Kunstcel Vlaams Bouwmeester, Waterwegen en Zeekanaal nv, Stad Dendermonde and the / und der Agentschap Natuur & Bos v.d. Vlaamse overheid.
Curator / Kurator: Ronald Van de Sompel
Project staff / Projektmitarbeiter: Lulu Cuyvers, Lucie Renneboog, Ibe Ryde

The book / Das Buch A Schelde Riverscape was realized in 2015 with / wurde 2015 realisiert mit Montse Hernandes i Sala and the / und dem Verlag Jap Sam Books.
www.tekenen-in-vlassenbroek.be

TEAM
VLAAMS
BOUWMEESTER

ZVIZZCHI
Made in Zvizzchi is a coproduction by / ist eine Koproduktion von Wapke Feenstra and / und Antje Schiffers / Myvillages.
The organizer in Russia was the / Veranstalter in Russland war die Professional Association of Cultural Managers (ACM), Moscow / Moskau.
The / Der International Village Shop and the exhibition at the / und die Ausstellung in der Galerie Bogorodskoe were part of the 6th Moscow Biennial / waren Teil der 6. Moskau-Biennale, **and were supported by the / und wurden durch das** Goethe-Institut Moscow / Moskau and the / und den Mondriaan Fonds unterstützt.
Thanks to the Netherlands Russian Year in / Dank an Nederland-Ruslandjaar 2013, Archstoyanie-Festival, Olga Gartman and / und Georgy Nikich.

BIBLIOBOX
Bibliobox in Leipzig was hosted by / war zu Gast bei Library GfZK / Bibliothek GfZK.
Bibliobox in Leipzig is curated by / kuratiert von Vera Lauf.
www.bibliobox.org

IMPRINT / IMPRESSUM BOOK / BUCH

Cover / Umschlagmotiv:
Kristina Brusa, Leipzig

Translation / Übersetzung:
Herwig Engelmann (E / D)
Uta Goridis (E / D)
Amy Klement (D / E)
Kathleen van Overzee-Mcmillan (NL / E)
Copy-editing / Lektorat: Miriam Wiesel
Design and setting / Gestaltung und Satz: Kristina Brusa, Leipzig
Lithography / Lithografie: Humme Leipzig
Printing and binding / Druck und Bindung: Pögedruck, Leipzig and / und Buchbinderei Mönch, Leipzig

Editor / Herausgeber: Myvillages and / und Stiftung Galerie für Zeitgenössische Kunst Leipzig
Concept / Konzept: Myvillages and / und Kristina Brusa

Bibliographic information published by the Deutsche Nationalbibliothek
The Deutsche Nationalbibliothek lists this publication in the Deutsche Nationalbibliografie; detailed bibliographic data are available on the Internet at **www.dnb.d-nb.de**

Bibliografische Information der Deutschen Nationalbibliothek
Die Deutsche Nationalbibliothek verzeichnet diese Publikation in der Deutschen Nationalbibliografie; detaillierte bibliografische Daten sind im Internet über **www.dnb.d-nb.de** abrufbar.

jovis Verlag GmbH
Kurfürstenstraße 15/16
10785 Berlin
Germany / Deutschland

www.jovis.de

jovis books are available worldwide in selected bookstores. Please contact your nearest bookseller or visit www.jovis.de **for information concerning your local distribution.**

jovis-Bücher sind weltweit im ausgewählten Buchhandel erhältlich. Informationen zu unserem internationalen Vertrieb erhalten Sie von Ihrem Buchhändler oder unter **www.jovis.de.**

ISBN 978-3-86859-465-2

ILLUSTRATIONS / ILLUSTRATIONEN

Antje Schiffers: 67a–d, 97b, 157a, 162, 231b
Evangelisches Schulzentrum Großbardau: 138–139
Kay Bachmann: 261a–h (invitation cards / Einladungskarten)
Wapke Feenstra: 15a–k, 104–105

PHOTO / FOTO CREDITS

ACM-Moscow: 71c, 212/213, 299a
Antje Schiffers: 50/51, 53, 57a, 64/65, 97a, 140/141, 153a,b, 156, 157b, 266/267, 272/273
atelier d'architecture autogerée: 33b, 35b
Barbara Schmidt: 72/73, 180b, 188, 293a
Emil Charlaff: 69a
Fetsje de Jong: 83b
Gea Zandvliet: 80a, 81a
Guillermo Mendo / CAAC: 71b
Imagen MAS / MUSAC: 70a
Isabel Rosario: 143a
Jennifer Balcombe: 36, 37, 38/39, 112–113h
Julia Rößner: 29b, 187, 189a,b, 199, 201a,b, 203a,b, 204, 206/207, 208a, 210a, 223, 224/225, 229b, 231a, 235c, 236, 237a, 245, 246/247, 259a
Kathrin Böhm: 6/7, 20/21, 23a–b, 30/31, 33a, 35a, 70c, 136/137, 147, 149a–e, 176b, 220/221
Liesbet De Visscher: 168/69, 194a,b, 195b, 196, 283
Luis Durán Aristoy: 10/11
Mascha Jakuschin: 288/289
Peter Mutschler: 20/21
Private Collection / Private Leihgabe: 144/145
Romke Kooistra: 84b
Ruben van Vliet / Fries Museum: 71a
Sebastian Schröder: 12, 102/103, 227a, 228, 229a, 235a,b, 237b,c, 238/239, 241a, 242/243
Susanne Altmann: 69b
Thomas Sprenger: 94/95, 122/123, 143b, 150/151, 160/161, 174
Valentina Bonomonte: 182
Wapke Feenstra: 16/17, 18a–h, 25, 26/27, 29a, 54/55, 57b, 58/59, 60/61, 63a–b, 69c, 70b, 78/79, 80b, 81b–d, 82a,b, 83a, 85, 108–109a–i, 110–111a–i, 112/113a–g,i,134/135, 176a, 178a,b, 180a, 183, 184/185, 192, 195a, 197, 208b, 210b, 227b, 232/233, 241b, 248a,b, 249b, 253a,b, 254a,b, 255b, 257a, 258b, 259b, 260, 280/281, 291a,b, 293b, 295a,b, 296a,b, 297a,b, 299b, 300/301
Wenzel Stählin: 249a, 250/251, 255a, 257b, 258a
Wimke de Boer: 84a